By His Hand

My Memoirs

By Patsy Nix

Fort Collins, Colorado
2024

Table of Contents

My Childhood 1
High School and College 16
Marriage, Family, and Farming 47
The Fort Collins Farm 72
The Kids Leave Home 103
Moving Off the Farm 113
Our Senior Years 134
Life After Tom 172
Acknowledgements 199
Family 200
In Loving Memory 201
Family Photo Gallery 202
Our Grandchildren 204
My Poetry, Songs and Prayers 206

My Childhood

The year was 1937. My brother and I were walking barefoot down the dusty road in Lafayette, Colorado. We walked barefoot in most kinds of weather to save our shoes. As we headed toward downtown, scuffing the dirt over our toes, we heard a neighbor say, "There go Walt Bennett's kids. They will never amount to anything." My brother and I turned toward each other and said, "We will show them and everyone" We sealed it by licking our thumb, placing the thumb in the middle of our other hand, then pounding that area with our fist and spitting on the ground. That's the way we sealed promises in those days. But that is not where my story begins.

Earliest Memories

I was born in Riverside, California, in 1928 to Leota Alice and Walt Bennett. At two years of age, Denver, Colorado, became my home. My first recollection of life was sitting with my brother, Billy, on my mother's bed as she hugged and kissed us. Mother was confined to bed with severe head and body pain accompanied by vomiting. She became worse with each passing day. My father was absent because he was serving time in prison for crimes he had committed. There was little talk about him except from my maternal grandmother. She told us our mother's head injury was caused by beatings our father lashed upon her during his fits of anger. We were not allowed to speak of him. (When I was 15, I wrote to the Denver Death Records Department and found out that my mother died from a brain tumor.)

Bill and me 1928

Can one remember life's happenings from age three? It is possible, because I told stories to my Aunt Reatha, my mother's sister, a few years later, and she was astonished as I repeated every detail of what my mother said, and the way I ran screaming after the ambulance when they came to take her away, and how my six-year-old brother caught up with me in the middle of the road where we sat, clinging to each other with deep, shaking sobs until Uncle John scooped us up in his arms and took us back to the house. My beautiful twenty-three-year-old mother died the next day.

My mother Alice

Aunt Reatha took me to a big building three days later. When we entered, there was music playing. We were led to a room where my mother was lying in a bed with covers just up to her shoulders. She looked so pretty and peaceful. Reatha said I could kiss her. I remember that her face was very cold when Reatha said, "Now Patsy, you do not need to cry anymore because your mommy is going to heaven to live with God and everyone is very happy there." I asked for my brother and was told he had already gone to live with our grandma and step-grandpa. How could that be? I distinctly remembered mommy saying, "Billy, take care of your little sister." How could he take care of me if he was gone? Again, my Aunt Reatha said I did not need to cry because I was coming to live with her and Uncle George, and that Billy would be happy at Grandmother's house. Those words, "you do not need to cry" would forever be etched in my entire being. I remember the funeral where someone sang "The Old Rugged Cross" as I choked back the tears.

Aunt Reatha and Uncle George Take Me In

Reatha told me that she and Uncle George would be my parents from now on, and I soon began calling them Mommy and Daddy. I lived with them for the next six years. I developed a special bond with Reatha. We lived on Humboldt Street in Denver. Daddy worked at Gates Rubber Plant. When I was four, I was allowed to get a puppy, which delighted me. I chose a big, clumsy puppy that I named Sandy. Daddy said he hoped we could afford to feed him; he was a St. Bernard! We wrestled together and when Sandy grew bigger, I rode on his back a lot.

We had a large backyard with two tall trees, so we had plenty of playing room. There were times we fell asleep together as I nestled into Sandy's furry side. Sandy helped my sadness over missing my brother. There were funny episodes with Sandy because he was so clumsy. One momentous time, Sandy and I were riding in the rumble seat of the two-passenger car Daddy drove. It was a tight squeeze. As we pulled out after a stop, Sandy toppled out to the pavement. He rolled and rolled but was not hurt. Daddy and two other men struggled to lift him back into the rumble seat. Sandy did not like the junk man who went up and down the alleys with his horse and wagon, yelling for anything people did not want. Sandy did not like him coming close to our yard. One day, the junk man got down from the wagon to retrieve something Daddy had put in the trash. Sandy frightened him so much that he climbed one of the trees in our yard begging me to take my dog in the house. I thought it was funny, but Mommy explained to me that even though Sandy would not hurt anyone, I should not have laughed. My new mommy, Reatha, taught me many things and gave me lots of hugs.

Our house was one block from a neighborhood grocery store. When I was five, Mommy asked if I would like to go to the store for her, and I asked, "all by myself?" I felt very grown up as I walked to the store. There was so much to look at in the store, especially the huge bin of penny candy that sat near the cash register. After I paid Mr. Grover for the loaf of bread, I told him I had two pennies and would like some candy. It took a long time for me to choose a Tootsie Roll and a butterscotch. Mr. Grover stood at the door as he waved goodbye and told me to be careful crossing the street. Later, I found out that Mommy was hiding behind me to be sure I was safe. The few times I went to the store, Mommy would say something about trusting me to be responsible.

Age 5

We were going to see Grandmother which meant I would also see my brother. I could hardly wait, and it seemed to take a long, long time to go from Denver to Lafayette. Cars moved quite slow on the roads. When I saw Billy, we hugged, then grabbed each other's hands and began to dance around in a circle. We got so dizzy that we both fell down. We went outside to play with Uncle Bob who was just two years older than Billy. So many people lived in that small house: Grandmother, Step-Grandfather, Billy, Uncle Bob, Uncle John, Uncle Russ, Step-Uncle Gib, Art, and Step-Aunt June. I did not want to leave., and on the trip home, I replayed in my mind all the fun I had.

A sad day came when we moved from Humboldt to an apartment complex closer to Daddy's work. I counted 15 outside stairs as we moved into our apartment. Mommy explained to me that Sandy could not come because dogs were not allowed. Although she told me not to cry, I could not hold back the tears. After I was tucked into bed each night, I pulled the covers over my face and cried for Sandy and my brother for a long time. I was careful that Mommy did not hear me. Attending Kindergarten occupied part of my time, and I made friends with Tara who lived downstairs. I loved school, and the teacher told Mommy that I was a fast learner. Right after that I got into trouble. All the grades were together on the playground for recess. I was swinging when a fifth-grade boy knocked me off and took the swing. I threw a rock that landed on his forehead which sent him to the school yelling and crying. I was back in the swing when a teacher said I had to go see the principal. As I was led to the principal's office, I was lectured by the teacher about throwing rocks and how dangerous it was and that I could have put the boy's eye out. She had me by the arm, walking very fast. When we reached the principal's office, the boy I hit with the rock was sitting in a chair, and I had to sit next to him. It was a big chair and my knees hurt as my legs dangled over the edge. We both got a lecture about how to treat others. I remember saying that I had skinned elbows and knees but did not make a fuss. The principal took off his glasses and gave me a staring look. Then both of us injured students apologized to each other. When I got home from school, Mommy reinforced what I had already been told. After I was in bed, I overheard her and Daddy discussing the situation. They were laughing and said the principal told them he liked my spunk. I had no idea what "spunk" meant, but I guess it was funny. I needed Sandy so I could tell him about everything. Tara and I became good friends. We played together outdoors and at each other's apartments. Even though we had fun playing dolls, school, jacks, cards, grocery store, etc., I still thought a lot about Sandy and Billy.

My Uncle Bud worked in a coal mine, but he was also a trained boxer. We went every weekend to watch him box. I learned to yell and scream and tell Uncle Bud to use an uppercut and knock the guy out. It was fun to watch, but I did not like the smoke-filled arena where I heard my first cuss words. When I used some of them later, I got sent to my room with a threat to wash my mouth out with soap. Yuk! Little girls did not talk like that! Little girls should be seen and not heard! Unfortunately, my Uncle Bud was killed in a mine accident which created sorrow for everyone. He was so nice, and I missed him a lot!

The security and trust I felt for two years came crashing down one day. Mommy had gone to the store. I was playing when Daddy called me to sit on his lap. He began to fondle me and touched me near my panties, tearing them. I knew things were not right, and I was frightened. Suddenly a voice from inside of me said, "Tell him you have to tinkle." I told him and he said to hurry back. The voice also told me to run downstairs to Tara's, which I did. I knocked on the door and asked if Tara could play, and her mother invited me in. I stayed there until Mommy came to get me. That night as she prepared to put me in the tub, she asked how my panties got torn. I told her that Daddy did it. She wrapped a towel around me, and we walked to the living room where Daddy was reading. Mommy said, "George, if you ever lay another hand on Patsy, I will call the police and you will be lucky if I don't kill you first." She led me back to the bathroom, hugged me, and said that she would never leave me alone with Daddy again, and that I was safe. I heard that still, small voice inside of me other times. It was not until many years later, I came to understand that it was God speaking through His Holy Spirit. Not long after, Uncle John was visiting us. Daddy was at work and Mommy said she was going to run an errand. I ran to the open window, hysterical, crying after Mommy. Uncle John caught me before I fell out. Mommy returned and explained to me that Uncle John would never hurt me and said she would go to the store tomorrow. She kept her word, and I was never left alone with Daddy for the next four years I lived with them.

During my fifth year, Mommy and Daddy would drop me off for Sunday School. Sometimes when they came to pick me up, we would attend church services together. My Sunday School teacher made God's Word come alive for the children in her class. One thing she stressed every Sunday was that we did not need to be afraid because Jesus was always with us. She taught us how to pray, and my favorite song was "Jesus Loves Me. "

Mommy and Daddy went to nightclubs frequently, and usually took me with them. Daddy would drink and tell the band director that I could sing a lot of songs. I did listen to the radio every day and learned many songs—my favorite being about the cowboys. I did not like being lifted to the bandstand to sing while people touched me and said how cute I was. Most of them were drunk and loud like Daddy. On the way home from the nightclubs, I crouched down on the back floor of the car thinking we were going to run off the road because Daddy was swerving all over while he and Mommy argued. One night, as Mommy tucked me into bed, I told her that I did not like those smelly people rubbing my head and hugging me. She promised that it would not happen again. The next weekend, I woke up during the night and called out to Mommy. There was no answer, so I got up, turned on every light in the house and searched for her. No one was home except me. I could hear my Sunday School teacher saying I did not need to be afraid because Jesus would always be with me. That thought comforted me, so I turned off the lights and went back to bed. The next morning, I told Mommy what happened, and I could see tears in her eyes. She promised that I would never be left alone again. She kept her promise.

We Move to Fairplay

Near my sixth birthday, Mommy told me that Daddy got a job in the mountains and that we were moving again. I asked where and if Tara would be able to come play. Mommy explained that it was too far for Tara to come play unless her folks brought her to pay a visit. We moved to Fairplay, Colorado. This time we did not have an apartment, but a tiny one-room cabin with an alcove for Mommy and Daddy's bed. I slept on a cot. Our heat was a potbelly stove, and we had a small table for eating. Our drinking water was brought in from outside in a pail. I was told that it was delicious pure water from a well that every cabin used. There were five cabins. All the dads worked in the gold mine. I became adjusted to my surroundings but missed Tara and our trips to downtown Denver where it was such fun to ride in department store elevators and eat from vendors' food carts on the street. The elevator operators wore uniforms with funny hats and announced what was on each floor. They opened the elevator door with a handle. I also missed the weekly movies and the popcorn. My favorite thing was looking out over the city from the top of the Daniels & Fisher Tower, especially at Christmastime. It was the tallest building in Denver, and one could see for miles from the top.

In Fairplay, we kids had a huge field to play in, and I liked the sound of the river that ran past our cabin. Also, we got to ride the burros that came down the river. They were very tame. I asked who owned them and was told they belonged to the mine. Teams of burros pulled the heavy carts out of the mine. There were three teams so when one team was tired, they were turned loose in the river and another team took over. The only thing we could not do was play in the water. It was gray instead of pure water like I had seen before because the mine sent the tailings downriver. I asked many questions about how the gold was mined. Daddy explained it all to me and made some drawings to enhance my understanding. Sometimes he would work the midnight shift. One day, he told me that the men were talking about taking the children down in the mine and asked if I wanted to go. I was hesitant until Mommy told me that two children would be allowed to go together with their dads and that other dads worked with Daddy. I said, "yes." I was told it was cold in the mine so when the time came for me to go, I was dressed very warmly. When we reached the entrance, I was given a cap that had a carbide lamp on top to help us see as we took the platform way down into the dark. There were no sides to the platform. It was scary, not like the elevators in Denver's department stores. When we reached the bottom, Daddy took me by the hand and led me through a narrow passageway. Then, we came to a larger area where there were a lot of glistening walls. I asked if the shiny stuff was gold and was told that some was and some was "fool's gold" which meant that it was fake. Daddy led me to a place back from the wall with Leland (one of the children), who had come down with his daddy. Then all the men went to work on the shiny wall. They swung heavy pickaxes to break off pieces which they placed in one of the cars that the burros pulled. The men grunted as they swung their pickaxes. Even with carbide lamps, it was very dark so a few lanterns were placed where the men were working. Leland and I sat close to each other because we were cold. After a short while, Daddy said it was time for Leland and me to go up top. So we got back on the platform. We were each given a piece of the rock from the wall. I was glad when Leland's daddy told us to sit down on the platform so it was not as scary going up. When we reached the top, there was a man who said he would take us home because his shift was later. After a long walk, we got into the man's car and took the bumpy, narrow road back to the cabins. I was excited to show Mommy the glistening rock, but I had no desire to visit the mine again.

I was happy because we were going to see Grandmother and everyone again. I picked wild strawberries and gooseberries for Grandmother. On the way, I got hungry and ate a little. I had a fun time again with Billy and my uncles. We ran races, played hide and seek, dug a hole that was supposed to become a cave in the vacant lot, and shot baskets through a hoop that hung on the garage. I was quiet on the way home because I missed my brother.

We Move to Empire

I had finished first grade when Mommy said we were moving again. This time, our home was Empire, Colorado, another mountain mining town. Our cabin was one of four, about the size of the one we left. Daddy continued working in the mines. I missed my friends and again I was told not to cry. I readily made friends wih some of the other kids, especially one boy whose parents owned the general store not far from the cabins. I liked playing with Buddy. Shortly after moving to Empire, Buddy and I were playing in the store when two men dressed in suits entered asking for Daddy. I piped up and said he lived in one of the cabins. I was hushed by Buddy's mom, and she said that I was new in the area and did not know the people yet. She told the men she did not know anyone by the name of George. The men left and later I told Mommy about it. I asked if Daddy had done something bad, and she said that I was too young to understand. I never did find out the circumstances. All I knew is that I did not trust Daddy.

I loved the columbines that grew in vast numbers. One day I picked some for Mommy, and she said it was against the law to pick wildflowers, especially the columbines, Colorado's state flower. To this day, my breath is taken away with the lovely groves of columbine encountered while traveling in Colorado's beautiful mountains.

In the fall, I started second grade. The schoolhouse was larger than the one in Fairplay and had a bigger potbelly stove. We walked to school except when it snowed. The schoolhouse was downhill from the cabins, so we rode our sleds, but it was not much fun to pull them home. There was a boy in my class who walked with braces. Some of the kids made fun of him. One day at recess, he was knocked to the ground by one of the boys. I went over to help Timmy up when the same boy pushed me down. That really made me mad, so I gave him an upper cut like I saw my Uncle Bud throw in the boxing ring. He ran screaming into the school. When the teacher came to see what was going on, I was still trying to help Timmy get up. Miss Crew helped stand Timmy up and asked for an explanation. Both Timmy and I told her what had happened, and I asked if I was going to be sent to the principal's office. Miss Crew said she was also the principal, and she did need to talk with me. She was kind and congratulated me for helping Timmy. She also said that I could really hurt someone with a punch like that and hoped I would not do it again. Miss Crew said that she would be talking to the boy who caused it all and would talk to the students about how we should treat each other. After that, whenever any of the boys started something, I discovered all I had to do was double up my fist,

Since there were mountain lions and bobcats near the cabins at night, no one went to the outhouse. Instead, we relieved ourselves in the coal bucket. One night, I used the bucket and the next morning my bottom was covered in blisters. I was in a lot of pain. Mommy felt badly and said it was her fault for not emptying the ashes. When my urine had hit the hot ashes, they splattered, causing the burns. I could not go to school for two weeks. I laid on my stomach with bandages on my bottom that had to be changed often. It was embarrassing because all the women in the neighborhood came to see my blisters. It was difficult to read and do schoolwork while lying on my tummy. When I went back to school, I sat on a pillow for quite some time.

One day, Mommy and Daddy told me some happy news. I would be having a baby sister or brother in July. Time passed and sometimes Mommy would be in pain. I did not understand it all, but I heard some of the women say the pain was not normal. Mommy had seen a doctor who traveled to surrounding towns, but the time had come for her to visit a doctor in Denver. She seemed better after that. I helped more with the cleaning and carrying things for her. I even emptied the ashes from the stove into the coal bucket. By the middle of June, I was told it was time for Mommy to go to the hospital. Daddy went with her, and I was cared for by a neighbor. Two days later, Daddy came home and said Mommy was not coming home, but would be joining my real mommy in Heaven. She had died on the operating table. My heart hurt as I tried to understand it all. I asked what happened and if the baby was all right. Daddy said that the doctors had made a big mistake, and Mommy was not expecting a baby at all. The few times she was checked by a doctor, he thought he heard the baby's heartbeat, but it was sounds given by the tumor. I tried understanding all of it, but I could not wrap my mind around what had happened. I did not even know what a tumor was or how I was going to get along without Mommy. I stayed at Buddy's house for the next two nights and his mother was so good to me. Later, we went to the mortuary in Denver. No one had to tell me I could kiss Mommy. I kissed her several times until Daddy pulled me away. I turned around and there was my grandmother, uncles and Billy. I ran to Billy, and we hugged each other tight. Now I had two mommies in Heaven. Once more, I fought back tears at the funeral as "The Old Rugged Cross" was sung.

After the funeral, I heard the adults talking about where I would stay. My grandmother said there was no room for me at her house because there were already too many people living there. It made me very sad. I decided if Daddy offered to keep me that I would tell how he had fondled me. I really wanted to go to Grandmother's house to be with my brother. A decision was made that I would stay with Grandmother's cousin in Denver. Her name was Ethel. Uncle John drove his car and came home with to Empire with me and Daddy. Buddy's mom came with a telegram that said I would be going to Ethel's house. The next day, I put my belongings in a sack: my clothes, Shirley Temple doll, some play dishes, crayons, the gold mine rock and a book. When we got there, Ethel said she did not know how long she could keep me. Uncle John told me not to worry and that he and Billy would come see me later. As I unpacked, Ethel was mumbling about not needing a child around. I could tell right away that she did not like me. I did not like her, either. That night in bed, I cried, and Ethel told me to shut up and go to sleep. I remember thanking Jesus for being with me. My stay at Ethel's was to last only two weeks. She was a very fat person who ate a lot of chocolates every day without offering me one. She kept them high in the kitchen cabinet. One day, when she went outside, I decided to eat a chocolate. I climbed up on the counter, opened the box and took one. Later when Ethel took the box down, she could tell a chocolate was missing. She went into a tirade about my being a thief and said she would tell my grandmother to come and get me. I hoped it was true! I apologized to Ethel. All she did was glare at me.

Life in Lafayette with My Brother

I was so excited that I was going to live at Grandmother and Step-Grandfather's house with my brother and uncles. Uncle John and Billy came to pick me up. When we got to the house on Geneseo Street in Lafayette, Grandmother and some of the boys greeted me. There was a small back porch with a cot, along with some canning equipment that became my room. Grandmother's house had two bedrooms, a living room, and a middle room that most likely was designed to be a dining room. Grandmother rested in her rocking chair, and we kids played games there. We were not allowed to sit on the sofa in the living room, but we could sit on the floor and listen to the radio. The kitchen had a large table with a pantry in the corner and a coal cook stove on the other side. The five youngest children, including me, stood to eat since there were not enough chairs. My chin was table high. The sink was large with cold running water. The outhouse stood quite a distance away next to the chicken house and garage.

Behind the house was a huge vacant lot where we played games and dug tunnels. We thought if we dug deep enough that we would reach China. In one of the tunnels, the boys hid while they smoked Indian weed in corncob pipes. I tried to smoke, but it was not for me. We played many games in the lot and in the street until dark when the weather was nice. Some of the games we played were: Blind Man's Bluff, Kick the Can, Red Light/Green Light, Crack the Whip, Keep Away, Red Rover, Run-Sheep-Run, and of course, Hide and Seek. We fashioned empty cans until they fit on our shoes and clomped around on them. Marbles was a favorite game as well. I practiced until I could shoot as good as the boys, and how I loved winning the agates. I loved wiggling and squirming my way into the middle of a truck tire. When I was secure, a member of my team gave a push and away I went down a hill, hoping to be first over the finish line without toppling over. When it snowed, we built forts for snowball fights and played Fox and Geese and Shoot the Rabbit.

Grandma and Step-Grandpa

Step-Grandpa worked in the coal mines, always had a pipe in his mouth and talked in a grunting way. His wife had passed away a year after my biological grandfather passed away. The two couples had been friends, so he and Grandmother decided to get married. My step-Aunt June was nice, but she was eight years older than I, so we did not have much in common. She and two of my uncles shared the second bedroom. The other boys—Billy, Bobby, Gib and Art—-slept on the large feather bed on the front porch. Once a drunk man, walking home from the nearby tavern, came into the back porch where I was sleeping. As he was groping his way in the dark, I got up real quick and ran to my grandparents' bedroom. After that, I slept with Billy and Bobby and the other boys on the front porch. We nestled down in feather mattresses that helped keep us warm. In the wintertime, Grandmother heated large rocks in the oven, wrapped them in towels and put them in bed with us. I don't remember getting cold even when we woke with a layer of snow on the top covers. The boys found out that I was not afraid of the dark and would ask me to go to the outhouse with them at night. I did that for a while and would stand out in the cold air, shivering. At Halloween, some people would give pennies instead of candy. I got the idea that I should start charging the boys a penny each time I accompanied them to the outhouse. To my surprise, they paid up. Later, Uncle Bobby and Billy asked to borrow some pennies, and I figured out they needed to pay me an extra cent in interest for every five pennies they borrowed. We used magazines for toilet paper in the outhouse. We called the Sears and Roebuck catalog "Rears and Sore Butt"!

Before school started, my grandmother said that I should use my own last name. I had been using Daddy George's last name. I asked Grandmother what my name was. She said it was Bennett and showed me how to spell it. My brother and I walked hand-in-hand to school, and he introduced me to my teacher. I could not believe the size of the schoolhouse. Made of light brick, it was two stories high. I was surprised when the teacher took me to the auditorium which was also a gymnasium. It was there all the kids learned different dances, performed plays, sang and danced to music, and played games like dodgeball. The combined Junior/Senior High School was in the same block as the elementary school. It was a huge building made of brick. In back was a football field with bleachers. I was allowed to attend the football games with the boys. After the first game, Grandmother asked what I liked best, and I told her the fight that happened after the game. I hid under the bleachers to watch. Lafayette was playing Louisville. They were tough rivals and a fight always broke out after each game, no matter who won. Speaking of fights, there were plenty in town as men and boys from different nationalities provoked each other. I would hide behind bushes or buildings to watch the fights and only engaged once when a guy kicked my brother while he was down. I ran from cover and tackled him. A whistle halted the fight while Billy led me away. He told me to never do that again. The guys had a pact to whistle if a woman or child was nearby. A second whistle meant to start the fight again. Dumb!

I read a lot while sitting on the floor of our middle room. Once in a while, I could bring a book home from school. The only books in our house were sets of encyclopedias and Aesop's Fables. I read them over and over. Grandmother made a few comments now and then, but she never really talked to me. I was having a difficult time trying to figure out why. Reatha had talked to me a lot, and I missed her. One day, while I was reading, Mrs. Lambert from across the street came to visit. I overheard my grandmother say that she could hardly bring herself to talk to me because I was so much like my mother. Then she told Mrs. Lambert that her grief ran very deep. When I was a year old, Grandpa died. Two years later, my mother died. Then, Uncle Bud was killed in the mine accident and three years after that, Reatha died. I realized that in an eight-year period, Grandma had lost her husband and three children. This helped my understanding, but it was still difficult to deal with. I missed both my moms a lot.

I also missed hearing the stories about Jesus. It had been over two years since I had been to Sunday School, even though I said my prayers every night. I told Grandmother that I wanted to attend Sunday School. She asked which church. I heard from a friend that there were three churches in town. I told her I wanted to go to the Methodist church. She approved but wanted me to know that some of the children who went there had much better clothes than mine. That did not bother me, and I was excited for Sunday School again. Several family members and some of my school friends made fun of me. I went early every Sunday morning and asked Reverend Brown if I could play the piano. I had never played but was able to pick out hymn melodies with one finger. He was so kind and understanding. He said he would unlock the church earlier if I wanted to come play the piano. I told him about my kindergarten Sunday School teacher and how I always remembered that I never had to be afraid because Jesus was always with me. Reverend Brown hugged me and also taught me how to react when people teased me about going to church. He said to pray for them because they probably did not know about Jesus. In fact, he said that we needed to pray for everyone who said or did mean things. He heard me singing and asked if I would sing a solo for church. We picked out the hymn, "I Would Be True." I especially like the part about being brave, a friend, forgiving, and looking up to laugh and love. I sang other hymns during the next two years which I memorized so I could carry them in my heart. The Baptist church had Vacation Bible School, which I attended in the summer. I learned more about Jesus and memorized many Bible verses. I like the upbeat hymns. Sometimes we stood up and clapped, which was great fun.

Step-Grandpa worked in the coal mine at Jamestown. Things were financially tough for the majority of families because of the stock market crash, the Great Depression, and the dust bowl days from 1929-1939. I really did not mind wearing dresses made from printed flour or feed sacks, but the panties really scratched. Grandmother canned a lot of vegetables from the garden. I helped her and remember what a job it was to make sauerkraut in the large pots. When the garden was picked over, there was always enough left that we kids were allowed to make Bum Stew in a big pot over an outdoor fire. It was called Bum Stew for the bums who would ask people for vegetables and cook them near the railroad cars which they rode from town to town. The only time we had fruit was once a month when the WPA dropped off a sack of oranges or grapefruit. Grandma rationed them to one a day. We only had canned milk for our cereal. Grandmother would let us drink a little sometimes. The boys liked it, but I thought it was yucky. There was a cheese factory not far from our house where we would gather the reject pieces. We ate a lot of beans, sometimes for every meal. The covers were fanned at night because of all the tooting. The breakfast oatmeal was very good, and there was usually a bowl left over. There was never food to eat between meals, but we took turns eating the left-over oatmeal as a treat. Grandmother tried hard to prepare nutritious food for us, but we lacked some vitamins. Each of us kids developed boils. They were ugly, painful bumps that left scars. Grandmother would place a poultice on a rag and secure it to the boil until it was ripe and came to a head. It was a relief when she would squeeze all the pus out. One of our neighbors thought they were caused by so many cuts or open sores. Another said it was because we bathed in the same water. Our bathing water had to be heated in large containers on the coal stove. It was then poured into a round tin tub. Because I was the youngest and only girl, I was allowed to bathe first (Aunt June took body baths from a large pan). The boys accused me of peeing in the water, but I never did, even when I felt like it to get back at them for their orneriness.

When I was in fourth and fifth grade, my brother decided that I should become an athlete. He said I was a good student, but now I needed to stretch myself. Tackle football with the boys in the gravel road left scars that are still visible today. One time, I was tackled so hard that I got a bloody nose and skinned both knees. I sat there, whimpering, when Billy said, "Get up, you big sissy and fight." No mercy was shown me by any of the boys. The day I was switched to quarterback, I ran over the line of scrimmage twice to pass the ball, and all the boys yelled at me. I asked what the line of scrimmage was, so Billy showed me. I practiced until I could throw good passes. Billy's instruction did not stop there. I don't know how many times I swung at the baseball before I could hit it over the fence to satisfy him or aimed at the basketball hoop before I could beat some of the boys in a game of Horse. Uh-oh, I had not learned to race yet. After some false starts, Billy said I needed to practice my timing. Most of the races were done barefoot which not only produced cuts and bruises, but also made our feet tough. We kids went barefoot most of the time to save our shoes. I grew to love playing all the sports, but whenever I beat the boys at school, they got upset. I asked Bill why I had to learn everything. He said, "To know that you can do anything." I did not realize at the time that my brother was preparing me to live in a man's world.

Billy and I wrote plays to entertain the neighborhood. With help from Bobby, Gib, and Art, we built an outdoor stage from old lumber. Occasionally, a neighbor would offer their big porch. We charged a nickel for admission and always drew a big crowd. Billy was very good on the trumpet. He could listen to a piece on the radio and then play it. I sang and danced, while the other boys were the actors in our skit. Grandmother laughed a lot at our skits and clapped as we practiced in the house. It was nice to see her laugh. We also earned money by emptying ash pits into a big cart that we pulled to the dump, a long distance to the other end of town. The ash pits were igloo shaped, made of concrete with a hole in the top where the ashes were dumped and a door at the bottom where we scooped out the ashes with a shovel. It was a dirty, dusty job which paid a dollar. We covered the ashes with canvas to keep them from blowing out as we pulled the cart.

All the kids in town looked forward to Saturday afternoon at the movies that cost a nickel. We saw the serials first. It was either Buck Rogers or Flash Gordon. Buck Rogers traveled around in his rocket ship. He had ray guns and robots. He was out to save America both in a comic strip and in the serials. Flash Gordon led missions to outer space whose ultimate purpose was to save the universe. He had superhuman speed and strength. He also began his escapades in the comic strips. We read the comic strips over and over and over. We pretended to do all the things that we saw. serials were exciting to watch and were the forerunners of Star Wars and Superman. We played a lot of cops and robbers with rubber guns. The rubbers were made from old inner tubes that we mostly picked up on the roads. When I got shot in the legs and arms, it really stung. I told Grandmother I needed to wear pants and shirts like the boys. She just smiled and said girls were not supposed to dress like the boys. I asked my brother if he thought some day we would travel to outer space and have our own rocket ships. He said, "yes, it will all probably happen for us to see."

I was very happy to share the indoor bedroom with June when I was in the fifth grade. Uncle John joined the Marines and Uncle Russ joined the Army. Something else good happened. Miss Tracy, my teacher, encouraged me to sing more. She persuaded my grandmother to support my performing for different organizations in Lafayette and Boulder. I loved our visits in the car and enjoyed the food that was served wherever I sang. Sometimes, I would sing for intermission at the high school concerts and plays. Miss Tracy bought two dresses that were worn only for performances. I loved how I felt when I put them on. On one occasion, Grandmother said I could not go because the sole of my shoe was loose and flapped when I walked. Grandpa was supposed to fix it on the shoe last, but he had forgotten. (His shoe last was a roughly shaped foot form made of iron in which shoes were repaired. It was called a last from the old English word 'laest' which means 'footprint'.) Billy took my shoe, went out to the shed and came back 30 minutes later. By using the shoe last tools, wire and nails, he repaired my shoe and said to Grandmother, "I fixed Patsy's shoe. Now she can go sing." He was always taking care of me, just the way our mother asked him to when she was dying.

Billy was my hero, and I am here today because of him. Our swimming hole was a lake, north of town. One day while swimming, an undertow pulled me down deep, and I was helpless. Because I kidded my friends a lot, none of them believed my call for help when I was able to surface for a second. I tried surfacing again sticking my arms and hands up as far as they would go. Yelling for help only sent water pouring down my throat. Then I felt like I was floating on air. My brother was halfway across the lake and recognized that I was in trouble. He was a fast swimmer and with the help of a friend pulled me from the water. I was unconscious and did not respond. One of the kids ran across the road to a house. A man came running to the lake while another summoned the fire department. I remember how much it hurt to breathe after the firemen used some kind of pump on me (CPR had not been invented). The firemen

Billy and me 1939

congratulated my brother and the man who helped by turning me on my side and hitting me on the back. It was three days before I felt like moving much and a few years before I felt safe in the water again. Later in life, I wondered if that incident could have been one reason for the respiratory problems I encountered.

Moving to Boulder

After finishing fifth grade, Grandmother and Grandpa told us we would be moving to Boulder. It was closer to the coal mine where Grandpa worked. I hated leaving my best friends, Madeline, Arlene, and Anna. I almost cried at the thought of leaving Miss Tracy, my classmates, and friends at church. The house in Boulder was located near to where the Boulder Canyon Road began. There was no big yard or vacant lot where we could play, so we used the street. We stayed out until dark like we had before, playing Kick the Can, Run-Sheep-Run, Red Rover and other games. We were not far from the city ball diamonds so we played ball when they were not in use. One very good thing was that we had hot and cold running water and an indoor bathroom. We were all getting too tall to sit with our legs doubled up in the tin tub, so we were happy for a real bathtub.

I made friends with a girl down the street whose name was Bernice. Her nickname was Brownie. I found out she attended the First Christian Church, so I asked Grandmother if I could go there. Grandmother said that way back a relative had been a pastor of a Christian Church, and she gave her permission. I really enjoyed the Sunday School class. Grandmother taught me to crochet that summer. I made doilies and hot pads. Although Grandmother did not talk much, I enjoyed the time with her. Snow White was playing at the movie theater, and we kids were able to go. During the movie, I began to feel sick with terrible stomach pains that made me vomit. Grandmother fixed some terrible tasting tea and sent me to bed. I woke up during the night feeling much worse, so I went downstairs and called for Grandmother. She gave me more tea and said I could sleep on the couch. I wanted my mother and begged God to send her back to me. I had so much pain that I thought I was going to die, and I did not want to die. I went to the neighbors the next morning to call the doctor. Dr. Jim had removed my tonsils, and I liked him. As I talked with Dr. Jim, he recognized I needed help. When Grandmother found out she was upset because of the cost but agreed to send my brother to pick up some medicine. I began to feel better physically. Even though I knew that Jesus was with me, I had an uneasiness that I did not understand.

I did my work and received good grades, but the teacher could tell something was troubling me. She asked what was wrong, so I told her about my persistent uneasiness, and that Grandmother rarely talked to me. The next week, Miss Condon introduced me to Mrs. Daniels, who was very kind and listened to what I had to say. Her position was like that of a social worker. After two sessions with Mrs. Daniels, she told me there was a doctor who could help me more. Mrs. Daniels had already told Grandmother that I needed extra help. I was introduced to Dr. Conley. She was very pretty and hugged me when we were introduced. The Boulder School District and Boulder County provided help and funds for kids like me. I will be indebted to each for the rest of my life. No one ever mentioned the word psychiatrist in those days because people were said to be crazy if they talked to one. Dr. Conley explained to me that my brain and heart could not hold more trauma. She was careful to identify each big word she used and said that without question, I could be helped. I asked how that could happen. She said it was simple. "We talk together until the fuzz in your brain turns into liquid honey." That sounded good to me, and I remembered something the pastor said about God's Word being like honey. Dr. Conley said that God will certainly play a part in our conversations. I had ten meetings with Dr. Conley. I had pushed down my feelings and buried all the hurt. Dr. Conley and I talked a lot about my feelings and vehicles to help me cope with unpleasant situations. I came to understand my grandmother more. In fact, I learned a lot about human nature, how everyone has problems and so many do not have the ability to cope and overcome what life throws at them. Dr. Conley said because I was so observant, my understanding was beyond my age. I was able to forgive Daddy George. I talked a lot about the people who had helped me. Dr. Conley said she knew I was confident and that I would use the tools and insights gained to help others. I never forgot that and called on God throughout my life to use me in that way. I never saw Dr. Conley again, but I thought about her through the years with gratitude. I cannot say everything from that time on was perfect. Dr. Conley said the old things would rear their head again, and I had to work hard to express my feelings. Some people were still saying that little girls should be seen and not heard. Grandmother began to talk to me and the other kids more. Grandpa even grunted more words to us.

It was not long before we moved again to an apartment complex on Pine Street. I counted 15 steps on the outside even though the front door opened to street level. I had my own bedroom again, for which I was grateful. I became acquainted with Joann who lived next door. We were the same age and became best friends. We walked together up the hill to Mapleton Elementary School. The school building was made of stone which was beautiful, and it was larger than the school in Lafayette. It had a round fire escape. I hoped we would have a fire alarm so I could slide down.

During 6th grade, Miss Condon asked me to lead the songs for music class. Joann and I attended North Side Junior High the next fall. Seventh grade was an adjustment since we passed from class to class, had several different teachers, and the school was very large. Lockers for our coats, books and schoolwork were never locked.

I made new friends in each class. Many of them were boys. I liked playing sports with them and the way they tended to the tasks at hand without gossiping. Billy was a sophomore in high school, and he said I understood boys from being around him and my uncles. I learned to stick up for myself. I learned what made boys tick in different situations, studied their emotions and why they could be preoccupied with girls. They only cussed when Grandmother and Grandpa could not hear them. Once in a while, I would say a cuss word under my breath. I knew I would get whipped with a cane if I said it out loud. I did get tired of hearing that little girls should be seen and not heard.

Mrs. Reilly, our music teacher, asked me to the front of the class to lead a song and said that I would help from then on. During art class one day, I got into trouble. The class was learning to make designs with ink. When Miss Lory left the room, one of the boys decided to roll the roller of ink over my face. Of course, I rolled ink on his face and soon the entire class got involved. Miss Lory put stuff on our faces, and we had to rub the ink off with brown paper—which hurt! Parents wanted to know why our faces were so sore and red when we got home. Even though we got into trouble, I had fun. Several teachers said I had a sense of humor. I did enjoy playing harmless jokes on my friends, and I laughed a lot. I enjoyed Junior High and liked having different teachers for each class. Joann and I studied together. Our favorite place was the roof outside my bedroom window when the weather was nice. Sometimes we crawled out there at night just to look at the stars and share secrets. That summer, Joann and I decided that we would read through the Bible. Every night we crawled onto the roof outside my bedroom window and took turns reading by flashlight when we needed to. After reading, we would discuss what we thought it was about.

Grandmother was not feeling well that summer. She had diabetes, so we pitched in to help more with the chores. I was learning to cook and made my first pie. My brother was the only one who tried to eat a piece because he did not want to hurt my feelings. I had kneaded the dough too long so the crust was like a rock. Joann and I took turns staying overnight and read lots of books. Sometimes we read to each other. Grandmother, Grandpa, and Joann's parents became good friends, and we all got along with our other neighbors. We went fishing and on hikes with the boys. Billy taught me the art of casting, but most of the time I did not catch any fish.

Joann and I were ready to start eighth grade. Except for art, music, and physical education, we had new teachers. I was friends with all the girls, but Jennie and Polly were at the top with Joann. I went to their homes often after school to cut out paper dolls, play games, or just talk. Grandmother even let me attend Saturday movies with Ike, Bud, and Bill, who were good friends among the boys. Sometimes the whole gang would get together to swim or hike. The best hiking place was above Chautauqua where we also watched plays or musical events on the weekend. Other times, we packed lunches and hiked near the mouth of Boulder Canyon, wading in the creek. Boulder had an indoor pool called the Hygienic Swimming Pool. I would stay mostly in the shallow water where I could touch bottom. My friends knew about my fear of deep water and began to encourage me, but not in the way one would think. They said that I was a good swimmer and there was no excuse for me not to jump off the diving board. I did have the courage to jump off the diving board, surface and get to the side—quickly. The next time I was on the diving board the boys followed me on, saying "if you don't swim the length of the pool, we are going to dunk you all the way." And then they pushed me off. I think I broke a speed record swimming to the shallow end. All the kids at the pool cheered. I did swim after that but not with the confidence I once had.

After math class one day, Bud came up to me and said I had blood on the back of my clothes. He was so kind and asked two other boys to walk beside me while he walked behind. We headed to the gym where I could talk to my PE teacher, Miss Collins. She welcomed me into her office where she helped clean me up, gave me a robe, a clean pair of panties, and a pad. Miss Collins explained about menstruation, drove me home, waited while I changed and took me back to school. My grandmother said very little but showed me how to pin strips of sheet to my panties. When I returned to school, I thanked my friends. Bud told me the same thing had happened to his sister. The next semester I was in health class. The Boulder School District had a curriculum designed for eighth graders. Our text was a book titled, *Being Born*. It had illustrations and enhanced our education about the process of being born as well as the proper names of sex organs and a lot of other facts. The teacher handled it in such a way that there was no snickering or "yuk" remarks. I discussed it with my brother, and he said to always watch my behavior and company because he would not always be around to protect me. I observed that he did not always hang around with the right crowd. He said it was different with boys. Right then, I took on the role of "older sister" and let him have it. There were other times in our lives that I became the one to give advice to my older brother, like the time he and my uncles drank too much. I never knew where they got the booze, but after the experiences with Daddy and his drinking, I came down hard on Billy. I told him, for the first time, how Daddy and his friends gave me homemade wine sweetened with honey when I was seven. The wine made me dizzy, and I staggered around while daddy and his friends laughed. I was scared. Mommy gave me crackers and milk and put me to bed. I was sick all night and had no interest in drinking alcohol.

On December 7, 1941, the Japanese attacked Pearl Harbor, and President Roosevelt declared war, joining the Allies against the Axis power in World War II. He said we were in for a long haul. Boulder was a small community, so everyone was acquainted with each other or their families. Boys older than 18 and men of certain ages were drafted into the Army if they had not joined the other branches of service. We glued ourselves to the radio for news every day and night. It wasn't long before we were watching war action on the newsreel at the movies.

The end of school was approaching. All the students were glad. Our summer was full of activities, not just ones that we or our friends planned, but those planned by the church.

Toward the end of summer, Grandmother became very ill. It was not long before that we heard the diagnosis of cancer. Treatment had not advanced since my two mothers died from the same disease. Morphine was used sparingly. Doctors were cautious in administering it because they feared people would become addicted. I was responsible for cooking more meals and all of us kids took turns helping Grandmother. She would become so thirsty and cry out in pain a lot. We cut pieces of ice off the block in our icebox, put them in a dishtowel and pounded them into smaller pieces with a hammer, and gave them to Grandmother. She was always so grateful for those slivers of ice. We also took turns placing cool cloths on her forehead. The time came when she no longer ate. We kids would cover our heads at night trying to drown out her terrible screams of pain. We told Grandpa that he needed to put Grandmother in the hospital, and he finally gave in. While standing at the door as she was carried out by ambulance attendants, Grandmother reached out to touch me and said that she loved me and the boys. We all cried and hoped her pain would get better at the hospital. Billy and I were also remembering when the ambulance came to take our mother away. Grandmother passed away and was buried in Lafayette. Billy and I held hands during the funeral. Neither one of us wanted to remember Grandmother's terrible pain, and we tried not to cry. I thanked God that she was in heaven with her first husband and children.

Before school started, Billy and Bobby joined the Navy. Gib joined the Army. Billy had to have Grandpa's signature because he was not eighteen. June went to live in California. Art, step-Grandpa's youngest son, Grandpa, and I moved to a one-bedroom apartment a few blocks away. Art slept with Grandpa and my bed was on the couch. It was my responsibility to get up at 5:00 a.m., fix Grandpa's breakfast and pack his lunch. On the weekends, I did the laundry in the bathtub on a washboard. Sometimes my knuckles would get sore and bleed after washing the clothes Grandpa wore in the coal mine. My teachers began to ask if I smoked. Of course I did not smoke, but Grandpa was never without his pipe, so my clothes smelled of tobacco.

High School and College

I started the ninth grade in September 1943. Homeroom teachers announced that it was time to elect a head girl and a head boy. I was nominated by several friends which I thought was so nice. All at once, I began to get nasty notes in my locker. I figured out that some of the girls who were from better homes were leaving the notes, because they would make snide remarks in passing. They did not want me to be elected head girl. Some of the bullying notes read, "We know you are probably illegitimate" and "You wear the same two dresses all the time." "Why don't you ever wash your hair?" "There is no way you will be elected head girl so you may as well give up. " "Most of the kids in school hate you and the teachers think you are pitiful." The notes kept coming and because I remembered what Reverend Brown said, I began to pray for the girls who wrote them. My friend, Jennie, happened to see a couple of the notes and took them to her mother. Mrs. Jenkins brought them to the principal, and I was summoned to his office. Mr. Jackson wanted to know about the other notes. He told me to please ignore them and not pay attention to unkind words. He added that sometimes girls do mean things when they are jealous. He sent a note to the teachers who talked to all of us about good conduct and manners relating to the campaign. The girls poured on the dirty looks and remarks after that, but they did not leave any more notes. The day came for my speech along with the others who were running for head girl and head boy. My speech brought a standing ovation. I was elected by a large margin. The girls who had treated me so poorly sucked up to me after that. So much for jealousy and dirty politics!

Foster Care

One night in October, Grandpa asked me to get in bed with him after Art fell asleep. I said no, that if he touched me I would tell everyone including the police. I knew Jesus was with me, but I did not sleep much that night thinking that any moment Grandpa would come to the couch. I did know where to hit and kick him if it happened. Billy had taught me how to defend myself. I told my best friend, Joann, what had happened. When she told her parents, they said Grandpa was too nice and would never do anything like that. That next day, I told my friend, Polly, who invited me to her house after school. Mrs. Bee, Polly's mother, questioned me further about Grandpa and said she believed me. She advised me not to spend another night in the apartment but to sleep at their house. When I explained I had to get Grandpa's breakfast, fix his lunch, and pack lunch for Art and me, she promised to wake me early enough to do all those things. I told Grandpa that I would never sleep in the apartment again. I was so grateful to Polly and Mrs. Bee. Two weeks afterward, Art and I came home from school and found that we were alone. Grandpa left a note saying he had moved to Wyoming and that we were on our own. We had no money and only a small amount of food in the ice box and cupboard. Mrs. Green, the landlady, said we could stay for one week. After that, she had to rent the apartment. Art and I told our homeroom teachers and on Sunday, I planned to share our predicament with my Sunday School teacher. Before Sunday rolled around, my homeroom teacher, Miss Bell, asked me to go home with her. I was happy that Art found a home with some friends.

So began my short time with Miss Bell. I shall forever be grateful to her for the kindness, guidance, food, comfortable bed, and the clothes she purchased for me. I went to visit her through the years until she passed away. I also stayed with Mrs. Anderson, the school secretary. After three weeks, I was summoned to the principal's office where Mr. Jackson introduced me to Miss Mollinger, the District Nurse, who told me that I needed a more stable home instead of moving around. I said, "Does that mean I will be put in an orphanage?" To my relief, she said no. I would be going to a foster home. After a meeting with a social worker, I was off to the home of Mrs. Werner. I liked her immediately. She was caring for Jimmy, seven years old, and a 6-month-old baby named Bonnie. I loved children and assisted Mrs. Werner in their care. The first week of my stay, Mrs. Werner told me to invite friends over for games and dancing. Her living room had a wood floor that was perfect for dancing. We kids at Northside Junior High were fortunate. Miss Collins and Mr. Lefferdink, our physical education teachers, taught us all kinds of dancing. Dancing would become a lifetime pleasant activity for me.

My Sunday School teacher, Mrs. Gillstrap, was happy that I had a nice foster mother. She had heard how I helped out with the children and asked if I would be willing to teach a first-grade Sunday School class. I was delighted to respond positively. I poured over the materials and songs and called to tell Joann. We were still reading through the Bible which helped me a lot. The next thing I knew, Mrs. Gamble, the choir director at church, asked me to sing in the adult choir. It was not long before I was singing solos at church again. I felt so close to God and knew He was leading me BY HIS HAND.

Helen Pease, one of my friends, told me that her neighbors inquired about me. Helen said that Hap and Mae Watkins had never had children. They knew about my background and were interested in meeting me. Since they attended First Christian Church, they had seen me and heard me sing. A time was arranged with my foster mother, and on a Friday after school, Helen and I rang Hap and Mae's doorbell. When we stepped through the door, many of my friends were there yelling, "Happy Fifteenth Birthday." I stood there in total shock. I could not imagine someone who had never met me doing something so kind. My mind raced trying to remember the last time I had a birthday party. We all had a great time eating ice cream and cake while I opened my gifts. After my friends left, Hap and Mae said they wanted me to come live with them. They had a small, beautiful house with two bedrooms. As they showed me the bedrooms, they identified the second bedroom as theirs but said if I would like to have that one, they would move into the front one. I was having difficulty taking it all in. They also said that if I did not want to stay with them after a period of two weeks, I could return to Mrs. Werner's. I was overwhelmed with Hap and Mae's kindness and selflessness. I had been with Mrs. Werner for two months. She did not want me to leave but agreed that a home atmosphere with two parents would be advantageous for me. It was difficult to leave Mrs. Werner, Jimmy, and Bonnie. I hugged each several times.

Hap drove up in a green Plymouth sedan. He put my suitcase in the trunk and opened the passenger door for me. I was moving again! At dinner time, we talked about school and what my future plans entailed. I shared that I wanted to be a doctor or a teacher. They emphasized that I was home, and they expected me to stay with them through college. They had a parrot called Polly. I walked to her cage and stroked her under the chin. Hap and Mae were amazed because Polly offered to bite everyone else. I taught her to whistle "Yankee Doodle." She would say, "Polly wants a cracker." She could pronounce her P's quite well. However, Polly called me Yahtzee. When I was doing homework, she would yell, "Yahtzee", drawing it out. Usually, I would take her into the bedroom, cover her cage and close the door. I could still hear a faint call of Yahtzee. Each time I returned Polly to the living room and uncovered her cage, she would place her bill under a wing and say in a low voice, "Polly's a bad bird."

I went to a lot of social dances the rest of the year and made many new friends. I played pool at Polly's, went ice skating, to the movies and on lots of hikes, played ball, attended the boys' basketball games, and read the Bible with Joann. My girl friends and I would stop by the drug store to get a cherry Coke every Friday after school. We would plan what we wanted to do over the weekend. John and Gene came to my house to do homework during the week. Joann and I stayed overnight at each other's homes nearly every weekend. We continued reading through the Bible. I loved teaching my Sunday School class. On Easter Sunday, April 25, 1943, I accepted Jesus as my Savior and was baptized.

Hap announced that with so many friends, I needed more room. He and two of his friends dug out a basement room. They hauled the dirt with a wheelbarrow and dumped it in the alley for another friend to haul away. The men worked hard. The room was perfect and also got us kids out of Hap and Mae's hair. It was not unusual for five or six kids to come over to do homework together during the week in that basement or to hang out with popcorn and games on the weekends. I was so appreciative for that wonderful gift. Hap and Mae continued to show their love and concern for me in many ways.

Mrs. Grey called one afternoon to ask if I could stay with her son, Kyle, Friday after school and all day Saturday while she was at work. She had called some adults, but everyone was busy with their own families, plus many women were working as their husbands were in the military. Her son was a classmate of mine and he suggested me because he knew I was trustworthy and would not tell other kids at school. Hap and Mae called and asked her to come visit. She explained that her son had been circumcised and needed to stay in bed for two days. Hap and Mae agreed, and I did my best to make Kyle comfortable as I tended to his needs. I also read to him and helped with his homework. We played guessing games and listened to the radio. While he napped, I took a walk or did my homework. When he did not like the scrambled egg sandwich I fixed, I told him my brother had put ketchup on his. That was successful and he asked for another one. Kyle told me I was an excellent nurse.

In May, we kids added another activity to our busy schedule. We collected paper for the paper drive. It was a program launched by the British Government to encourage recycling materials to aid the war effort. The paper was used sometimes to make war posters.

My friends, Jennie, Ed, Reese, Nancy, Dolly, Mike and Jean agreed to collaborate on writing a play for the end of school. It was the story of a poor girl who had a lot of bad luck but ended up successful on Broadway. We took each page and idea to our English teacher who helped us a lot. We incorporated lots of singing and dancing, enlisting help for additional actors and stage crew. The musical had three acts. Several students built stage sets and operated spot lights. The kids insisted that I take the leading role. We performed the musical for the entire school, again and on the weekend for the community. Both performances received standing ovations. I thought it might be fun to become a playwright.

My Uncle John came to see us. Home on leave from the Marines, he came to find out if I was all right. For the first day, Hap and Mae were concerned that he would want to take me to California where his wife and baby lived. We spent a lot of time talking. Uncle John took me shopping and purchased several clothing items for me. He was pleased that I had such a good home, lots of friends and that I loved being with Hap and Mae. When he left, we hugged tightly, and he said how proud he was of me.

Hap tried to interest me in playing the accordion, but I had wanted to play the piano for years. Even though the living room was small, he purchased a tall, black upright piano. I had my first piano lesson at 15.

I enrolled for second-year Latin in summer school, which enabled me to take additional music classes in the fall. I went from Latin class to my new job at the Kress Five & Dime Store. Every new employee had to start in the pots and pans division. By the time school started, I had worked my way up to the candy counter and got a free piece of candy each day plus my 50-cent-per-hour pay. I also got a job cleaning a large two-story house on Saturday for Mrs. Malm. I found out she taught voice, so I traded some of my pay for voice lessons. I think because of that Mrs. Malm worked me hard. She had a son named Carl who was a real drip. He didn't want much moved in his room. When I cleaned it, I promised not to tell anyone what I saw. One of my friends, Rene, began voice lessons with Mrs. Malm. She suggested that we sing a duet on one of the floats for the Boulder Pow Wow. We had fun practicing and making cowgirl outfits. Later, when Rene and I gave a recital, I began to have some trouble with my throat. I managed to sing the recital but had to rest my voice for a while.

Home on leave from the Army, Uncle Russell came to see me. Like Uncle John, he was pleased to find me so well taken care of. Uncle Russ was a paratrooper destined for Burma. Shortly after his visit, Uncle Gib and Uncle Bob showed up at the Kress Store where I worked. They would be leaving with their outfits soon. I appreciated my uncles who were interested enough to check up on me. Billy came to tell me goodbye as he had been assigned to a carrier in the South Pacific. It was difficult to see him go. I prayed daily for my uncles and brother to be kept safe.

All communities had air raid practice and many built concrete bunkers below ground for safety in case our country was attacked. Watching what was happening in Europe on the newsreels at the theater gave upfront views of the terrible bombings, destroyed buildings and lost lives. We continued the paper drives for the war effort. During the war, everyone was issued ration books. Meat, cooking oil, sugar and canned goods were rationed. The Japanese cut off imports from the Philippines, and cargo ships from Hawaii were diverted to military purposes. Gas was rationed, mostly to keep drivers home because Japan had cut off rubber supplies from the Far East. Families were allowed four gallons per week of gasoline if they could prove they did not own more than five tires. Gas was not issued without a windshield sticker signifying family, truck driver, or doctor. Butter was rationed. We received a brick of white stuff. In the package was a bead of yellow coloring. We punctured the bead, poured it over the white stuff which was like lard and mixed it with our hands. It was the color of butter but did not taste like it! Silk was also rationed because it was used in the manufacturing of parachutes. No more silk stockings! Someone invented liquid leg makeup that did a fair job of looking like stockings. After it was rubbed on, we girls helped each other draw the straight, black line up the back. All hose had that line up the back. The leg makeup served its purpose unless you got caught in the rain, which created a streaky mess.

Every high school student and many in the community were upset when our Japanese friends were interned in prison camps. They were loyal Americans! The only thing we could do was travel to their camp in the eastern plains of Colorado to visit them and speak words of encouragement through the fence where they were housed. America lost 500,000 lives before the war was over, and six million Jews were murdered by the Germans.

Years later, my husband and I, along with some family members, visited the Dachau concentration camp in Germany. It was difficult to believe that such atrocities occurred. We were all silent as we visited the barracks where experiments and torture took place, and the gas chambers and ovens where so many innocent people were killed because of their nationality. There were pictures of shoes and clothing at the huge grave sites where bodies were dumped and covered. As we approached the exit from Dachau, we began to weep and pray that this atrocity would never happen again.

It was time for summer vacation. There was swimming, tennis, roller skating, movies, church youth group, hikes, and picnics, as well as Chautauqua shows and mountain drives with Hap and Mae. We also went to Bennett's dude ranch on vacation (no connection to my Bennett family). I rode a swell horse named Speedy every day. Rene came with us, and Speedy passed her horse in every race.

All the summer events came to an end. It was time to start high school. Sophomores were ordered to bow down to the nude Art Deco bas-relief sculptures of the Greek gods "Wisdom and Strength" found at the top of the school entrance and nicknamed by the students as Minnie and Jake. I could not believe that previous students voted for them instead of a swimming pool. I was a muddy mess after the sophomore girls were initiated, as we had to perform athletic feats in the mud, such as racing and throwing balls. The next week, I was selected to be in the Cubs, the high school pep club, and was also elected a council member.

I was in the a cappella choir and the girls chorus. My throat grew tired after singing all period, and the director said I should not be clearing it so much. He recommended that I seek medical advice. After an examination by the family physician, I was sent to a specialist in Longmont who gave me two options: surgery, which might destroy any singing ability, or treatments. After talking with Hap and Mae, I chose the treatments. Once a week for seven weeks, I sat with packed sinuses and throat in front of radiated heat. Besides the feeling that I was choking, the heat was very intense. I was concerned about my brain being affected and asked God for that protection. As always, He held me throughout those seven weeks. During and after treatment, I refrained from yelling at any games and had to stop indoor roller skating. I was to stay away from anything that would cause irritation, which was very difficult. I could still participate in the choirs half the period if I did not strain my voice. By second semester, my condition improved as I proceeded with caution. Grateful to God, by spring I was able to participate in the school musical. I never again yelled in full voice at any athletic events.

During my sophomore year, my cousin, Ronald, contacted me. Since he was related on my father's side, I had never met him. After getting acquainted, he asked if I would like to meet my fraternal grandmother. Hap and Mae gave permission. My grandmother and grandfather migrated from Kentucky in covered wagons, stopping to homestead in Longmont. Their first home was on Atwood Street with their twelve children. Three died in infancy. They later moved near the saloon they owned at the corner of Ninth and Main. Grandmother was four feet ten inches tall, cute as a button, and tough as nails. She kept a shotgun close by to practice shooting rattle snakes that she nailed from a long distance. Grandfather had died before I was born. Grandmother remarried and operated a grocery store after selling the saloon. Two years later when my boyfriend met her, he declared that he was going to marry into a family of midgets. I met some of my aunts and uncles and Ronald's sister, Shirley. I enjoyed seeing them several times, but unfortunately both Ronald and Shirley died from cancer in their thirties.

Grandma Bennett

First Boyfriend

I had been dating different boys for movies, bowling and other activities. Of course, the parents dropped us off and picked us up after night dates. Even when we attended the midnight movie, parents were gracious about picking us up. Some students were allowed to drive their parents' cars. We usually walked everywhere, even in snowstorms. On my sixteenth birthday, Ray asked to take me to a dance. He was a swell junior, quite handsome and an athlete. My friend, Neva, was dating Tommy. Judy was dating Dick. We three couples triple dated for practically every event and especially enjoyed picnics near Estes Park. We had great times together, but I was not too fond of Tommy (I thought he was conceited and a ladies man). Hap and Mae told me they liked Ray a lot and trusted me to go to out-of-town events with him. Our favorite places were Elitches in Denver, the Jitney Dance Hall for Teens in Longmont, Eldorado Springs, Estes Park, or driving around with friends. Occasionally, we dared to drive up to the old Goat Lady's place that was shrouded in mystery. Boulder was a small town—around 12,000 population, not counting university students. We knew practically everyone in town or at least whose family they belonged to. Lots of kids still gathered at my home for games and food, and we would go in numbers to movies or to get hamburgers. One of the best places in town was the Alba Dairy where we downed delicious thick malts that cost ten cents.

Joann, Helen, Rene, Wanda, Becky, Doris, Neva, Naomi, Jean, Lilly, and many more girlfriends palled around and spent overnight together. Sometimes, Ray, Tommy and Dick would come over to play cards or the four of us would ride around. In March, all students were invited to a free movie in celebration of the 1943 State Championship Football Team. Two days later, students got out of school again because of a bad snowstorm. Several of us ended up playing in the snow all afternoon. We built a fort and had a war with snowballs while the snow was still whirling down. It took a long time to get out of my wet clothes. Hap and Mae thought I would get a cold. Every time I was sick, Hap would bring garlic cloves to me. That was his cure for almost everything. I liked garlic in food, and was especially fond of Kosher dills, but I did not like it raw. Most of the time, I would chew it a little, drop it under the bed and throw it away when Hap wasn't looking.

During my sophomore year, I was invited to attend the annual conference of delegates from high school councils in the state. The main topic was how to improve our schools. It was held at Colorado A & M College in Fort Collins. There was a banquet and dance on the last night. It was a fun evening since I already knew a few of the Fort Collins students from athletic events. A few days after the conference, I sang a song in the vaudeville contest and won the cup, which was very exciting.

I sent for my birth certificate so I could get my driver's license. To my surprise and others, my name was Alice Marie. My mother had liked Patsy better than Alice (her middle name was Alice), so she called me Patsy. Everyone in the family assumed my name was Patricia, and when I lived with Reatha and George they had me sign their last name on my school records, Patsy Caldwell. Later, everyone knew me as Patsy Bennett. When I enrolled in college, I used my legal name as Alice Marie Bennett, but no one ever called me Alice. Sometimes it was confusing to others.

I was active in the Girl Reserves at school. The Dean of Women was our sponsor and provided some wonderful guidance and programs for us. Girl Reserves stressed being gracious in manner, impartial in judgment, dependable, sincere, eager for knowledge, and having a reverence for God. I made some wonderful new friends in that group. Hap and Mae let me know that they could not enlarge the house anymore.

Ray's brother belonged to the Sigma Nu Fraternity on campus. We went to a formal dance there which was such fun. The band was swell, and Ray looked handsome in his tux. The next evening, we joined some other kids at the movies and on Sunday, Ray went to youth group at church with me. He had been backing out, but became a regular after we began dating.

A marker had never been put on my mother's grave in Longmont, so I saved money to purchase one. Between my job at the Kress Store, cleaning houses, and babysitting, I soon had enough. Hap, Mae, and I went to visit my mother's grave with flowers. The marker was beautiful, and I was so pleased that we could now identify her burial plot. Each time I visited, I remembered how beautiful she was and how much she loved Billy and me.

On June 6, 1944, the invasion in Europe began. We were all on pins and needles, praying for victory so our military men and women and those of our allies could put an end to the war and go home. The media and photographers spared nothing in the current events which made us all feel sick in the pit of our stomachs while watching the newsreels at the theater or reading Life Magazine. On the cover of one Life Magazine was my Uncle Gib with helmet off, smoking a cigarette, resting until his unit was ordered to advance. His facial expression told the story of war. The invasion marked the beginning of intense fighting that lasted for nearly another year before Germany surrendered. I continued to pray for the safety of my brother and uncles who were fighting in Europe and the South Pacific.

After visiting Mother's grave, Ray, Tommy and Dick came over. We played cards and worked on puzzles. Mae decided to fix a waffle supper for us. I could not believe how much those three boys ate and still devoured a large dish of ice cream and cake. After that, the four of us piled into the front seat of a Model A owned by one of our friends. It was a fad to see how many bodies we could squeeze into the front seat of a car and still drive it. I was on the floor and pressed the gas pedal with my hand. Tom had the longest arms, so he steered. Marie, who was on the floor with me, operated the brake. The other kids who could see out the windows were lookouts and gave directions which way to turn or when to stop and go. My feelings about Tommy did not change that much, but I liked his folks a lot. Mrs. Nix would always thank me and compliment me after I sang solos for church.

It was time for the prom. Ray gave me a corsage of white and pink carnations with a huge gardenia. I was very fragrant all evening. Joann's brother, Don, had been killed in the war. When the band played, "I'll Be Home for Christmas", I joined Joann in the hall where we held each other and wept. Ray and Joann's date joined us, wrapped their arms around us and shed tears, too.

My favorite player on the basketball team was Lilly Mae. We scored a lot of points together and became fast friends for life. Lilly was from one of the three black families in town. I was friendly with everyone at school and gave no attention to the color of their skin or how they worshipped. I knew God expected that of me. At lunch the next day, Gale announced that she was having a slumber party. As she began to rattle off who was invited, I was among them. She further announced that Lilly was not welcome because she was black. I stood up with my tray, glanced down the long table and said if Lilly was not invited than I would not come. Seven other girls, including Lilly, joined me at another table. Wow! That caused some angry words, snide remarks and hateful stares. Most came from the same girls who had written the nasty notes to me in junior high school.

The time drew near for church camp at Sylvan Dale Ranch. The ranch was located along the Big Thompson River outside of Loveland—a perfect setting. Youth from Disciples of Christ churches across Colorado attended, with a few from Wyoming. There were twelve from our church. Neva and I rode up with Harry, Wendell, Bob and Joe. My cabin mates were great. Our camp director was a gentleman we addressed as Daddy Dobbs. I sang for vespers and especially enjoyed Morning Watch. I wrote some poetry while outside in God's beautiful country. After classes, we rode horses, played games and shopped at the Dam Store. During free time, Joe, Harry, Neva and I went on a hike. The last night began with a banquet, followed by consecration and the friendship circle. God was alive and present during those times. I was elected secretary for next year. I delivered pictures from youth camp to my friends, including Joe Nix, Tommy Nix's younger brother. Mrs. Nix invited me in and asked me to stay for dinner.

The Nixes had moved from their home on University Hill to an acreage in North Boulder. Before preparing dinner, we sang a lot of songs. Mrs. Nix was a wonderful pianist and loved to sing alto. I was peeling potatoes when Tommy came home. He untied my apron string which irritated me because I still did not like him very much. After dinner, the family and I gathered around the piano and sang some more. Mr. Nix had a ten-chair barber shop on University Hill close to where they had lived. But their move gave them room for the horses and Tommy's egg business. Mr. Nix also had a herd of Hereford cattle that were pastured in Superior. Joe was a class behind me and more like a little brother.

My junior year in high school was about to begin. It was September 1944. I helped register the seniors, juniors, and sophomores. After Ray registered, he was quite indifferent. Perhaps he was upset with the song I wrote for him about his acting like a baby, never on time, and the way he ignored me. I had just sung it for a contest and took second place. That night Dick and Tommy came over and invited me to the movie. Mae asked about Ray. Dick said Ray did not want to come. I knew our nine months of dating was coming to an end.

After youth group on Sunday, Tommy was waiting to give me a ride home. He asked me for a date, and I told him I was not sure I liked him. Two days later at school, Tommy asked me for a date again and asked if I would at least give him a chance. I said O.K. The next weekend we went dancing at the Jitney in Longmont. He was a great dancer, and we had a lot of fun. He was a perfect gentleman. The next Monday, Tommy was waiting after my first class to walk me to the next one. We had another date for the movies. After six dates, I asked Tommy why he had not tried to hold my hand, and he said he respected me too much. Well, I thought maybe he was all right after all. I enjoyed being treated with such respect. I was elected to the Junior Council and became the secretary. I enjoyed working with the students and both Deans of Students.

Dick and Pat, and Tommy and I double-dated to movies, hayrides, swimming, and hikes. Tommy and Dick were best friends, and the two of them were always pulling shenanigans. They were hilarious. Pat and I never knew what to expect from them. It was nice to see that side of Tommy. Pretty soon, the catty girls were saying that they would cause a breakup between Tommy and me. Golly gee, I wondered when those girls would get tired of being mean. I began praying for them again. I still hung out with the guys and gal friends I had since junior high. We went to the football games and to get hamburgers afterward. Tommy played end on the team. Tommy's parents chaperoned some school dances. I enjoyed visiting with them. That weekend, I had a date with Eddy who was a barrel of fun. The kids who went with us told dumb jokes and we laughed ourselves silly. We had fun riding around and got talked into playing a game of Ditch 'Em where you try to hide from another car. Eddy gunned the motor and off we went through an alley and up the street. Then he parked the car on a dark street, and the other kids went driving by without noticing us. We won! I was glad it ended because it was a dangerous game, and I thanked Eddy for not going wild with his driving. The next day, Hap and Mae said they heard that some of the kids played Ditch 'Em and spoke about what could happen if a tire blew out while going fast with a carload of kids. That did it for me. I had visions of a wrecked car and injured bodies. I never got in a car again when Ditch 'Em was mentioned. Mrs. Nix asked if I would like to write a letter to their daughter, Mary Jane, who was a Lieutenant serving in the Army Nurse Corp. She had been overseas a long time. I was delighted to write to her.

Our choral director scheduled the a cappella choir to sing for the two junior highs in town. It was wonderful to see my junior high teachers, especially those who were so kind to me. Most of the athletes were in the choir, so Tommy asked me for another date. We went to the movie. When we came out, Tommy's truck was gone. Dick and Pat, D.D. and Bill, Tom and I went to the police station to get his truck. Tommy had parked in a "No Parking Zone." He did not have enough money to pay the fine so the rest of us chipped in. We teased and teased him for two days and someone spread it around school. So, he got teased some more. He received a little of his own medicine because he was such a big tease.

Uncle Russ married a lovely woman named Betty. He was stationed at Buckley Field in Denver, so I was able to see them often. I got a letter from Billy, the first in two months. I was glad to hear that he was okay. He bought War Bonds with some of his pay and sent them to me for safe keeping.

Practice for "The Messiah" began. There were usually over 200 voices which made it a thrilling experience. Our Triple Trio continued to perform throughout the state and for local events. I also sang for several community groups, assemblies at school, weddings, and for church services.

Bill Come Home on Leave

Our girls' basketball team beat the seniors in a tournament. Hap and Mae were at every game, and I could hear Hap yelling at the top of his voice. He was hoarse for two days. Our high school held a lot of dances, and I loved dancing with Tommy. (Sometimes the kids would clear the floor just for us.) When we got home, Bill was there. It had been over two years since we had seen each other.

Bill home on leave, 1944

We stayed up half the night talking. He had a 30-day leave which made me very happy. Bill went with Tommy and me to Christian Endeavor. Afterward, he, Tommy and I drove to Lafayette to see old friends. That was a real treat, especially for Bill. On the way home, Bill and I talked about the time we lived in Lafayette. We spoke about having one bike to share with three uncles. We took turns riding it and especially enjoyed going fast over a place we called the "Lindy Loop" which was rutty and had small hills. We laughed about how the boys took advantage of me being the only girl.

Our first basketball game of the season was with Manuel High School from Denver. Tommy was going for a layup when one of Manuel's players bit him. Tommy almost took a swing at him, but the ref blew the whistle and called a foul on the kid. Tommy came out of the locker room after the game sporting four stitches.

Getting to Know Tommy

The next school day, Tommy asked if he could walk me to class. I thought he meant one class, and he showed up at each one. I told Tommy I would go to the movies with him, Dick and Pat. Walking me to class became a habit for Tommy. Most of the time, I liked being around him. It would be another two weeks before he reached for my hand to walk down the halls. I sort of liked it, so I did not discourage him. Tommy even picked me up for school sometimes which was a good deal during the cold weather.

Uncle Bob came home on leave, so he and Bill chummed around and went on several dates with girls they had known. We were all invited to the Nixes for

Tommy age 3

dinner a few times, and I became more fond of the entire family, including Tommy. He had just spent $200 on chickens. He got up early every morning to take care of the chickens and milk the cow. His egg business was very successful. Girls at school made no bones telling me that when they dated Tommy, he spent money on them. I thought, *La-dee-dah*! My interest was in what made Tommy tick! Art also came home on leave. I was so happy to see him. We had fun finding civilian clothes for Bill, Bob, and Art to borrow while their uniforms were laundered or cleaned.

Tom, Dad, Mom, Mary Jane, Joe

Hap and Mae let me have the car on my next date with Tommy. Besides going to a party, we spent a lot of time talking. I wanted to know more about him. We drove out to Baseline Lake and walked along the shore before going home. The moonlight was bright, and our conversation was good. I found out how devoted Tommy was to his family. I also found out that he lacked confidence in himself. He felt he did not measure up. I began to encourage him whenever I could. Our dating was rocky from time to time as I tried to understand Tommy's moodiness. Whenever we had arguments, I accepted dates with Eddy which did not set too swell with Tommy. We did triple date with Bill, Bob, and their dates on several occasions which we enjoyed. December of 1944 rolled around, and time drew near for Bill, Bob and Art to leave. It was wonderful having them home. Hap and Mae along with the Nixes were so kind to provide lodging, food, entertainment and fun evenings while they were on leave. It was difficult to say goodbye. I shed a few tears and Bill said to remember it was O.K. to cry.

Tommy and I sang in the "Messiah," went to the Christmas dance at school, CE party, and on several dates with groups of friends. Hap, Mae and I were invited to the Nixes for Christmas Eve. We had a wonderful meal and enjoyed singing carols around the piano. I went home with several nice gifts including a stuffed Panda Bear from Tommy. I pretended it was Tommy as I kissed it good night. That was nothing new because I kissed my pillow at night pretending it was John Payne—a tall, dark, handsome movie star. Before we returned to school in January, Tommy and I went to movies, put puzzles together, danced at the Dark Horse Inn at Estes Park, and went with his dad to feed the cattle. As Tommy and his dad checked on each one, I listened to their conversation, trying to learn the lingo. I made a big mistake and called one a bull heifer [a bull is male; a heifer is female]. I never lived that comment down as Tommy and his dad delighted sharing my mistake with others. I checked out a book from the library about cattle and did not make another mistake!

Tom and Patsy 1944

Tommy and I practiced for the Christmas Pageant at church. He never took an active part in our youth group before, so it was nice to have him participate. The next week after the pageant, the Nixes had a party. We visited and drank hot chocolate around the fireplace. I really liked Mr. and Mrs. Nix and was enjoying Tommy's company more and more. Tommy came to see me twice at work the next day. The second time he asked me to go dancing at the Jitney in Longmont. We only sat out one dance to get a drink and had a whale of a time. We went to a New Year's Eve party at Billy Jean's. Afterward, Tom asked if I would wear his football. The State Championship Football Team players were all given gold footballs that could be worn as a necklace or on a key chain. I was thrilled with Tommy's gesture. I bought a chain at work and had the store deduct it from my pay.

Tom's parents had a cabin near Nederland. They invited me for a weekend. The cabin had three bedrooms, a large kitchen/dining area, a potbelly stove, and a huge fireplace. We had fun dancing to music played on the phonograph, playing cards and tobogganing down a steep hill, careening across the lake at the bottom. Our speed across the lake was very fast and we had to lean way over, more than once, to miss the trees as we shot off the lake into the woods.

On New Year's Day 1945, Hap and Mae had several guests for dinner. Tommy asked if he could read some of my diary. I didn't think much would interest him, especially the silly and serious girl talk, but I agreed. After several pages, Tom commented about how many friends I had, especially boyfriends. Of course, I explained that most of the boys were just friends. I giggled because he acted jealous. Back to school on January 2, I was anxious for basketball season and a whole raft of other activities. The school voted for attributes that different students possessed. Tommy was voted as having the best personality in his class and being the best athlete. I was voted as having the best personality in my class. All the students were gearing up for semester tests. They were not held before Christmas vacation because there was too much going on. It was a real bummer.

Going Steady

Mrs. Nix invited me to the Stock Show in Denver. Tom, Joe, and Mr. Nix were showing some of their Hereford cattle. What an experience! I stayed with Tommy most of the time and nearly froze as the cattle had to be groomed in outdoor pens that were packed with snow. The only heat I felt was from their breath. Mrs. Nix commented that it seemed bad weather showed up every year during the National Western Stock Show and Rodeo. It was my first rodeo. Afterward, my hope was that none of my future children would be interested in the rodeo circuit, especially bull riding. Two days later, Tommy asked me to go steady. My answer was "Yes."

Tom and Patsy 1945

On January 22, 1945, Hap became very ill. The family doctor thought something was wrong with his spleen. After visiting a specialist, Hap was diagnosed with Aplastic Anemia which was not good news. He received two blood transfusions the next week and felt better. I was praying for God to heal him. I even asked God if I was a jinx because of my mom, Reatha, and grandmother all dying. Hap was one brave man and rarely complained. One could see the blood preparing to ooze through his skin. The transfusions kept him alive while we all prayed for a breakthrough. Mr. Nix had begun to buy old homes and remodel them on the weekend or when he could break away from the barber shop. One purchase was an old antique house. It was filled with antiques from top to bottom that no one claimed. Mr. Nix enlisted Hap's help which was a blessing. Hap worked at his own speed and came home feeling like he had accomplished something. The doctors believed that lead from paint caused his illness, probably because his work had been repairing and painting cars. Hap continued having transfusions every week.

I had two birthday parties for my 17th birthday. On March 2, several of my friends organized a huge get-together. Their folks fixed such good food, and all the kids had a hilarious time eating and playing games. The Nixes had a dinner party on my birthday, March 3. Hap and Mae were able to come, plus some other friends and adults. Tommy's sister, Mary Jane, was still an Army nurse in the South Pacific. She sent me a doll and a defense stamp book. I received other nice gifts plus a beautiful heart-shaped necklace from Tommy. Later, I had it engraved with both our names on it.

The Boulder High School boys' basketball team was picked to win the state championship. Every conference game was exciting. Tommy remarked about his bird legs. I hollered out at one game, "Come on bird legs!" Soon the entire pep club and kids were yelling the same. After the game, Tommy made me promise I would not do that again, so I called him "Peaches." He had several boys calling me "Wiggles." I tried to walk very straight without wiggling my hips, but it was not worth the trouble. I usually rode to out-of-town games with the Nixes and Tom rode back home with us. I stayed with Uncle Russ and Aunt Betty during the state tournament. We lost the first game by two points to Manuel High School. Everyone had tears in their eyes. That loss threw us into the consolation bracket. The Pep Club and everyone from Boulder filled the rafters with cheers during the next two games as the team fought their way back. Tommy's play during the tournament was outstanding. He was elected by his teammates to accept the trophy. Later, he presented it to the school on behalf of the team. After the school dance, a bunch of us attended the midnight movie. That was the only time we were allowed to stay out late. Most of the time, I was home by 10:00. Hap had a clock collection. He had built a shelf in the family room to hold them. Of course, Tommy and I waited on the porch until 10 p.m. was straight up. The minute I stepped in the door, the clocks began banging and chiming. I could hear Hap's laugh from the bedroom every time. He synchronized the clocks so I would hear bang, bang, ding, ding, ting-a-ling-a-ling, gong, gong, etc. If I didn't make it to my bedroom by the last ding, I was in trouble.

Tommy continued to attend church and CE every Sunday. I sat in the balcony with Tommy and a group of friends when the choir was not singing. One Sunday morning, we were passing notes and got the giggles. Rev. Link stopped the sermon and said, "When the young people in the balcony are quiet, I will continue with the sermon." Yikes! *Wah Nah!* Every head from downstairs turned to look up at us. We all felt like hiding under the pews. After that, only a few notes passed between us, and we were careful not to laugh out loud. We thought our parents would have a *cable*, but they never said a word. I guess they figured the embarrassment we felt was enough.

Every year, the youth group looked forward to our weekend at Hewe's Kirkwood Inn which was located on the back side of Long's Peak. The weather was perfect. Cold and snowy! I shared devotions and led our singing the next two nights. Some of each day was spent with Bible study, discussion and planning ministries. Part of it was packed with ice skating, sledding, tobogganing and snowball fights. Later, the warm fireplace was a welcome sight.

Hap and Mae were a source of encouragement to me. Whatever I wanted to do or whatever I was involved in, they were right there to support and cheer me on. Mae said that the world was waiting for me because I had something important to offer. She said that my kindness, desire to help others and my sense of humor blessed others and God. I knew that I had been blessed by God, and He had a strong presence within me. I felt like God led me BY HIS HAND all the way as He continued to prompt me with that inner voice. Hap and Mae put up with friends gathering at our home, girlfriends spending overnight practically every weekend, my endless activities and fun times with my friends—and countless dates with Tommy.

My class was leading in the paper drive again. I had a lead in the Spring Operetta, so much of my time was occupied with rehearsals. Tommy and I spent as much time together as we could. By now, I knew that I was in love with him. I was taken by his sense of humor, honesty and how he respected me. We had great times together along with some good arguments. I balked when he became a little overly possessive and the moodiness would set in. I liked the way Mr. and Mrs. Nix stuck up for me. I really fell in love with them first.

Our school was saddened by a classmate's death. He had been killed in an automobile accident. Our triple trio sang for his service. It was the first time I sang for a funeral, and I was to sing for countless others throughout my life.

A shadow hung over our school whenever someone in our community, especially one of our friends, was killed in the war. Every week, I wrote letters to my brother and uncles. I also penned some to Tom's sister, Mary Jane, as I prayed for all to return safely home. The newsreels at the theater were as graphic as ever. I was so grateful that we did not have to run from bombs or experience the destruction of our country. At our council meeting after school, we discussed other ways we could help out with the war effort. Time was drawing near for Tommy's physical. He had joined the Navy. Track season was upon us and Tommy broke the high school record in the high jump. The coach taught him a new approach to the bar. Later it was called the Fosbury Flop. Before each sporting event, Tom could never eat. He said he got butterflies in his stomach.

It was time to elect a head boy and head girl for next year. Friends asked if they could campaign for me. After some urging, I agreed. The same girls who left bully notes for me in junior high were at it again. They spread around school that I was pregnant. The dean of women asked me to come to her office. She asked why some of the girls would spread such a lie. I shared about their behavior in junior high and added that it would be quite difficult to pray for them this time around—but I would. Hap and Mae were furious. As sick as Hap was, he suggested a conference with the principal and the girls' parents. I talked him out of it knowing the consequences it could have on his health and the school atmosphere. The girl running against me would do a super job, so when I lost by four votes, I was happy for her. Hap asked why I did not cry, and I told him it wasn't worth it. Besides, God always gave me strength to persevere. That was most likely one thing that irritated some of the girls. At times, they called me "goody two shoes" which was a way of poking fun at me for being so involved in church and trying to do what God expected of me. My favorite Bible verse became, "I can do all things through Christ who strengthens me" *Philippians 4:13*. I had a great year working with the head boy and girl as council secretary and enjoyed planning school dances, assemblies, other activities, and working with community leaders.

Occasionally, the theater owner would reserve the theater just for the high school students. One night they were hosting a jitterbug contest at intermission. Hap and Mae asked me not to participate because Tommy and I would be up on the stage. They could see us dancing with my skirt flying high when Tommy threw me around his hips. We agreed. It was difficult to stay in our seats when the contest time rolled around. There were four couples on the stage, but the kids started chanting, "We want Patsy—We want Tommy." They would not stop. The theater manager stepped to the stage and said, "Will Tommy and Patsy please come to the stage so we can get on with the contest?" We did not move, and the chanting began again. We finally decided to dance. The kids cheered every time Tommy did the splits, whirled me around, or slid me through his legs along with several other gyrations. We won the contest and were awarded a year's pass to the movies. When Tommy took me home, he said, "This is really great. I will only be here a short time to use the pass and you will be taking all your friends to the movies while I am gone." That was true. Hap and Mae were still up when we got home, and we were prepared for a verbal lashing or being told we could not date for the weekend. When we shared what happened, they said, "Congratulations" Then the clocks began to bing, bang, bong! Of course, Hap gave out with his wonderful laugh, and Tommy said a quick goodbye!

Tommy Joins the Navy

In April, I wrote a poem for Tommy which he carried in his pocket during his time in the service. I also composed a song which took first place in a contest. I sang it as a farewell to him at the last school assembly. The principal gave me a hug and said he wished someone would write a song for him like that. It was amazing that the principal and teachers were never negative about high school students being in love. Wartime forced us to grow up quickly. Several of our classmates had already been married, and others followed suit after graduation. I sang for several of the weddings.

Wonderful News!!! GERMANY SURRENDERED on May 8, 1945. Horns were blowing, church bells were ringing, sirens blew, people were yelling, hugging, kissing, and jumping up and down. School was dismissed, and Boulder was planning a parade. The entire town showed up to celebrate. However, everything was not good as we gathered to hear the names of our fallen soldiers while extending sympathy, thanks, and hugs to their families. I spent extra time with Joann and her family that day, still wondering if my brother and uncles were safe. After the parade, most of the high school students headed for Baseline Lake to swim. Tommy and I took in a movie.

The Nixes had a party on May 21, 1945, for Tommy's birthday. It sure was swell, but I kept thinking about his leaving soon. Seniors were out of school for the last week, but Tommy came to eat lunch with me twice. He either walked with me or gave me a ride home every afternoon. He got orders to report and would not be here for graduation exercises. He took it in stride saying that some of his classmates got married and did not have time for a honeymoon. His folks and Hap and Mae talked to us about next year. They were concerned for both of us but suggested that since I would be a senior in high school, they were interested in my taking part in activities and not sitting at home. Tommy agreed but later asked if I would be true to him even while dating. I assured him that I would. On May 22, we went to Elitches in Denver with Dick and Pat. We rode a few rides, but spent most of our time on a bench, holding hands, talking and hugging until the dance started. The next night, Tommy and I went to the movies with his folks. On his last day, we went to the Sunrise Dance and in the afternoon we went on a picnic with several friends. I rode with the family to Denver where Tommy was to board a train for the Great Lakes Naval Training Base in Illinois. Not many words were exchanged on the way home. Mrs. Nix shed tears. She had just said goodbye to her son, knowing that Mary Jane was tending to severely wounded soldiers somewhere in the South Pacific. Mary Jane had been overseas for 30 months without leave. At graduation Tommy's name was read followed by "United States Navy." All the kids cheered as they did for each guy who had left for the Navy, Army, or Marines.

Tom and Mary Jane

Missing Tommy/Preparing for Senior Year

Tommy and I began our daily letter writing to each other. I received one from him right away describing the landscape as the train rolled toward the training base in Chicago. The next letters described changing from civilian clothes into the Navy uniform, getting a real short buzz haircut, and marching until near exhaustion. He described training in firefighting, chemical warfare, identifying anti-aircraft and how the eyes burned for days after walking through tear gas. However, when his commanding officer found out that he was an athlete, he was assigned to the basketball and track team. That would prove to make his training a little more tolerable. He was also selected for the 200-voice Great Lakes Naval Training Choir. They sang for three services every Sunday and made several recordings. As one might surmise, our letters were filled with expressions of love and how much we missed each other. Tommy said he now understood why letters from home were so important to service men and women. He would reminisce often about past events, especially spending time on our favorite hill or walking over the bridge in the moonlight. He spoke about dancing and spending time with our friends at the movies, attending church, going on hikes and just hanging out. We vowed that we would share everything with each other, even if it might be embarrassing or make us feel ashamed. He admitted that he cried some nights because he was homesick. In fact, he described his barracks as a "bawling dorm." Some of Tommy's letters were comical as he described learning to march with rifles, mistakes made, and getting inoculated twice because he did not step out of the line in time. When he was on KP, he and his buddies had to cook 4,950 steaks and then do the dishes. He would also write a "gosh darn" for having to wash his clothes. My letters described what I did each day and what was happening around town. I sent him newspaper clippings about high school athletic events, the church bulletin, and a monthly devotion called, "Understanding Myself." It was expensive to make phone calls, so those were few and far between. But they were so exciting when they did occur. I really missed him!

I left my job at the Kress Store and began work at the Mercantile Bank. Because I had won national honors for bookkeeping, typing and shorthand, the teachers had recommended me for the job. I filled in for the bookkeeper, tellers, and secretaries when they took vacations. I learned a lot and was treated swell by everyone, including the customers. Operating the large bookkeeping machine was a challenge that I enjoyed. Some nights we stayed very late when the teller's till did not add up. At times we spent over an hour searching for a penny difference. I told my boss it would be easier if someone just put in a penny. Those skills became very important later in my life. Tommy announced that I would be in charge of all bookkeeping during our married life since I was so well trained!

I took several of my friends to the movies during the summer on the free passes. I missed Tommy, especially dancing with him at The Jitney or the Dark Horse Inn. None of the guys danced like Tommy. I loved teaching my Sunday School class of first and second graders. One Sunday in July, I was there by myself. The children in town were staying home because of the polio scare. My summer schedule was filled with the usual events. I was grateful for all my friends and overnight stays with girlfriends. Marie, Helen and I sang for several community gatherings. We had so much fun and laughed a lot when we were together. Hap and Mae always had to ask us to be quiet whenever they spent the night.

Joann and I finally completed reading through the Bible. We were helped most by the stories in the New Testament as we tried to understand everything Jesus said and did for everyone. How He could die on the cross for everyone in the world boggled our minds. His life showed us how to love others.

Mrs. Nix asked if I would go with her and other war mothers to sing for the wounded soldiers at Fitzsimmons Army Hospital in Denver. My heart went out to those soldiers who had given so much for our country. During three different performances, my mind was on Tommy's safety. I had an idea that I could organize a performing troupe of high school students to entertain the soldiers. When school started in September, I ran the idea past our principal who approved wholeheartedly. Several students volunteered. I organized two different teams of vocal and instrumental soloists, duets, dancers, cheerleaders, athletes and magicians who entertained every six weeks. We were able to bring smiles and laughter to most of the soldiers. We worked hard for smiles from the tuberculosis patients who were wheeled out to the balcony area. When we entered the amputee ward, we were approached by John who had lost both arms and had hooks in place of hands. He was traveling around the ward trying to cheer everyone up. He asked who would join him in a game of ping-pong. I said, "sure." The table was brought into the ward and the game began. John beat my socks off as he switched the paddle from hook to hook and delighted in cheers from his buddies. What an experience! I never forgot John and his determination to help others instead of sitting on the "pity pot." We needed written permission from parents and permission from the principal to entertain in the psyche ward. Doctors, nurses and attendants expressed appreciation for our program. Afterward, they played music on the phonograph. One of the patients asked me to dance. A nurse explained that he had been shell-shocked (a term that later was replaced with PTSD), but he remembered dancing with his girl, and I would be safe. Our chaperones said, "OK." Charles was a very good dancer who smiled a lot as he whirled me around the dance floor. When the music stopped, he bowed and thanked me. Some of the other girls also danced with patients. Our entertainment troupes gained much respect for those wounded soldiers, and we appreciated what they sacrificed for all of us. My desire to become a doctor was even stronger after meeting all of those soldiers, but I knew that medical school and farming would not mix if I were to marry Tommy.

We had a lot of company in June. It was good that Mae's sister, Anna, and her husband, Elmer, lived in town to help accommodate everyone. Relatives from Iowa and California loved the mountain trips and the concerts held in the band shell downtown. It was also interesting to sit on the benches in front of the courthouse and "people watch." I changed piano teachers in June. Mr. Bean was the organist at the Presbyterian Church, and I looked forward to my lessons. My former teacher was good, but she had body odor that would almost knock one off the piano bench. Whew! I learned so much from my new teacher.

Four of Tommy's friends joined the Navy and were sent to Great Lakes Naval Station. On a few occasions, they were able to get together which was great fun for them. Each of the guys who left for the service received letters from each other's parents and other adults. Tommy corresponded with former high school chums, especially those in the service. I mentioned earlier about the interest adults in our community took in young people. We were supported and well taken care of. Growing up in small towns was a pleasure, even though the busybodies knew everyone else's business.

In July, Hap left for the Veterans Hospital in Cheyenne. I prayed that God would give direction to the doctors for his treatment. Mae went with him, so I stayed with Helen and her folks. Three days later, Anna, Elmer, and I drove up to see Hap. He looked so pale and was getting ready to receive a blood transfusion. They also pumped his body full of folic acid which is given to patients for anemia. Two weeks later he was back home looking and feeling better.

Tommy's grandma, Mollie Purdy, came to visit. Grandma, Mrs. Nix and I went to a horse show. Mr. Nix won first prize for his horse, Captain. That night the Nixes and Grandma came over with homemade ice cream. It was so good, and Hap ate two helpings. Grandma was a riot and liked to play jokes on people—right down my alley. She and I created a lot of mischief together.

Tom home from boot camp

On August 5, 1945, Tommy arrived home from boot camp. He looked so handsome in his uniform, and I was so happy. What an exciting day! The week passed too fast! We went dancing, took drives to Lakeside in Denver, went to the movies and spent time with friends. Tommy also spent quality time with his parents and grandmother. On his last day, we all went to see the cattle before we took him to Denver where he boarded the train at 9:00 p.m. for California. Three days after he arrived at the base in Shoemaker, Tommy became ill and was placed in sick bay. He said something about getting "cat fever" which was the Navy's term for the flu. He became quite ill which required a 10-day hospital stay. I was praying for his recovery. He was able to write a couple of letters to me and his parents. In fact, his nurse wrote most of the letters to me for him. He did not let his parents know how sick he was, and I promised not to tell them. He was allowed to take it easy for a few days when he returned to base. I received word that Bill had been injured when several torpedoes struck the ship he was on. The ship was destroyed, and only a handful of sailors survived. He was in a hospital in San Diego and later received the Purple Heart. I thanked God that he survived. Because his injuries were severe, he was sent to a hospital in Illinois and later Iowa. A cute nurse, Janey, who helped him, became his wife.

WHOOPIE!! JAPAN SURRENDERED on August 14, 1945. The official surrender took place on board the USS Missouri in Tokyo Bay on September 2, 1945. So that day was declared VJ Day. The war was over! School was dismissed on September 2 and a big parade was held in Boulder. A bunch of us headed for Baseline Lake again. Lora and I went to the movie, and she spent the night. She was a swell girl, and it was fun being with her. At that time, I had no idea she would one day be my sister-in-law. I was so excited to know that Tommy would not be involved in combat. He wrote that there was still a job to do. His sentiments were beautifully expressed. He told how he really missed me during Boot Camp, but nothing compared to now and how his love for me was different, deeper with more understanding. Looking at my picture, Tommy commented about my blue eyes and beautiful smile that showed kindness and sincerity. He said he wished he could write poetry to express his love for me and that he was trying to memorize the poem I wrote for him. I told him his words were like poetry. I was a member of the Junior Red Cross and continued folding bandages for the Red Cross because there was still such need for them.

Sixteen youth from our church left for camp at Sylvan Dale. The first night vespers were so uplifting and provided a spiritual atmosphere. I found myself wishing that all youth could experience this type of connection with God. Besides Bible study, devotions and personal meditations, we played games, hiked, sang, and ate good food. Consecration night always left us with that still voice of God reminding us how much we were loved and what He expected of us in our daily life. So beautiful! I consecrated my life to serve God in the church and in Music Education. My friend, Bob R., and I were elected co-presidents for next year. I corresponded with several friends I came to know from different towns in Colorado and Wyoming.

My summer job at the bank, which I enjoyed a lot, came to an end. We kids made good use of the time before school started. We bowled, swam, hiked, played tennis, shot pool, roller skated, played ball, had wiener roasts and saw movies. On August 30, Hap and Mae left for the Veterans Hospital in Illinois in hopes they could provide a cure for Hap's anemia. The Nixes had sold the home and acreages they owned. They were waiting for the builders to complete their new home just two blocks from us. Hap and Mae invited them to stay in our home while they were gone which worked well for everyone. Mr. Nix teased by saying they could read more of my letters from Tommy. I shared many of those with them. During their month's stay, Joe was like my little brother. Every night, he shared his problems, especially about the two girls he was dating. He could not decide between Mareta and Lora. I became better acquainted with Mr. and Mrs. Nix and grew to love them even more. I so appreciated their help. Tommy and I were pleased that our parents were good friends.

In September 1945, I helped register students. That night, I went to Lakeside with Ken. He was a good friend, active in his church, and we shared the same values. Ken and Tom had played basketball together. I stayed in Denver at Uncle Russ and Betty's. Their twin babies were so darling, and I could not hold them enough. Uncle Russ contracted malaria while serving in Burma, and he carried that illness for years. When school started, I really missed Tommy walking me to class and holding my hand. Tommy was moved to Treasure Island, waiting for further orders. Seven of my friends, Ken, Roy, John S., Harry, Bob, Dick C., and Wayne made sure that I did not miss out on any school dances or events during my senior year. I was so fortunate to have such good friends, but it did raise the hair on those jealous girls a few times. They could not understand why the boys would ask me out when they knew I was going to marry Tommy. The guys just smiled and told them that I was a heck of a lot of fun. I did drop John because he tried to get a little too friendly! Ken, his parents, and I, went to Denver one evening to hear E. Stanley Jones, a nationally known Methodist preacher. I reached up on my neck to feel Tommy's football, and it was gone! Ken and his parents, plus some ushers helped search for it, but our efforts proved futile. I was sick at heart as Ken tried to cheer me up on the way home. When I was getting ready for bed, the football and chain fell on the floor. They had been caught in my bra. I called Ken immediately, and his parents told me the neighbors could probably hear him laughing.

Tommy scribbled a note saying that he was on the USS Lexington Aircraft Carrier heading for Hawaii, so we would not hear from him for a while. I missed running out on the field to hug Tommy after the first football game of the season and dancing with him afterward. I knew how much I missed him and realized how much more he missed me and his family being so far away. His letters attested to it. I got six letters from Tommy by the time the Lexington had pulled into Pearl Harbor.

I accepted an invitation to attend a slumber party, even though most of the girls who had written the nasty notes and told lies about me would be there. I did like Patty who was hosting the party. Her parents were attending dinner and a dance at Colorado University where Patty's dad was a professor. We all took blankets and pillows and prepared to sleep on the living room floor. Some of the girls talked Patty into getting liquor from the cabinet. All but Katy and I began to get plastered. I threatened to put a washcloth in one dirty mouth, and she quieted down. Katy and I took a few to the bathroom where they threw up. We were finally able to get everyone to bed. Some of the girls were crying. All of a sudden, one of them asked if I would sing the Lord's Prayer. There were a bunch of "ditto" echoes or "please sing it." I have to admit, it did tickle my funny bone a bit, and I promised to sing if they would all be quiet. The next morning, those girls looked like something the cat dragged in, and they could not thank Katy and me enough. Everyone made a pact that we would not rat on each other.

Slumber parties were popular during high school. As a sophomore, I was at Barb's slumber party. She lived out in the country, and I really liked her mother's home cooking. We were playing games when one of the girls said we should play strip poker. Well, I did not fare well. I only had my panties left when we heard Barb's mother coming down the hall. All the girls jumped on top of me. When Mrs. W. opened the door, the girls told her we were playing pyramid. I nearly suffocated by the time they piled off me, and I never cared to play any kind of poker after that. However, decades later, Matt, one of my grandsons, taught me to play Texas Hold 'Em with only chips at stake!

I continued to enjoy teaching my first and second grade Sunday School Class and Christian Endeavor. I was also asked to serve on the church board, which I enjoyed. The adults made me feel like my opinion mattered.

Hap and Mae came home on September 27 from the Veteran's Hospital in Illinois. I was so thrilled to see them, and Hap looked good. I was grateful that the Nixes stayed with me for the month. Timing was swell as they were able to move into their new home. After arriving home, Hap was able to drive the ambulance for one of the funeral homes to transport people who had died. Mae accompanied him a lot, and I went on a few calls with him. Each of us tried to comfort those who had lost a loved one. Sometimes it was just a squeeze or a hug. The most difficult transport was a baby who had lived only an hour after birth.

The specialists in Illinois recommended that Hap check into Colorado General Hospital in Denver. I thought how weary he must be of doctors and hospitals, but he never complained. Mae was a beautiful woman who had kept her girlish figure and was strong in her faith and support of Hap. She did break down as we cried together before they left again. I convinced Hap and Mae that I was old enough to stay by myself. After all, I had a lot of girlfriends who would spend the night with me. The specialists at Colorado General followed the same protocol as the others in allowing Hap to become very weak before they gave him a transfusion. A Japanese intern challenged the specialists in saying that the only way to save Hap's life was to give him transfusions plus some other medications as fast as they could. The specialists threw up their hands and told the intern to take over if he thought he could do better. Hap's veins endured over 50 transfusions in a short amount of time. God provided a miracle because Hap's veins did not collapse. We were grateful to the intern and the many people who prayed for Hap's return to health. Although he did not have the stamina and energy as in the past and needed transfusions occasionally, Hap lived twelve more years which was unheard of for his disease. He worked at the courthouse in the Driver's License Department while Mae took a job as receptionist at the County Hospital for six months. They received some funds for being foster parents, but their desire was to help pay for my college education. I told them to stop worrying as I was able to save money and would apply for a scholarship. I loved my job at the floral shop where I learned to arrange flowers, and I could not fill all the babysitting demands. I took over mowing the lawn, shoveling the snow, keeping the car gassed and helped Mae with more household duties. I performed those duties joyfully for my parents who had done so much for me.

Tommy and I continued our daily letters. I lived for his and he for mine. We were two lovesick teenagers. I felt worse for him because my life was busy with school, community, and church activities, and with family and friends. That is why I did not say much when Tommy took up smoking. He said every sailor on the ship smoked, and it did help pass the time as he daydreamed about me and talked to my picture. He told me that other guys would try to talk him into going out to pick up girls, etc., but that he always declined. He did go to the USO to play pool and to dance but left early before he "got into trouble," as he put it. He wrote how he would never do anything to make me or his parents ashamed of him, and he thanked me for helping him grow as a Christian and a man. I felt blessed and humbled. Tommy always said how glad he was that I was being true to him, and I always said how much more difficult it was for him to remain true under the circumstances. It was comforting for both of us to know we were trustworthy!

On November 2, 1945, Mary Jane arrived home. Such a swell gal, and I loved being around her. She had been an Army nurse overseas and in the South Pacific for 36 months. The last part of her assignment was caring for soldiers who had the most serious wounds, so it was not easy for her to talk about it. Those nurses had to build a shell around themselves in order to cope with the horrors of war. On the other hand, she was excited because she had fallen in love with a doctor in her unit who would be stateside within the next two months. Mary Jane and I got well acquainted riding the horses owned by Mr. Nix. We would take them from one pasture to another. Tommy and I had done a lot of horseback riding together. I liked the moonlight rides best.

I was home for a week in November with the flu. Hap fed me garlic again! When I returned to school, over half (around 250 students) of the student body were still home with the nasty stuff.

Several of my friends came out to the house, and we all piled into one car to go riding. We figured out how to sit so we would not get crushed. I sat on a lap, and someone sat on my lap. We sat three across. The guy on the bottom had to take deep breaths, and when we counted to three, we all changed butt cheeks.

Our senior girls basketball team cleaned up on the sophomore and juniors. Lilly and I were referred to as the "mighty twosome." Of course, the rules did not allow us to dribble the entire court, so we had fun when we could set up some scrimmage time with the guys. Lilly and I made quite a pair. She was black, and I was a blond-headed Irish girl. I would have claimed her for my sister any day.

Two of my friends from our church youth group joined an organization called *American Youth for Democracy*. I received an invitation to attend a meeting that was held at Colorado University. I left before the meeting was over because things did not feel right. The next day, they urged me to return, and I declined. The next week they asked if I would sing for the meeting which I did. Afterward, I left. That quiet voice from within was urging me to leave. Three months later, Hap, Mae and I attended a concert by a well-known singer who was performing at the Mackey Auditorium on campus. He had a fabulous voice and gave three encores. He had also been in the movies and was well known. As Hap, Mae, and I made our way to the foyer preparing to leave, my two friends from the youth group broke through the crowd followed by the performer. I was introduced as he said, "It is a privilege to meet you, Miss Patsy. I know of your talents and leadership qualities. I want to invite you to return to New York with me, join my organization and perhaps perform in one of my concerts." I became frozen, wondering how this happened while that still voice within let me know things were not right. Hap and Mae, standing near me, were astounded. Before they could say anything, I told them not to worry. I thanked the very tall, wonderfully talented man and told him that I preferred to graduate from high school before I could consider such a generous offer. My two friends stood there in disbelief. The next day, they asked how I could turn down the once-in-a-lifetime opportunity. We all learned later that the AYD Organization was backed by the Communists. As time wore on, it was my understanding the talented performer was asked by our government to leave the United States or be deported. I felt sorry for my friends who had learned the hard lesson that things are not always what they seem to be. They had been swept up by dangerous brainwashing techniques. I thanked God for discernment from that quiet voice within me. Actions by people who believed in Communism were prominent in the late 40s and 50s. McCarthyism took over the news media and Congress as Senator Joseph McCarthy interviewed countless American citizens who were thought to be involved in communist activities. During that time, someone burned the awning on Mr. Nix's barber shop and wrote "bigot" on the windows. That very night, the Nixes and I were at the newly built Negro Baptist church where Mr. Nix was being honored for his significant contribution toward the building. He had also accepted responsibility, given to him by a judge, to supervise a Negro parolee. The parolee, Mr. D, had discovered a man in bed with his wife and killed him. Mr. Nix gave Mr. D a job in the barber shop where he was employed for 20 years.

December was busy with rehearsals for our school play and the yearly performance of "The Messiah." I visited the Nix household a lot and enjoyed palling around with Mary Jane. Our school trio continued to give performances in Boulder and throughout the state. I received a letter from Tommy saying that the Lexington was headed for the United States. All the planes had been flown off the ship and replaced with cots for soldiers who had been in combat for months. Tommy later told how they all stood up, cheered and saluted as the ship passed through the Golden Gate Bridge in San Francisco.

I was thinking it would be more than swell if Tommy could come home for Christmas. On December 16, his side of the ship won the draw for leave. I thanked God for answering my prayer. Tommy was home by the 19th, and we all got together at the Nixes to celebrate. Tommy and I went to two Boulder High basketball games. I was so crazy about him. The Nixes were invited to our house for Christmas Eve. I was grateful for the fun time and especially for the long wool coat, a present from the Nix family. During Christmas break, I went to the cabin near Nederland with the Nixes. As usual, we had a great weekend. Tommy and I were invited to so many dinners, and we were together every day or evening. The time had gone much too fast, as Tommy had to leave January 12. Darn it all! I was plenty ashamed because I hurt Tommy's feelings on his last day home. We did make up before he left. The Nixes and I made the trip to Denver and told Tommy goodbye—again.

Lilly Mae decided to try out for the talent show. She asked me to give her voice lessons and to accompany her on the piano. After a lot of practice, we made it! I never ceased to be amazed by the talents of my special friend. Lilly and I looked forward to basketball, softball and running around the track during our senior year. We were friends for life!

I remained busy with school, church, and community activities while performing individually and with the trio. I loved my job at the florist and continued earning extra money by cleaning houses and babysitting. In February, I decided to enter the Elks Most Valuable Student Contest. It was a contest that awarded a college scholarship, and the competition was heavy. I enlisted the help of a friend to create a portfolio showing my accomplishments through drawings that depicted educational experiences including my grades and notes from teachers. Other pages showed my church and community involvement, activities, and job experience. Added to that were letters from a variety of adults that included the high school principal, teachers and one from Hap and Mae. I figured if I could win this scholarship, Hap and Mae would not have to worry so much.

By this time, Hap was feeling better, for which I was so thankful. I offered thanks to God many times. Hap told me the reason he fought his disease so hard was for me. He did not want to add to my loss of loved ones. I could not express my thanks and love enough to Hap and Mae, and to God who led me BY HIS HAND, showing His love, mercy and grace every day. My friends remained faithful in keeping me busy with high school events, dances at The Jitney and trips to Elitches. On every occasion I found myself wishing that I was with Tommy, but I was appreciative of those kind boys who were also a barrel of fun. Since Hap was feeling better, the kids began to frequent our home again to study, play games, or just hang out.

Hap, Mae, and the Nixes had a swell birthday party for me on March 3. Tommy sent me a pen and pencil set and a sweet letter. He asked if I would love him as much when he reached 50. Fifty seemed very old to us. I told him, of course, and beyond! In Tommy's next letter he said if he did not know me better, he would think I belonged in an insane asylum. I had written him a letter in shorthand. He reciprocated by drawing a lot of Japanese symbols in his next letter.

It was time for the girl's state basketball tournament. Ten of my friends plus our chaperone made reservations to stay in a suite at the Shirley Savoy in Denver. We girls were really excited to stay in such a nice hotel. We won our first game by two points in overtime which was really exciting. We beat East High School by three points the next day, which lined us up to play Longmont for the championship. We came home with the trophy!!!

Taylor, Mary Jane's fiancé, came for a visit. He seemed nice and Mary Jane was very excited. We did not get to visit much because Hap, Mae, and I left for Iowa for spring break. I met all of Hap's family and especially enjoyed Nancy, Hap's niece who was my age. I missed reading Tommy's letters and knew there would be several when I got home. WooEEE! Seven letters awaited me.

Elaine, Wendall, Harry, and I went calling for the church. We met some very nice people who liked our visit and church information. Our youth group made visits three times a year. When we finished, we usually played pool or games at the church.

Our choir director asked me to be the assistant director of our operetta. I was having difficulty with my voice again so I did not audition for a part. I loved directing and the cast was very cooperative. I found that if I memorized all the music, I was a more effective director and conductor. All the performances went well. In between operetta rehearsals, a group of us from the choir put on Snow White for two grade schools. Those little kids liked the performance and were so cute with their questions.

Hap and Uncle Elmer took me to Denver to get a graduation dress. I enjoyed being with them. They were an absolute stitch, making comments about some of the dresses I tried on. I finally decided on a pastel green dress and found some jewelry to match. Of course, I needed a pair of shoes to match and tried on some high heels, trying to pose like a movie star. The three of us laughed a lot as I tried walking in them. I finally chose a pair of whites with low heel. We ate at the Daniels & Fisher Restaurant before heading home.

Neva and I palled around and had many nights at each other's homes. We spent a lot of time writing letters to Tommy and John. We had some wonderful speakers and guests at our Christian Endeavor meetings, which would be part of my report to the church board each month. Mary Jane decided to join the church choir, so she and I had another thing in common. She was such a swell gal, and I enjoyed her company. Tommy said he was glad that I hung out with his sister. Mareta and I were very busy singing duets for many events during the month of April at school and in the community. She was so much fun that we spent most of our time laughing. We had a comedy routine for the annual Vaudeville that brought down the house. We went to Fitzsimmons to sing for the wounded soldiers, accompanied by Mrs. Nix and another War Mother. Sometimes it was difficult to hold back the tears.

I continued placing mementos in scrapbooks that I started in junior high. Tommy enjoyed looking at them since he was part of many events. I went to the prom with Wayne. I had a good time, but was missing Tommy more all the time. The Elks informed me that I had won the local scholarship contest, and my entry would be sent to the state competition. They had a special banquet to present me with the $150.00 check. Wow! $150.00 was a lot of money! When I took it to the bank, I asked if I could hold $150.00 in bills before it was deposited. That same evening, I performed for the Safeway stores executive meeting in Loveland. I never sang for money, but I was given $25.00 in an envelope. I felt rich and smiled all the way home. Later, Mae and I went shopping for a suit. It was a gray and white pinstripe which was very popular, and the fit was perfect. I wore it on a date with Tommy after he came home. He whistled, picked me up and twirled me around.

School was winding down. I was asked to sing at the recognition assembly. I was presented with the Girls' Athletic Association Pin and a certificate of achievement for grades, music and other activities. The best gift was a great surprise. I was presented with a scholarship from the Elks as I had won the state contest. May 21 was Tommy's 19th birthday. Since his ship was docked in California, Mr. and Mrs. Nix were on their way to spend some time with him. I was secretly wishing I could be a stow-away in the car. A group of us went to Lakeside in Denver. We traveled by caravan. I never got into another Roll-A-Plane or Loop-The-Loop after that. I threw up, twice! We had picnics, hikes, went to Estes Park to dance and play pool, and swam at El Dorado Springs. We nearly wore ourselves out. I was asked to sing "The Lord's Prayer" at the end of Class Day. There were lots of hugs and tears. The next day, we seniors checked out our caps and gowns and picked up our yearbook, the "Odaroloc" (Colorado spelled backward). We thought that was clever. Graduation was on May 29. More smiles and tears! The next three weeks were busy as I sang for seven weddings. One was for Joann and Hal. Joann and Hal lived in Boulder for the next year and had a darling baby girl. I loved that precious baby as I rocked and held her. Tragedy struck as their baby became ill with chicken pox that escalated into meningitis which was fatal. Such grief and sorrow!! Joann and Hal moved to Frederick and later had two sons. We kept in contact with each other, always reminiscing about how we would climb out of my bedroom window, sit on the roof to look at the stars and share secrets. That was where our reading through the Bible began.

On July 1, I went to work for Mr. Douglas at Colorado University as a stenographer. I worked there until noon and then left for my job at Fashion Bar, a women's clothing store. I learned a lot during breaks from the married women who worked there. I was not expecting to be educated about so many aspects of married life.

The Nixes arrived home after visiting Tommy. Grandma Purdy came back with them, and I was delighted as she and I planned our mischievous moves on the family. She was such great fun and a real dickens. Hap and Mae invited them to dinner, so I was able to hear about their time with Tommy

On June 15, Tommy called me. It was so wonderful to hear his voice. When I went to bed, every word he said was on my lips and in my head until I fell asleep.

Mary Jane had gone down south to meet her fiancé Taylor's mother who grilled her about everything, which proved to be very uncomfortable. Taylor's mother told her about a former girl Taylor was going to marry but the girl did not measure up to her standards. Mary Jane felt so uneasy about the visit and realized, for the first time, that Taylor was very attached to his mother. I remembered hearing stories about people falling in love while serving during the war and having a different experience upon returning home. Sure enough, Taylor called Mary Jane on July 15 and broke the engagement. Oh, how hurtful that was for Mary Jane, her family and all of us. She had been given three bridal showers by this time and had to prepare to return all the gifts. I accompanied her on several of those returns. She was so brave as she went about the task. Many people asked her to keep their gifts for the future, but Mary Jane could not see a future at that time.

It was time for the Boulder Pow Wow. Mr. Nix let me ride Stardust in the parade, and she did not wince or get upset at the crowd one time. Mary Jane rode alongside of me and later we attended the rodeo. By this time, I was comfortable around the cattle, and I loved riding horses. The next day, I went with Mr. Nix to check on the cattle, and one of those Hereford bulls took out after me. Mr. Nix yelled and waved him off with his hat. Guess I wasn't so comfortable after all!

Tom Comes Home

Tommy was asked to stay in the Navy and receive a higher commission, but he told the CO that he wanted to get enrolled in college, see his family, and he had a girl waiting for him. We were waiting to pick him up at the airport in Cheyenne. He and I had a bet that if he would quit smoking, I would stop biting my nails. He arrived at 4:00 and as I jumped into his arms, one of my false fingernails came off on his uniform. Grandma Purdy went crazy with laughter. Well, the bet was off for the time being. Tommy was home, and I didn't care about anything else. A couple of days after Tommy came home, he, Mary Jane and I went to Lakeside and then paid a visit to Uncle Russ, Betty, and their cute twins, Karen and Sharon. It was great to have them in my life. Uncle John settled in California with his family and checked on me once in a while. Gib and Bob kept in contact, and Art came home after being discharged from the Army.

Tommy announced that it was time for people to address him as "Tom." He felt Tommy sounded too juvenile. His mother continued to call him Tommy for quite some time, and his friend, Dick, called him 'Lil Tommy Nix in jest many times.

Tom and I were together as much as possible—horseback riding, attending weddings of friends, bowling, going to movies, walking across our favorite bridge, and just hanging out at each other's homes. Tom hauled hay and helped his dad with the cattle until the time came for him to leave for college.

Someone told me about a job opening at the university library. I applied for it because I could not work for Mr. Douglas while taking classes. I was hired as an Assistant Student Librarian. I learned a lot and got to see many friends while working. I was still employed at the Fashion Bar on the weekends. My friend, Mary Alice, also worked there so we palled around a lot. Tom and I fell into several arguments along the way. Some, my fault, and others, his fault. I was puzzled at his attempt to control everything, then becoming upset when it did not work out to his liking. I asked him where that came from. I knew that it was easy for him to become involved in a fight, which he blamed on always having to step in and protect his little brother. I also knew that I loved Tom's tender heart, that he was so well liked by others and such a tease. I began to ask God if this was the man I was supposed to marry. Tom and his dad urged Mary Jane to enroll at Colorado A & M. She decided she would major in Occupational Therapy, a good fit for a nurse. She and Tom left for Fort Collins.

College Life at the University of Colorado

In September 1946, I prepared to take my entrance exams for Colorado University. They were not too tough. The next day, I registered and paid my fees. I liked my counselor, Mr. Durn. The weekend before classes began, Tom and I attended the Christian Youth Fellowship picnic, two football games and played a couple games of rummy.

On the second day of classes, I had my first piano lesson with Mr. Hardy who was very encouraging. Music classes were held in what was the old chemistry dissecting building. Every once in a while, there was a waft of lingering odor that filled the air. Monday, Wednesday, and Friday my classes were all day until 5:30. Sometimes I walked the three miles home, but other times I was glad to ride the bus. I liked being a university student and enjoyed the beautiful campus. I was elected to serve as an officer on the music council which I enjoyed. There were many GIs working on their degrees. Some of the wives were also going to school, which made it difficult for those who had babies. So a group of us decided to help out. There was space at the end of one hallway where we took turns babysitting between classes. We held and fed those cute babies, and rocked the buggies with our feet if we needed a little extra time to prepare for the next class.

I received a letter from Tom who was busy with classes and starting a job working in a cafeteria at the corner of Laurel and College Avenue. He liked it, mostly because he got all the food he could eat. Later, Mary Jane told Mr. Nix that Tom's hours at the cafeteria were interfering with his studies. Tom was not too pleased, but he made a deal with his dad that he would forgo working for the first quarter.

I sang at two weddings on one weekend. Many more classmates were walking down the aisle. I had a great time at each wedding, but I missed Tom. During the next weekend when he was home, we watched Boulder High's football game. As usual, Joe's playing was outstanding, but Boulder got beat. We went to dinner at the Sigma Nu house. Tom and Ray hung out at the Sigma Nu house when they were in junior high and high school where they did all kinds of chores for the guys. It was only natural that both of them joined the Sigma Nu Fraternity in college. Whenever Mary Jane came home for a weekend, Tom had a ride. Most of the time, he hitchhiked to Boulder and took the train back to Fort Collins. So many times, we were having an argument when he left. We were both at fault, but what got my goat were the times he became so possessive and demanding.

The music students had frequent gatherings which was great fun. I was invited to many of the girls' dorm rooms and was glad I did not have to live in such cramped spaces. Marion, Lorraine, Cam and I became close friends. We had fun studying together and hanging out at my house. I was rushed by two sororities and invited to join each. With the hours I was carrying, performances I was a part of, and my responsibilities at church and Sunday school, I declined and joined the

Associated University Women. The programs were educational and wholesome, and the organization was all about helping others. I was excited to be part of a Big Sister program in Boulder which sought to help children facing adversity. We were mentors who partnered with under-resourced families to provide mentorship with encouragement and support. I was able to understand most circumstances because of my background.

I had a part in the opera, *The Bartered Bride*. It was great, and the stage was huge. I was excited because the director of choirs at CU had been the choral director at Boulder High. He selected students for the first Modern Choir. Singing modern music sprinkled with music from other eras was a ball. We girls wore formals, and the guys wore black suits with white shirts. We gave many performances around the state and community and sang over the radio. I made many more friends in that group. We had reunions every year until our director passed away 35 years later. Besides the large chorus and Modern Choir, I was to be part of one more musical group. Our director was looking for a trio whose voices blended well. Gloria, Lee and I performed throughout the state to help recruit students for CU.

Since I was fifteen before the opportunity arose to take piano lessons, I had to put in a lot of practice hours to keep up with students who had played for many years. I also had to keep my academics up to snuff. Even though I was busy, I really missed Tom and was so happy when he could come home for a weekend. He came for the high school homecoming.

I spent time with Mr. and Mrs. Nix whenever I could and, as always, enjoyed their company. On November 3, it had snowed so deep that Tom did not get on the train to come home until 11:30 at night. Tom wanted me to come for the Aggies homecoming the next weekend. My friend, Cam, was from Fort Collins and had already invited me to stay at her home for that weekend. I could hardly wait! Cam invited Tom, his roommate Don, and me to dinner. We went to the rally and dance afterward. Mary Jane and her boyfriend, Bob Rinker, joined us for the dance and the game which was played the next day. A few weeks earlier, Bob had seen Mary Jane at church and wanted to meet her. He followed Tom into the student center one day and joined him in a game of pool. Bob asked about Mary Jane. Tom told him she was soured on men, but told him where Mary Jane lived and wished him good luck. On his first visit to Mary Jane's apartment, he took a box of candy. She put the box back in his arms and told him she was not interested. After being so hurt by Taylor, she was not ready for dating. On Bob's third try, he took a bouquet of flowers. Mary Jane told him to give them to someone who would appreciate them. He calmly said, "I am not giving up. Why don't you invite me in and tell me about it. I am a good listener." It worked!

Our freshman class won the tug of war against the sophomores. I was one of five girls on the team. My hands hurt and I was all scuffed up, but we won! Afterward a bunch of us invaded The Sink, a hangout for students, to drink Cokes and sing dumb songs.

Joe continued to play top-notch football at Boulder High. The team carried him off the field after two of the games. He was still dating Mareta and Lora, not knowing which one he liked the best! I would smile as I heard about his dilemma—often.

Tom would surprise me on some weekends by telling me he could not come home and then show up. On one of those weekends, Cam and I had gone to the movie. Tom had called ahead asking the ushers to leave the seat next to me vacant. He quietly sat down and while I was engrossed in the movie, he proceeded to put his arm around me. The theater was dark, and I had no idea it was him. I slapped him. He never tried to pull that one again!

One of the most interesting and wonderful happenings occurred during my freshman year that had nothing to do with my classes and activities. The girls who had bullied me in junior high and high school apologized for their actions. They admitted they were jealous and asked where I got my strength. Some told me their deepest secrets and longings and even asked my advice. I told them of my favorite Bible verse, "I can do all things through Christ who strengthens me", and how I relied on God to help me as I kept praying for them through it all. Tears flowed from their eyes. I was grateful to God for touching the hearts of those women, not for me, but for them being released from the bondage of jealousy and lying that held them so tight.

Mae talked to me about becoming overly involved, and cautioned me to get enough rest. I did admit that once in a while I was tired and promised I would pay attention when I needed to rest. Hap shared some of his wisdom, too. Whenever he addressed me as "his little girl," I knew I needed to listen.

Before December rolled around, I was asked to join Delta Omicron, a National Music Fraternity for men and women. I enjoyed the group very much as we were all working toward a degree in music education or performance.

Lorraine and I became good friends and did a lot of studying together which made it easier for both of us. She also enjoyed chumming around with my high school friends. Lorraine was a super pianist and cheered me on as I practiced and played in recitals. We remained close friends even though she was in New York for her entire teaching career. We got together for several summers over the years. I felt like I had lost a sister when she passed away in 2012.

It was great to finish exams on December 1 which allowed me to spend five days in Fort Collins with Tom. The time was spent watching him play basketball, double dating with Mary Jane and Bob, attending the Sigma Nu dance, the movies and church services. A tinge of sadness overwhelmed me as I waved goodbye to Tom from the train. He ran alongside my window making funny faces.

Fashion Bar was very busy during the Christmas season. We stayed open late, and I worked 10–12-hour shifts. I did enjoy waiting on the ladies and on the bewildered men as they shopped for their wives, mothers, and girlfriends, describing their height and favorite colors

Tom came home on Christmas Eve. We met friends for hamburgers and Cokes and played games. After a delicious Christmas Day dinner, we played cards and, of course, went to the movie. Throughout our life up to that point, we saw every movie shown. I never grew tired of holding hands or feeling Tom's arm around me for those two-hour times. We enjoyed a couple of days at the Nix cabin with the Nix family and Hap and Mae. Memories of times in the mountains came flooding back from the two years I spent in a one-room schoolhouse. I remembered the many sounds of the river, riding the burros, building forts for snowball fights, sucking on icicles, running through the fields, hiding in the trees, trying to catch chipmunks, racing my sled, the warmth of a potbelly stove, and attending taffy pulls.

My brother Bill was working on his college degree in Education in Iowa. Little Pammy was born December 2, 1946. Janey continued her work as a nurse. It would be swell when we could see each other again.

Throughout the fall of 1946, I sang at the Tuberculosis Sanitarium in Boulder. Patients came from different parts of the country hoping for a cure in the dry air. It was sad to see so many ill patients. I sang acapella through a mask for the critically ill, and each time I went, some were missing. It was a dreaded disease that offered little hope at that time. I also wanted to be the best Sunday School teacher for first and second graders, so I enrolled in Christian Education courses through the United Christian Missionary Society. I did enjoy teaching and being in charge of our Church Youth Group.

In January 1947, Tom told his folks that we wanted to get married. His dad said, "We thought you would never ask." It was different with my folks. They wanted me to finish college first and tried several types of bribery to change my mind, like purchasing a grand piano. They also pointed out that they knew Ray still loved me, and he was going to be an engineer. They really did not want to think of me living the hard life of a farmer's wife. I told them bribery would not get them anywhere, that I did not love Ray, and I felt Tom and I had gone together enough years to know what we wanted, and—I would finish college. (I had to quit college when Ed came along in the middle of our junior year, but I did go back to school, 12 years and four beautiful children later. I went on to earn a master's degree at UNC in 1966.)

Tom pinned me with his Sigma Nu pin which was a way of saying we were almost engaged. I lost his pin two months later. The pin was expensive, decorated with diamonds and rubies. Oh my! It would take a lot of my savings to purchase another pin, but I ordered one right away. It came just before Tom came home two weekends later so he never knew. I did tell him after a few years had passed.

Art sent $75 to me. Was that ever a nice surprise! He was good to write letters while in the service, and now said he had a good job and thought I could use some extra money. That more than paid for Tom's pin.

Lee, Gloria, and I kept busy performing throughout the state. Our voices did have a perfect blend with Gloria on first soprano, me on second and Lee on alto. We also sang a lot in the community, at university gatherings, plus a tour for Foreign War Relief. Gloria was Jewish, but whenever she joined me at youth group or other meetings, she was a good sport about the food.

We're Engaged!

Tom and I had talked about getting married on June 22, 1947. The day we officially became engaged that spring, Tom was helping to run a track meet at Colorado A & M (later called Colorado State University). I rode to Fort Collins with his mom and dad. We were engrossed in watching a race, when a high school kid ran out on the track and interfered with the race. Tom grabbed him. The kid wiggled away and ran toward the bleachers. Tom caught up to him under the bleachers where we were sitting. They were rolling around on the ground wrestling and dirt was flying everywhere. After a short time, Tom had the kid by the neck and marched him out of the stadium, giving him a boot as he kicked him out. The crowd cheered. That evening at dinner when Tom placed the engagement ring on my finger, he still had dirt under a few nails. I thought it was funny, but his mom was not too pleased.

Tom and I thought we were going to live in the basement of his folk's house during the summer which we were not too excited about. On May 12, Mr. Nix told us that he knew the owner of a vacant house close to them and Hap and Mae. The owner said Tom and I could live in the downstairs until we left for college if we painted the walls. We had more fun painting and got into a paint fight one night. We were both a mess. It was dark when I got home so Hap and Mae had me disrobe outside the back door and carefully walk to the bathtub. Tom had to do the same thing. During the next month, friends gave me four showers: a kitchen, a bedroom, a miscellaneous, and a personal shower. My, I received so many nice things. After the showers were over, Mae held a trousseau tea where all my gifts were displayed for those who had attended the showers. I was busy writing thank you notes. Mr. and Mrs. Nix, Hap, and Mae helped to clean up the old house. Besides the paint, there was a lot of dirt on the floors and the yard was a mess.

More friends were getting married, and I sang for two during the month of May. University was out for both Tom and me, so we could spend more time on the house. I hung the curtains over the huge windows. It was finally beginning to look like a home. Lora and her mother gave another shower. It was for the bride and groom which was lots of fun. Tom's friends gave him a lot of spoof gifts. We laughed so hard.

Hap, Mae, and I went to Longmont to buy my wedding shoes. They had already purchased my beautiful gown and long gloves in Boulder. Gladys fixed my veil because it was too long. I was getting more and more excited with our wedding, just a week away. On June 20, Tom and I moved our things to the house. Tom took our travel clothes out to the Downing Farm where we would be changing for our honeymoon, a weekend in Colorado Springs at the Antlers Hotel.

Marriage, Family, and Farming

Wedding and Honeymoon

We said our vows in front of 300 guests at First Christian Church in Boulder on June 22, 1947. My dear friend Cam sang "O Promise Me" and "I'll Be Loving You, Always." Roberta was the organist. Mary Jane was my Maid of Honor, and Tom's dad was his Best Man. Groomsmen were Tom's brother, Joe, and best friend, Dick Rogers. My bridesmaids were best friends Neva Jackson and Mareta Ross. Tom's fraternity brothers threatened to kidnap him after the ceremony. They had done that to another couple. Unknown to me, Tom had borrowed handcuffs from the sheriff, and as we headed for the reception, he slapped them on us. In the picture where we are cutting the cake, they are visible. I told him I loved him with my whole heart, but hoped the Downings had the handcuff key. We were finally on our way. We did not own a car, so Mary Jane loaned us her Chevy.

Tom kept saying that we were going to have twin beds, but that was not my idea. He made arrangements at the hotel, and when the bell boy opened the door, there sat twin beds. Tom thought he would get a rise out of me, but I pushed them together and asked the bell boy to bring bedding that would fit. I knew marriage required adjustments, and I made the first one that night. I had visions of falling asleep in Tom's arms. He said he could not go to sleep like that. I called him a "touch me not." However, I discovered that night that he was a very restless sleeper. He moved a lot, throwing his arms around. Jeepers Creepers! I moved over as far as I could to keep him from hitting me. Since we inherited "early miscellaneous" furniture, we did not sleep in twin beds until 40 years later when we purchased extra-large electric twin beds. Even then, they were flush against each other!

We had a wonderful weekend honeymoon as we did sightseeing in Colorado Springs and ended up dancing at Elitches in Denver. We could not afford more than a weekend and needed to get back to work. The following weekend, we heard the most gosh-awful noise outside our house. It was coming from everywhere. We opened the door and found 50 friends and family circling the house beating pans with spoons, tooting toy horns, beating a base drum, dancing around and yelling in several different keys. They were caught up in a shivaree, which was a way to haze and roast the bride and groom. Tradition was that everyone was invited in, and the newlyweds had to host the party. I was glad they all brought food and drink because we had few groceries in the house, and I cooked on two small electric burners. Our living room and dining room were quite large in the old house we were renting, so everyone was comfortable sitting on the floor. The party lasted for two and a half hours as they roasted us and gave crazy advice. Dessert was a cardboard cake which we tried to cut while blindfolded. Then we cut the real one. On top were figurines of a farmer and the wife with a pitchfork. Such fun!! I don't know if folks still shivaree brides and grooms, but I can highly recommend it.

Early Married Life

We were very happy, and Tom came up with mischievous antics almost daily. I thought "oh no! I will be dealing with this the rest of my life." I did have difficulty sometimes knowing when he was kidding. Frustrated one night, I tied his PJs into knots. After he worked on the knots for a while, he jumped into bed naked. Foiled again!

We got things put away and proceeded to write thank you notes. I should say, I wrote thank you notes. From that day on, I did all the note writing, gift wrapping, etc. It was good because Tom always made a mess. His big hands and lack of desire got in the way. He would say things like "my nose is sore" or "I have a hip bind twist, so I can't help." One night his friends asked him to go out. I thought it would be OK, but he said, "That's a good way for a married man to get in trouble." I loved him so much for that wise statement.

We had Hap and Mae and Tom's folks for dinner, and they were surprised that I put out a meal with only two electric burners. Tom always said that I invented one-skillet meals years before they became popular. We discussed buying a car we had seen advertised in the paper with Hap and Mr. Nix. They went with us to look at it. It was a honey—a 1934 Ford coupe that needed some work and paint. As the saying goes, "we bought it for a song", and Hap offered to have it painted. We chose cherry red. A short time later when Tom was driving, he did not stop in time and ran the front end under a truck. Needless to say, none of us were happy about that!

Tom's folks were acquainted with the Longmans who lived in Fort Collins. Mrs. Longman was trying to find an apartment for us. The Sheldon's offered to fix their upstairs for us. There was a large bedroom, a bath and the kitchen had been a sunroom. It had a nice stove and plenty of counter space and a sink with no running water. We were not bothered that we had to get water from the bathroom for cooking and washing dishes. The price was right at $10 per month. In visiting with the Sheldons, the four of us could tell that we would get along fine. We had to go through their kitchen and part of their dining room to go upstairs, but that did not bother anyone. Mrs. Sheldon said we could use her icebox. The icebox was a forerunner to the refrigerator. The deliveryman had a truckload of huge ice blocks that he loaded from the icehouse. He used mega tongs to carry the ice block into the house and place it in the wooden icebox. It was amazing how long that block of ice lasted.

We went back to Boulder satisfied with the apartment and the set up. I really did not know how to address Mr. and Mrs. Nix. I did not like introducing them as my in-laws. I had heard too many bad jokes about in-laws. Mr. Nix said, "Call us something, anything." Tom said to call them mom and dad. They had been like parents to me for some time. Hap and Mae assured me they would not be offended. Hap had asked me if they could adopt me during my senior year. Years later, I was sorry my answer could not have been different, but since I knew they did not approve of my marrying before college graduation, I declined.

The remainder of summer was filled with game nights at our place, plus times at Lakeside Amusement Park, swimming, horseback riding, church events, movies, watching ballgames, bowling, and playing pool with our friends. I was still involved in church youth camp, except in a more executive way than before, helping with planning and counseling. I really enjoyed my last year at youth camp. When consecration night rolled around, I was led to dedicate my life to serve God in Education and Music. I'll have to admit that pangs of being in the medical field sort of hung in the background. My chemistry high school instructor encouraged me to become a surgeon or to go into medical research. Years later, God made it possible for me to assist our family doctor in a way I could never have dreamed about.

Tom's brother, Joe, graduated from high school and left to play baseball with the All Stars. By this time, his relationship had grown deeper with Lora.

Fashion Bar gave a good discount to employees, so I purchased a beautiful wine-colored suit which served me for many years. Tom also bought some new clothes. We were ready to move into our apartment in Fort Collins. I had already been to Aggies to enroll and transfer my credits from CU. I was grateful that my scholarship also transferred. Another blessing was that I was hired as Assistant Student Librarian at Aggies. My boss at CU had called the head librarian at Aggies and encouraged her to hire me. Tom got a job working for the athletic department.

On September 10, 1947, Mary Jane and Bob were married in Fort Collins at the First Christian Church by Rev. Harrison. Tom and I were their attendants. Mom and Dad and Bob's mother witnessed the ceremony. I could not help but think how Mary Jane dreamed of a large church wedding when Taylor broke their engagement. However, Bob was head and shoulders above Taylor in every way.

I was busy getting things straightened up in our apartment. It was strange, at first, going through the Sheldon's home to reach our apartment. Tom had responsibilities at the Sigma Nu house. While he was gone for a few evenings, I lengthened the hem on my skirts since it was more chic. We were so welcomed at church, and there were activities for college students. We sang in the choir, and it was great attending services with Mary Jane and Bob. In fact, the four of us spent a lot of time together during the next two years playing bridge, attending concerts, movies, potluck suppers at church, car races, and athletic events, especially watching Tom play basketball. On occasion, all four of us spent weekends in Boulder.

Before classes and our jobs began, we opened an account at Poudre Valley Bank. We were able to deposit $400 from both of our saved earnings and vowed to leave it there except in case of an emergency. I prepared envelopes that we kept in the kitchen cupboard. They were marked Church, Rent, Groceries, Gas, School Supplies, and Miscellaneous. Once in a blue moon we had 50 or 75 cents in the miscellaneous envelope that enabled us to see a movie and buy popcorn. Those were special dates whenever they rolled around. On one occasion, we had to walk home because the car would not start. We were happy to walk the mile, hand in hand.

One evening, Tom asked me if I loved him more than anyone. I said, "no", and his head drooped until I added that I loved Jesus more than him. Then he asked, "Will you love me when I am 50?" Fifty was very old to a 19- and 20-year-old, but I did say. "I will love you way beyond that." We were very happy even though we had our arguments, and some were donnybrooks. I accused him of being a "know-it-all" more than once. We had agreed to kiss each other "good morning" and "good night" even if we were angry. Sometimes that made us burst out laughing, but we honored that gesture except for one situation that arose in the 1960s. Even then, I kissed Tom on the cheek.

Tom was a good kisser, and I asked him where he learned that. He said, "Dad showed me how." I said, "He showed you?" His answer was, "Yes, dad kissed both Joe and me to teach us, and then lectured us about stopping before we got into trouble." I thought, "jumpin' Jehosaphat!" I had never heard of that. I did appreciate other things his parents taught him. Tom had excellent personal hygiene, always turned his pants pockets inside out before placing them in the laundry, and usually laid his clothes out every evening for the next day. I never, in our 70 years of marriage, picked up one item of clothing after him. Friends would say, "You're kidding?" My answer was, "Nope, not even one sock."

I began typing all of Tom's school papers when we were in high school. I continued to help him in that way. In his writing he left out words, and his spelling was atrocious. Tom always liked lecture classes and could recall the lessons, but reading was not his favorite way to learn. It took me awhile to figure out that he was dyslexic. I read his lessons to him in bed every night. I became absorbed and interested in his classes, especially genetics, animal behavior and production, anatomy, and others. Tom told countless people he never would have made it through college without me.

Our jobs usually did not coincide. Tom worked for Charlie, a delightful middle-aged man from England, in the athletic department. He sometimes worked between classes and usually on weekends after athletic games and activities unless the basketball team played in town or out of state. I worked two different shifts at the library. Sometimes from 3:30-6:30 and often from 4:00-10:00 which was closing time. I rode the trolley home at 6:30, and Tom would pick me up when I worked until 10:00. One evening, he had put the potatoes on to cook. When I got home, he asked how long it took for them to cook. He got wide-eyed when I said about 20-25 minutes. He had put huge potatoes in the pot whole, and swore he would never try to cook again. He almost kept that promise. A few times when Tom picked me up at 10:00, he would find some of the male students asking me questions or to please get them one more book from the stacks. Tom would announce it was closing time, that I was his wife and to get lost. At Colorado A&M there were 10 boys to every girl on campus. It was not unusual to be the only female in some classes. Considering that the total enrollment at Aggies was around 3,500, it was easy to become acquainted.

I was asked to join the Sophomore Women's Honorary called "The Spurs." It was a combination pep/service club. We held fundraisers to help students' children and those in the community and planned parties throughout the years. We wore saddle shoes plus green and white skirts and sweaters with the Aggie emblem. I tried out for the basketball team and was placed on the first five. I had also played the same at Colorado University. Our games were on Saturday mornings and the crowd usually numbered 25-40. Women's sports were not supported very well until Title IX took effect in the 70s. Even then, it was several years before women's athletics were recognized. I also played shortstop on the softball team and forward striker on the field hockey team.

Bob, Mary Jane and I went to the basketball games together. Tom always played really well. In high school, he was a nine-letter man: Basketball, Football and Track. And yet, that old "not good enough" feeling would grab hold of him. I discovered that part of it came from his parents and Mary Jane's statements that Tom was a good athlete, but Joe was the all-around gifted athlete. Joe was three years younger than Tom, so was spoiled in some ways. He slacked off while Tom remained the obedient son. Joe would disappear when there was work to be done and somehow became involved in fights. Tom would step in to rescue him. One of those times was after a football game in Longmont. Tom, his parents and I came upon the fight and saw Joe getting beaten up pretty badly. I witnessed Tom's physical strength that night. He jumped out of the car, took care of the two boys that had Joe pinned down, plus a few others. The fight ended. Now, I understood why the guys said, "You never want to provoke Tom Nix to fight." I had mixed emotions as I saw gentle Tom turn into a barracuda.

Tom and I had a lot of fun together. We ran races, had food fights, played jokes on each other, and measured to see who could spit a mouthful of water the furthest. One night, Tom decided to show me some wrestling holds. I thought I could wiggle out of one and found myself flying into the dresser. The next morning Mrs. Sheldon asked if we dropped something. She was a very proper lady, and I almost laughed at her expression when I told her what had happened. We became very fond of the Sheldons, and I appreciated how much I learned from Mrs. Sheldon about gardening and canning vegetables and fruit.

When Christmas of 1947 rolled around, Mom and Dad gave us a Kelvinator refrigerator. But there was a catch. Dad was known to make decisions for his family when he found a good deal. Although he and Mom made a large down payment on the refrigerator, we had to take over the $10.00 monthly payments. I was not too pleased and was ready to voice my opinion when Tom stopped me. Hap and Mae gave us an automatic toaster and Joe gave us towels. Mary Jane and Bob gave us $15.00 which would go toward the first month's payment on the refrigerator with $5.00 in an envelope toward the next payment.

During the year, Tom and I met at the student union every noon to eat lunch together. Those were precious moments of uninterrupted talking and sharing. We usually had PBJs or honey and peanut butter, plus fruit and cookies I had baked. We sat in the car to eat unless the weather was too cold. We learned that frozen honey and peanut butter sandwiches were delicious. That gave me ideas to freeze bread, sandwiches and to experiment with produce that turned out pretty good. Mrs. Sheldon was interested in freezing produce, too, so I offered her space in our refrigerator freezer.

We loved our Ford Coupe, but it lacked proper windshield wipers, a heater, and a gas gauge. When driving to out-of-town football games we encountered a couple of blizzards. Young people thought nothing about driving in a blizzard or getting all wet watching games. When Tom could not see the road anymore, we would stop while I wiped the windshield with towels. I was wet before we got to the games. There was a hole in the floor of the car that provided some heat from the engine. I would tell Tom we needed to fill up with gas, and he always said we could make it a few more miles. I cannot count the times we pushed that little Ford to a gas station. I lovingly called Tom "Dumb, Dumb" while I slacked off so he would have to push harder. He would tell me to do my part, and I would answer, "I did my part when I told you we needed gas. "

We never missed a school dance or those held at the Sigma Nu house and had great fun at the formal dances. We were fortunate to dance to live big bands during high school and college. Even though jitterbugging was our favorite, we loved gliding around the floor to a waltz, a two-step or dancing the polka. Many times, other dancers would stop to watch us, mainly because Tom did the splits and many other gyrations he made up. The bands would usually play the Charleston which I loved. I taught the steps and moves to Tom. We planned to try it at the next dance. Right in the middle of the dance, Tom decided to make up his own steps. So much for that! Sometimes when the Aggies had a basketball game out of town, I drove home to Boulder for the weekend. I would spend time with Hap and Mae and the Nixes and get together with friends. On a few occasions, Tom and I would go home together for a weekend, which was always a treat.

I was learning to play bridge. Tom and Mary Jane grew up playing with their folks. Mary Jane, Bob and Tom taught me to play. I had my cheat sheets which told me how many points I had to have to open or answer a bid. Early on in one game, I passed. So did everyone else. Mary Jane asked to see my hand. I laid down 9 spades, an ace of hearts, a jack of diamonds, and two small clubs. Mary Jane said, "You idiot. You big idiot. You cannot pass with a hand like that." I counted points and did not have enough to open. I had not learned about pre-empt bidding or how many points a singleton was. It was a good thing my feelings were not easily hurt, or I may not have played again. I really learned to play well from Tom who was a whiz. We enjoyed playing in several bridge groups throughout our married life and often won. As for Mary Jane's words—well, that was how the Nixes talked to each other and always loudly which was due in part because Mom was so hard of hearing. I was brought up in more quiet surroundings, and, of course, with that antiquated statement that girls should be quieter and more ladylike. Even though it was my nature not to be loud, I jolly-well learned to hold my own with the Nix Clan. So did gentle Bob when the occasion arose. I always believed that God smiled when He put opposites together in marriage to fight it through! Bob and I had mutual respect which led to a wonderful in-law relationship. In gatherings, when there were loud expressions of opinions, we would look at each other, smile and hold up fingers designating how many minutes we thought it would last.

I used the Better Homes & Garden Cookbook. Most women did. When my first one wore out years later, I received a later edition for Christmas. Tom complimented me on the gourmet meals I fixed. However, after two weeks, he said, "Honey, the meals you have prepared were very delicious, but I am really a meat, potatoes and gravy man." I was OK with that because it made menu planning and cooking easier. Tom loved his desserts. One time, I made a three-layer chocolate torte cake that he even ate for breakfast!

During spring quarter, Dr. Bueche, Music Department Chair, asked if I would like to teach and direct the choirs at Fort Collins High School. Miss Bauder, the director, had broken her knee. There were no music substitutes in Fort Collins, so the music staff and Dr. Bueche selected me. I was carrying 20 hours and asked Dr. Bueche about my classes. He assured me that he would talk to my professors and get all my assignments that I could pick up and complete in the evenings. He also said the job would pay a little. Evenings turned into half nights since I still kept the same hours with my library job. But—I loved teaching high school students. The advanced choir was preparing a concert. Miss Bauder was out for six weeks. The first week I taught, I went into the teacher's lounge to get my lunch out of the locker. At that time, Miss Hixon came in stating that students were not allowed in the teachers' lounge and what was I doing there? I said, "But I...," and that was all I got out of my mouth. She took me by the arm, and I decided to surrender as she marched me into the principal's office. The principal was at his desk, looked up and asked if there was a problem. Miss Hixon gave her speech and then the principal said, "Miss Hixon, meet Mrs. Nix who is substituting for Miss Bauder." Miss Hixon was embarrassed. It was a logical mistake since I was only a year or two older than the students. Through the years, each time Mabel Hixon and I saw each other, we burst out laughing. I loved teaching the high school students. After the advanced choir concert, parents gave compliments, the students were proud of their performance, and I received notes from the principal and a few other teachers. Miss Bauder thanked me over the phone, and she was also pleased. I did not meet her in person at that time, but our paths crossed years later which was a blessing to me and my family. The opportunities in music that I experienced in public schools, Colorado University and Aggies (Colorado A & M) had prepared me well to teach the high school students. I did not want it to end.

Mr. Wood was my vocal and choral instructor. Tom and I became good friends with him and his family. I told Mr. Wood that even though Tom did not read music, he had a very nice voice. After hearing Tom sing, we signed him up for vocal lessons. Tom had ten lessons but had to quit because his schedule was so tight. During our married life and my career, Tom was my best supporter and cheerleader. His love of music was instilled by his mom.

Mary Jane, Bob, Tom and I loved it when we could work out our schedules for a picnic, a drive in the mountains, bridge games and the occasional weekends spent in Boulder.

Tom and I had good friends who lived in one of the Quonset Huts, part of the first Aggie Village student housing. The huts were made of a prefabricated metal. They were corrugated steel in a semicircular shape. Bill and Margo played bridge, so we spent a lot of time in their hut. The huts were hot in the summer and difficult to heat in the winter, but they were at a minimal cost for the GIs and their families. All conversation would end when rain or hail pelted the metal building.

As summer neared, Tom was thrilled to get a job with Gunthry-Callahan Construction. Their crew was working on building the Horsetooth Reservoir. The tiny town of Stout, a sandstone quarry town, had been buried during the project. Tom had been a ship fitter in the Navy, so he was an experienced welder. His job was welding equipment that broke down. Sometimes his work was on the huge trucks that hauled dirt referred to as "Yukes." They are the largest dump trucks in the world and would cost $6M per truck today. I called the drivers and those trucks "perpendicular monkeys." It looked as if at any moment they would tip over backward as they crept up the steep hills. Those drivers had to be brave. During the summer, I worked in the documents department of the library and found it very interesting. Tom and I did not see much of each other the first three weeks. He was on the graveyard or midnight shift, and I worked 8:00 to 5:00. We would meet each other coming and going until Tom talked with his boss and asked for a different shift so we could spend some normal time together. The boss was very understanding and only on occasion did Tom work the late-night shift. We not only had time together, but we were able to play bridge with Mary Jane, Bob and friends and help at the church. By this time, I was teaching children's Sunday School again, which I enjoyed. We always looked forward to the church potluck dinners which were delicious, and we left with take-home food.

Before school began in the fall of 1948, we were able to spend a week in Boulder with family and friends, which was a treat. My boss was so kind to give me that time off, and Tom had finished his contract with Gunthry-Callahan. Tom asked that his pay be held during the summer. We were thrilled to deposit $600.00 into our bank account.

Our junior year was very busy. I had been initiated into Hesperia, the Junior Women's Honorary, and was still active in sports, school, and church activities. In addition to my academics, I was excited to learn another form of dance, so I signed up for Modern Interpretive Dance which included performances. Besides playing on the basketball team, Tom had signed up for additional work hours and volunteered to help with the "newbie" freshmen at the Sigma Nu House. He was delighted to assign freshmen the task of carrying little baby pots half full of water and one goldfish to every class and football game.

One night around 10:00, some of the fraternity brothers dropped him off. In the loudest voice, he yelled, "You guys be quiet so you don't wake up my wife," which told me he had more than one beer. It was rare for him to party with the guys, after an experience early in our marriage. We had gone with a group of our friends to the Red Lion Inn located in Boulder Canyon. The wives and girlfriends of the other guys drove home, but Tom insisted he was OK. Halfway down the canyon, I asked him to stop. I took the key out of the ignition and went around to the driver's side. When we arrived home, I went in and got ready for bed. I went out to see what was keeping Tom and found him sound asleep on the back porch stoop. I covered him with a blanket and went to bed. He came in around 3:00 a.m., apologizing, and in his dainty way, threw himself on the bed, breaking the slats. That was not the first time we ended up sleeping on the floor. I told my friends we had "Early Miscellaneous" furniture, and that bed was from the earliest times.

Bill called the day after Christmas to tell us what fun it was to watch two-year-old Pammy open her Christmas gifts. Pammy spoke into the phone to wish Aunt Patsy Merry Christmas. So cute! It was good to talk with Bill and Janey. Janey was still working at the hospital and Bill was buried in his studies. He was looking forward to graduating next year and was hoping to find a teaching job in Colorado. That would be swell.

In May, I found out that I was pregnant. Wow! I was hoping to finish college first, but we were both happy about it. When I was three months along, we told the Sheldons. The next day they said as much as they enjoyed us as renters, having a baby in the house might be too much. We were OK with that because we would not have been comfortable with the situation.

For a year, we had purchased our milk from Mr. Toothaker who lived on an acreage at the corner of Vine Drive and Shields. Tom noticed that two college-aged students lived with him, so he asked about the situation. When told the students would be graduating, Tom asked if we could rent part of the house. Mr. Toothaker said we could enjoy the entire house if we would cook and clean for him as part of our rent. We were delighted. It was no coincidence. God was taking care of us again!

In the fall, I had a phone call. The man said, "Hi Patsy. This is your dad. I have my wife and two little girls with me. Can we come see you?" He was a stranger to me, who had never cared about my brother and me. I gave him directions to our house. He introduced me to Geraldine, his wife, and to Jackie (age 2) and Yvonne (age 3). Those little girls were so darling, and I fell in love with them immediately. I fixed lunch and took the girls outside to play. My dad led me to the car, opened the trunk, and the first thing I saw was a pistol. He said it was for his protection. He reached for a box and handed it to me. It was my brother's Purple Heart. Bill had been injured when the ship he served on was torpedoed. Our dad had visited him at the hospital in San Diego before Bill was transferred to a hospital in Iowa. He stole the Purple Heart and told everyone that it was his. I was so happy to return the Purple Heart to Bill. I never saw my dad again, and in later years, I tried to find my sisters without success. I heard they had been raised by two maiden aunts in Iowa. My thoughts returned often to those darling girls and what had happened to them.

Family Life

In 1948, it was unusual for pregnant women to attend college, but everyone was supportive. Mary Jane worked between her classes at the Student Health Center. I came down with a bad cold and flu symptoms. I made a point to visit the health center when Mary Jane worked so she could give me my shots. I continued with all my classes. Even in my sixth month, I did not show much because thoughtful Mary Jane had made a darling pink suit with a box jacket for me and a flared green jumper. I was determined to keep my weight in check, so I walked the three miles to the campus in nice weather. It worked as I only gained 17 pounds. The guys in my classes insisted on helping me up and down stairs, especially those in Old Main which were creaky and unsteady. I really was in good physical shape, but I kindly accepted help. The quarter ended on December 18, and my due date was January 8. The library staff sent me off with a baby shower. Since I was so close to my due date, the entire family would spend Christmas with us at Mr. Toothaker's. I scrubbed floors, washed walls, and baked a lot in preparation for Christmas dinner. Christmas Eve we were all gathered around the piano singing carols.

At 9:30, I told Tom we should go to the hospital. Thomas Edward Nix, III was born at 4:00 a.m. Christmas morning. What a Christmas gift! Tom was asleep in a bed down the hall. There was a lot of scurrying around by the nurses, and they put me completely out. The doctor had been at a Christmas Eve party and did not move fast enough to deliver my baby, so the nurses delivered 5-pound 9-ounce Eddy. Tom asked if Eddy was all right. He had long fingernails and had scratched his little face. Tom wheeled the baby buggy in the room. It was loaded with presents which we opened together. Later, the entire family took turns visiting and looking at Eddy through the nursery glass. After our hospital stay, Eddy and I headed home. I was in considerable pain not only from the stitches but from internal problems that occurred because I had not been cared for properly. After the family left, our precious friends, Dick and Peg, came to stay with us. Peggy was a real pro at taking care of Eddy and me. Learning to cook on a big coal stove was a challenge for her. We were so grateful for the love shown by Dick and Peg and said goodbye after a week.

On January 2, 1949, Northern Colorado and Wyoming were hit with a historic storm. Eddy and I had been home from the hospital one day. The upstairs where we slept was so cold that we huddled in blankets near the coal stove in the kitchen. The worst thing was changing the baby in that extreme cold because he would be wet from head to toe. Blizzard conditions stranded motorists between Fort Collins and the Wyoming border. The temperature dipped to 17 below zero and dropped to 50 below zero later! Patrolmen were delivering milk and food to travelers. Ted's Place (a filling station and store north of Fort Collins) took in as many people as their building would hold. The Town of Wellington rescued 80 people. Unfortunately, some folks did not make it. The death toll was in the 80s. Four feet of snow fell and the wind piled some drifts 30 feet high. It was the worst storm on record for the Northern Plains. President Truman declared the region a disaster. The U.S. Army Corps of Engineers launched Operation Snowbound. Roads were opened and more than 4 million head of livestock were fed. More than 158,000 cattle and sheep died. The states affected were Colorado, Wyoming, South Dakota and Nebraska. On January 5, the skies began to open up, and the sun peeked through on January 6.

Mr. Toothaker was nearing 90 years old, and he was glad to turn over the milking to Tom. We had a separator and when I gathered enough cream, I churned butter. At my first doctor appointment, I was told to feed Eddy every three hours. At the next appointment, Eddy was above the weight chart. I asked the doctor when I could go to four-hour feedings. He said, "My God, are you still doing every three hours? No wonder this baby has gained so much!" Well, I was a new mother, so what did I know? At three months, I ran out of milk which the doctor attributed to my doing too much work. I asked if I could give Eddy our fresh milk if I pasteurized it. He said yes, so I studied about pasteurization. Eddy did really well on that milk.

Because the floor was cold, Eddy was either in the playpen or baby buggy. I took him outside when the weather was nice. He tried to reach through the playpen slats to Wiggles, Mr. Toothaker's cocker spaniel. As I hung clothes on the line, I talked to Eddy about everything he could see. Consequently, his first sentence was "see the birdie." He walked round and round holding on to the playpen and walked on his own at nine months. When I ran short errands, Mr. Toothaker watched him. I can still see Mr. Toothaker rocking the buggy with his foot. Tom used his own approach to rock Eddy to sleep. He held him on his knee, keeping the rhythm as he sang "Boogie Woogie Washer Woman!"

Although I could have kept my job at the university, I decided to stay home with my baby. When Eddy was nine months old, I was offered the job as secretary of International Harvester which paid well. My friend, Juanita, took care of him. How fortunate that God placed her in my life. My job allowed Tom to quit his second job and concentrate on his studies. He was on track to graduate a quarter early.

About that time, Tom's dad found out that the Stearn's Dairy in Broomfield was for sale. He had the idea that Bob, Mary Jane, Tom and I should run the dairy which meant that Bob, Mary Jane, and Tom would drop out of school. Dad did not talk to me about it, but Tom told me, stating that it was a great opportunity. I said, "So you are going to quit school and not graduate? I do not agree that this is a great opportunity just to take on a huge mortgage and all that goes with it." Also, as much as I loved Mary Jane, she had a strong personality (like telling me how to peel potatoes). Tom said, "Dad is going to be very disappointed." I said, "That's OK. I did not marry your dad. I married you." Nothing more was said, except at a later time when Dad was helping me paint the kitchen.

He never mentioned the event but made the statement that he found out I would not let people walk on me. It tickled me, for I dearly loved him.

Our time at Mr. Toothaker's was wonderful. I had a huge garden, so we enjoyed canned vegetables and lots of Kosher dill pickles with garlic. All winter, we enjoyed the food. One night when Tom and I went to the movie while Mary Jane and Bob watched Eddy, Bob asked if Tom had eaten dill pickles. He had not, but he had chewed a piece of garlic. Every once in a while, Tom cupped his hand over his mouth and blew his breath my way thinking it would punish me. It did not work! On Saturdays, I baked pies, cakes, cookies, and bread. At dinner, I would ask Mr. Toothaker if he would like a piece of cherry, apple, or banana cream pie, and he always answered "Yes." That is the same answer Tom gave throughout our marriage.

People across the street had a small grocery business which was very convenient. They were so taken with Eddy that they encouraged us to go out so they could babysit. We took Eddy most everywhere, but he did not like the loud noise at basketball games. We decided to leave him with the Browns for some of those games, and also when we went dancing.

Tom's parents hosted Christmas dinner in 1949. Eddy smashed his little one-year-old birthday cake on top of his head and squished it with his hands. We adults played monopoly nearly all night and card games the next night. Later, it was nice to be with some of our friends before we headed back home.

Someone told us that time goes by fast after you have children. How true! And, yes, Tom continued his teasing and orneriness. However, I got the drop on him a lot. And, yes, we had our differences and arguments along with our love for each other. We were best friends! However, from time to time, Tom showed that feeling of not measuring up. He still needed lots of encouragement.

Our First Farm

The year 1950 was a year of newness for us. In March, Tom graduated from Aggies with a degree in Animal Husbandry. I thought that was an antiquated name for a major. After the Aggies name was changed to Colorado State University, they updated Tom's major to Animal Science. Dad had found a dryland farm for Tom and me to buy. It was located 5 miles east and 2 miles north of Hudson, Colorado. Hudson was a small farming community located 9 miles east of Fort Lupton and 7 miles North of Keenesburg. It was difficult to leave Mr. Toothaker. He was like our grandpa and the three of us shed tears. It was also hard for Eddy to leave Wiggles.

Off we went to the farm with $400 in our pockets. The mortgage was $1,000 a year. Mr. Dick Culverwell owned the land and assured us that they would work with us young people. Eddy had a large vocabulary at age two, having been around adults for the most part. We introduced him to Mr. Dick Culverwell. Eddy immediately called him 'Dickie'. Upon correcting him, Mr. Culverwell got such a kick out of it, and told Eddy he could call him Dickie from now on. The farm consisted of 128 acres without water rights. A few of the bottom acres were sub-irrigated, good for raising alfalfa. The house sat on a hill, had two bedrooms, an L-shaped living/dining room and a kitchen with a combination wood/coal cooking stove. There was a full unfinished basement with no inside entrance. It had a small back porch and a larger front porch. We began to gather our early miscellaneous furniture from family and friends. We ended up with a kitchen table and four chairs, a dining room table with chairs, a couch and one easy chair, a double bed and a single bed for Eddy. We had purchased a trundle table for Eddy which served for eating and playing. I went to the grocery store and asked for two orange crates. Turning them on their sides, I made a shelf in the middle. I threaded wire on overlapping material at the top and strung it around the crates, securing with nails where needed. Presto! We had a dresser.

The barn and corral were located west at the bottom of the hill, and there was a shed east of the house. A chicken coop was on the north side. There was a fence in the front yard and plenty of space out back for a garden. I got busy right away planting a garden. It became impossible because we soon found out that the jet pump on the water well could not furnish enough water. We had to run water in buckets and pans to have enough for use in the house. It took three days to draw water for doing the laundry. Crawling down the ladder and priming the pump was a royal pain in the butt, and it happened often. Flushing the toilet was another story, but we had no money to remedy the situation at the time, so we just rolled with it. It became a laughing matter when company came and we had to caution them about flushing the toilet.

Since we had no farm machinery, Dad loaned us the money to get started. The first tractor we had was a little Ford that we purchased from Montgomery Ward. Watching Tom pull the manure spreader was hilarious. That light tractor reared up its front wheels like a bucking bronco as Tom let out with expletives, language he had picked up in the Navy which often took the Lord's name in vain. I prayed for God to take that away from him. Tom planted the lower acres of the farm in corn. He was able to rent some water, but we mostly prayed for rain. In June, the Korean War broke out and Tom received a letter telling him to report for duty. Golly, we were just getting settled. I pulled Tom's reserve papers from the file and was happy to advise the general that Tom's time in the Reserves was up the end of May. Tom received confirmation, so we were able to breathe again.

People in the town of Hudson kept to themselves. The first time we went to town was to rent a mailbox. We spoke to people we met, and they just looked at us. Later, we introduced ourselves to nearby neighbors. Our visits with the Foos, Harkis, and Weimer families went well. There were three Foos families that joined together in farming. We discovered one lived across the road from the Harkis family and had never met. This was quite foreign to Tom and me as Boulder and Fort Collins people were friendly in town and in rural areas. We decided to suggest something we thought might draw folks together. I visited with each farm wife, explained a 'progressive dinner' and asked if they would be interested in meeting and visiting with neighbors in this way. They all agreed. What a feast and good time we had as we traveled to the different homes. We ended up at our place for dessert. As Tom said, "I had a college education, but those friends taught me how to farm." The Foos families operated a large dairy, and Tom was able to suggest more modern ways to help them. They recognized that we were struggling on our dryland farm and told Tom if he had any extra time at all, they could use his help. What a godsend!! We had a big truck, but had no racks for it. The Weimer family asked Tom if they could purchase racks for the truck so he could help them harvest their beets. They insisted on paying Tom. We were able to purchase a decent tractor.

One evening, Tom came in dead tired from struggling with trickles of water in the corn rows. He asked what I thought about buying a few milk cows. We had purchased 200 baby chicks that I cared for, and we figured that eggs and cream could pay for groceries. We had to wait awhile until we were able to purchase six cows and a bull. We talked about needing a puppy. Tom's folks saw an ad in the Boulder *Camera* about six collie/German shepherd puppies to give away. We figured they would be smart puppies. I drove up Boulder Canyon to see them. When I arrived, the owner walked me out back where I saw five puppies playing. I asked where the sixth one was. She said he always followed his mother out to herd the turkeys. I said, "That's the puppy I want. " I came home with a nine-week-old puppy that we named Smokey. Knowing he would cry for his mom and siblings, I made a soft bed in the clothes basket and wrapped our alarm clock in a towel, placing it next to Smokey. He only whined a little while before falling asleep. Of course, Eddy loved playing with him. The second week we had Smokey, we were milking and heard his tiny bark. We found him behind a cow, barking at her hoof. It is a wonder he did not get kicked. Eddy sat on a little chair in the corner drawing, singing and playing while we milked. When Smokey was four months old, Tom was cleaning the barnyard. The gate had to remain open for him to load the manure in the spreader. I went to keep the cows from getting out. No worry. Smokey placed himself in the middle of the open gate area and barked if a cow came near. He got double loving that day, and a bone to chew on.

We were right about the eggs and cream money. We sold our eggs and cream to the Safeway store in Brighton transporting them ourselves. Hudson had a small grocery store where one could buy staples, but I shopped twice a month at the Safeway store in Brighton.

We attended the Methodist church in Hudson for a month after we got settled on the farm, but we missed having communion every Sunday. We decided to attend the First Christian Church (DOC) in Brighton. Sixteen miles did not seem that far. We had attended services for two weeks when I was asked to direct the choir. The job paid $10 per month. I told Tom that I would sign the check and place it in the offering plate each month for our tithe. He said, "We could use that money." Tithing was new to him. I explained tithing, and as he grumbled I said we got along fine without the extra $10 per month before. I am sure as he walked outside, he let go with the expletives! There were Sundays that Tom said he had to work and did not go to church. Eddy sat in a nursery chair next to me. When he was naughty, I picked him up, held him in my left arm, and directed the choir with the other. Once in a while, Charlotte Harkis kept Eddy on Sunday mornings. I don't remember how long this pattern continued, but on one particular Sunday, when Eddy and I came home from church, Tom met us at the car and said, "Everything I did today went wrong. I think God is trying to tell me the work can wait on Sunday mornings while I go to church." I thanked God for an answered prayer.

It wasn't long before Eddy began to have severe sore throats while running high fevers. He nearly choked during one bout, and the doctor said his enlarged tonsils needed to be taken out. As much as we hated seeing a two-year-old undergo surgery, we agreed it was the only answer. We drove to Porter's Hospital in Denver. When the nurse came to carry Eddy to the operating room, I asked if they did not intend to put him to sleep first, before taking him to the OR. She assured us that he would be all right. After the surgery, the nurse handed Eddy to me. His eyes were wide open, but he was still under the effects of the anesthesia. He had gone to sleep with his eyes open from the fright of seeing the operating room, instruments, and everyone in white. We were so upset to think the medical professionals didn't use better judgment. I wanted to stay overnight but was not allowed to. Hospital rules were cruel in those days. Until Eddy was 8 years old, whenever he had a doctor or dental appointment, he clung to me and cried—they all wore white.

One night after milking, I had to return to the barn and told Eddy I would be right back. While I was finishing the cleanup, he came down to the barn and said, "Here I am with my little sweeper ready to help" He had been given a play vacuum for Christmas. He was always such a helpful child.

That summer, I found out I was pregnant, but it ended in a miscarriage of twins at three and a half months. The nurse told me that one twin was not developing. The physical and emotional toll was difficult for Tom and me, even though we knew we would see them again. Our church family surrounded us with love, help and groceries. Our farmer neighbors brought food and offered to keep Eddy.

Years later, I met a woman named Ann in the grocery store who was led to tell me her story of carrying quadruplets until it was clear that two of the babies were not receiving nourishment and would probably die, posing a threat to the other two babies. She and her husband had to make the agonizing decision for surgery to keep the perfectly formed ones. She told of feeling so empty and the longing she still had for those babies they lost. Although our experience was different, I shared with her about losing the twins, knowing they were in heaven, and how our darling Susie at age 3 stopped playing one day and suddenly said, "You know, Mommy, we get to see the twins 'cause they are waiting for us in heaven." Ann was overcome with the thought of seeing her babies whole in heaven as her tears flowed heavily along with mine. It was the first she had been able to cry in ten years. I later received a thank you letter from Ann and her husband, but it was God who intended us to meet that day in the grocery store. He also provided a grocery aisle with no traffic the entire time we were together. God did and does use our experiences and heartaches for good if we trust in Him.

I enrolled Eddy in Vacation Bible School at the Assembly of God Church in Hudson. The pastor of the church had helped Tom with work from time to time and shared with Tom that earlier in his life he had been a good-for-nothing drunk. He had cut all ties with his family and was living on the streets, when the Salvation Army came by and took him in. Their motto of food, soap, and salvation led him to Jesus and put his life back on track. The next day, Tom was fixing a piece of farm machinery, hit himself with the wrench, and let loose with the expletives including taking the Lord's name in vain. Eddy was with Tom and began to sing a song he learned at Bible School. "Thou shall not take the name of the Lord, your God, in vain." Tom fell to the ground weeping. He came into the house and asked if I would pray with him that he would not use the Lord's name in vain again. And he never did! Tom's mother and I had prayed five years for that answer. God was listening and chose words of a babe to answer our prayer.

Grandma Purdy and Eddy

Our house had only the kitchen stove and a small heater in the living room. I heard that the area needed a telephone operator and applied for the job. I wanted to earn enough to carpet our floors so it would be warmer for Eddy. Grandma Purdy offered to stay with Eddy for my two weeks of training. What a delight to have her around again, and she was just as mischievous as ever. Since I would work the night shift from 10:00 p.m. to 6:00 a.m., it would work well with Eddy's schedule. He would just be waking up when I got home.

Adolph Martinez, whose parents had moved to Commerce City, wanted to finish high school in Hudson. He had the opportunity to work for four different farmers, but he chose us. He was a blessing and quickly became part of the family. We set up a bed in the basement where he slept quite warm in a feather mattress and covers.

The old telephone boards held panels with individual metal drops that would ring when calls came in. I used a cord with a plug at each end to answer and ring calls. Every night at 11:00 p.m. the train would go rumbling by which sent all the drops in motion. It took a bit to get everything up and running again. At midnight, the Town Constable came by to see if everything was all right, then went on his way to check locks on all the businesses. I worked for four months to earn enough for the carpet. I was told I would receive better pay if I stayed, but I was glad to get back on a regular schedule.

Our Growing Family

After I had been told that I would not be able to carry a baby after losing the twins, Tom's response was that we would see Dr. Bonham. In earlier years, he was the Nixes' family doctor who had become a gynecologist with an office in Denver. After examining me, he commented that my uterus had become bound by adhesions, and instead of surgery he recommended trying to remedy the problem that day. He said, "Wait a minute because I want Tom to come into the examining room. I believe husbands need more information about what their wives go through." He explained to both of us that what he was about to do would be very painful. With some instruments, pulling and tugging (which seemed to take a long time), he was successful in loosening the adhesions. He was sure right about it being very painful. I was put on medication and an antibiotic. At the next visit, Dr. Bonham said it was safe to try for a baby again, warning us that if I did conceive it meant that I would need to see him every three weeks until the baby weighed enough to keep my uterus from tipping.

I was able to drive myself to the appointments and Eddy was content to color and visit with the nurse. Dr. Bonham gave us a chart to check ovulation which meant that there were times I would drive near the field where Tom was working and wave a flag. Well, after a while, that got really old and there is such a thing as "being in the mood." We decided to tear up the charts and depend on God for another baby.

God answered our prayers. On July 26, 1952, Susan Marie Nix was born. Susie was a good baby, except for being a mommy's girl. I ran out of milk at the three-month mark, just like before. Susie had a stubborn streak and did not want anyone to feed her except me. I kept encouraging Tom to keep trying, but he decided it took too long. Once in a while, Susie would drink from the bottle while Eddy held it, and after some coaxing, the grandparents were successful. Tom's dad would sing "Ka,Ka,Ka Katie" and change it to "Su,Su,Su,Susie." Her eyes would widen and her mouth would open, so he quickly stuck the bottle in. Dad loved spending time on the farm and usually came on the weekends. Having a ten-chair barber shop kept him busy most of the time, and he trusted one of the barbers he employed to be in charge on the weekends he spent with us. On one occasion, I went to our hayfield to get him for lunch. He was turning the hay since it got rained on the night before. He was on his hands and knees crawling around looking for his false teeth. To save money, he had gone to Mexico for his teeth and they never did fit right, so much of the time they were in his shirt pocket. Somehow, they had fallen out! We were fortunate to find them before they got covered up. Once in a while, Mom would come with Dad, and we would have several bridge games. Mom loved rocking Eddy and Susie, calling them her little lambs.

Being around adults, Eddy's vocabulary was quite advanced, and he loved to talk. He still does! Sometimes I would ask if he would like to ride on the tractor with Daddy. I would take him down to the field where Tom was working. After about 20 minutes, Tom would bring him back to the house. I told Eddy once that talking all the time was exasperating. He said, "I know I am annoying, but there are so many questions to ask." Eddy also had an imaginary playmate that he named Dodi. Whenever Eddy got into trouble, he would say that Dodie did it.

Our Ford Coupe with all our fond memories had bit the dust. We found a pretty good deal on a used Ford sedan which we needed with two children. It was blue, and everything worked on it, including the gas gauge! Since we drove to church every Sunday and I drove to choir rehearsal every Thursday night, we were glad to have it.

We borrowed money to purchase more cows. Adolph helped with the milking, so I was able to take care of the children and only went to the barn to wash the equipment. By this time, we were shipping milk in cans picked up by the milk truck. My arms were just long enough to clean the millstone that stuck in the bottom of the cans. The young man who drove the milk truck was missing an arm. Tom and I were amazed as he swung those cans onto the truck with one arm.

Smokey was proving himself to be more valuable each day except when he decided to chase the chickens, killing two. I did not think scolding him would be sufficient, so I tied one of the dead chickens around his neck which got pretty stinky after a couple of days. Smokey begged me to remove the chicken until I gave in on the fourth day. Afterward, I walked him down to the chicken coop. We went inside where he laid down with chickens running all around him as I told him that this was off limits. He never bothered the chickens again. Smokey was very protective of the children. One day, Charlotte was visiting with her daughter, Lynn, who was three years older than Eddy. Lynn was pushing Eddy down the hill on his trike, and he was squealing with delight. Smokey thought he was hurt. He knocked Lynn to the ground and stood over her until I told him it was OK. He did not even like it when Tom and I would give the children an occasional swat. He would run between us and talk to us. I loved it when salesmen would drive into the yard. Smokey would bark and run to their car door, sometimes putting his paws on the window. When they asked if my dog would bite, I said, "Yes, if someone tried to hurt me." Smokey never bit anyone, but we knew he would if we were in danger. One Thursday night, I was followed home all the way from Brighton by a carload of drunks. When I skidded to a stop in the yard, I ran to the house calling for Smokey. He was there so quick and proceeded to jump up on the car growling. The driver could not back up fast enough to leave.

Our Holstein bull would get out at the most inopportune times. Tom would either be way down in the field helping the neighbors or at a farm sale. Most of the time, I could jump quick enough to grab the ring in the bull's nose which changed his mood, so I could lead him back to the barnyard without incident. When I was not successful, Smokey was right there to show him who was boss. He saved my life twice from that bull and stood guard while I fixed the place where he had gotten out.

We had a huge, mean boar that attacked Tom one day. Smokey saved Tom from being injured badly by him. Visions of Smokey encircling those animals were amazing—a ring of biting their hoofs, heads, noses, sides—until they gave in as he herded them to their proper place. We had invested in some pigs mostly for the meat. It was wonderful to have beef, pork, and chicken so I did not have to follow through with writing 100 different ways to fix macaroni. Even then, especially if we had unexpected company, I would add breadcrumbs to hamburger so it would go farther. Of the utmost importance to us was seeing that our children received proper nourishment. I can remember a neighbor saying they could not afford orange juice or vitamins for their children and how did we do it? My answer was—wearing holey underwear, patching Tom's jeans and coveralls until it was hard to distinguish where the original material was, going bare legged to church when my last pair of nylons gave out, etc., etc.

Tom or I would sit with a sow while she gave birth. It was too easy for them to move around while in labor and smother the newborns. One evening, I had brought some little pigs into the house because of a bad storm. I placed them in a clothes basket in the kitchen. During the night I heard the pitter patter of their feet running around on the linoleum. I got up, put them back in the basket, wondering how they got out. So I stood there watching. Three pigs stood side by side. The others climbed on top of them lending enough weight to tip the basket over. Who said that pigs were dumb? The storm from that night escalated into a terrible blizzard. We only had a shed to protect the pigs. The storm continued to blast away. Milking and feeding took a long time. Later when Tom and Adolph went to check on the pigs, they were met with an unbelievable sight. The pigs had panicked, piled on top of each other, causing many of them to smother. One had to be there after the storm to smell the stench. Tom and Adolph with help from the neighbors wore scarves around their faces as they loaded the carcasses in our truck to be disposed of. Scrubbing the truck bed and sides with vinegar and Clorox helped some, but the smell finally wore out under the sun.

Susie was such a darling and paid so much attention to all the happenings around her. She did not have much hair when she was born, so I made a little bonnet for outdoors. She loved sitting in her little seat with Smokey beside her. Such a happy baby, always smiling.

Things were working too good now because I did not have trouble getting pregnant again. Susie would be thirteen and a half months old when the next baby was due. I was gaining an enormous amount of weight, and Dr. Bonham had given me some pills for energy. I asked if they would affect the baby, and he said no. I had climbed down the ladder to prime the well pump while carrying Susie, but it was difficult this time. I barely fit in that small enclosure. I could not figure out why I was gaining so much weight as I was watching my food intake. The kitchen got so hot during the summer. We figured it reached 100 degrees in midafternoon. Tom put a fan in the window of our bedroom, so the children and I were able to cool down some. Kenneth Lynn Nix arrived on September 2, 1953. Our good friend and neighbor, Dave Weimer, went to tell Tom about both the births of Susie and Kenny since he was milking or doing chores during their births. We did not have a phone, and the cost would have been $1,000.00 to bring the line in from a mile away. The Weimer and Foos families were so good to bring us messages.

Kenny exhibited intestinal problems. The doctor showed me a technique to help with his bowel movement. He mentioned that surgery was not a good option. In addition, Kenny had what they called colic, and he cried a lot doubled up with pain. We tried our best to comfort him. To help out, Hap and Mae would come to take Eddy home for a few days. The Tureck family lived up the road from us. Elsie really loved Susie and kept her during the day from time to time. Susie was potty trained at 14 months which helped a lot. I was so grateful for family and friends. During Kenny's 8th month, he began to feel better. As he tried to walk, we noticed a curvature in his left leg which threw his foot in front of the other one. The doctor placed him in shoe braces. The braces had a wheel crank which we moved slightly during bedtime every night to straighten his leg. He had a 90-degree curvature of the tibia. The braces did not stop Kenny from doing anything or going where he wanted to go. He was a very determined little boy! It was a happy day when he was able to walk.

Dr. Bonham had said three children were enough, but we were to welcome David Robert Nix on August 10, 1955. I had called Tom's parents knowing the time was near, and they came to stay with the other children. When Tom finished the chores, I told him we needed to leave for Denver right away, and that he did not have time for a bath. When we reached Colorado Boulevard, there was a stopped train on the track. We prayed it would move quickly. When Tom came into the hospital after parking the car, a nurse asked if he would like to see his son. Whew! We just made it. There were two young fathers pacing up and down, awaiting the arrival of their babies. They asked Tom how he managed to do that! David was a good baby and slept all night. I could not believe it. I kept getting up during the night to see if he was breathing. Susie was like a little mother, especially with David. David was named after our good friend, Dave Weimer. His middle name was Robert, and Susie began to call him Robbie. I would prop David up with a pillow in a clothes basket and sit him on the table as I was working in the kitchen. I sang to all the children a lot, but David picked up singing almost before he could talk. When he was six months old, I needed surgery, so my cousin Goldie, who lived in Denver, took care of him during that time. While in the hospital, I was missing Tom and my children. After the first week, I asked Dr. Bonham if Tom could sneak the children up to my room. What a surprise to see all of them except the baby!

When I returned home, Kenny had pulled an anvil onto his little foot. It looked awful. He was always into something and was accident prone. He would also steal David's bottle and drink it. I tried fixing one for him, but he wanted David's. Kenny was hyperactive, but the adults in our family laughed at his antics. Hap, for whom Kenny was named, always said, "Ain't he cute." I often wondered if those pills I was given while carrying him caused his physical and emotional problems.

Lora, Judy, and Joe came for a visit. Tom's brother Joe and Lora married young and were having difficulties. Lora had been with her parents in Texas but returned to Boulder where she and the children lived in a motel. She filed for divorce and Joe was soon drafted. It was not easy for Lora to discuss her problems. I asked if I could pray with her. Afterward, she expressed what happened and how miserable she was. I went to the barn where Tom was milking and told him about our conversation. He suggested that I go to the neighbors and call his parents. They had certainly heard Joe's side of the problem, but not Lora's. Tom and I shared more about Jesus with Lora while Mom and Dad were on their way. She told us later that she left a different person. God was at work again! Lora became a sweet witness for the Lord. When Mom and Dad arrived, they embraced Lora and ended up taking her and the children home with them. Lora was expecting their third child. Joe was remorseful, missed his family, and asked Lora to bring the children to California where he was stationed. They reconciled and added John and Jack to their family.

It was evident that Kenny lived in his own little world which added greatly to Tom's frustration. Tom began to have outbursts of anger, mostly directed at Kenny. When Kenny was four, Tom slapped him on the face, which caused a huge bruise. I asked Tom to promise me he would never hit our children on their face again. He promised and kept it. I also asked Tom where all that anger came from, and he could not tell me at that time, but he eventually told me that Mom never disciplined Tom and Joe but would tell Dad if they misbehaved. There would be no questions asked as Dad grabbed the belt and used it, sometimes unmercifully on the boys. Tom was targeted the most. One time, Mary Jane accused Tom of stealing some pennies from her. Tom did not do it, but Dad beat him so badly that he finally confessed to make him stop. Tom told his dad about it years later. I had seen my step-grandfather use a cane on my brother and uncles. In those days, the norm was to beat kids until they behaved. We were worlds apart in our discipline, something we had not discussed thoroughly, except Tom said he would not discipline Susie because he did not want to hurt her. Having witnessed beatings with belts and canes along with babysitting and teaching Sunday School, I chose a different approach to discipline by denying privileges or sending the children to their rooms. I did apply the back of my hand a few times when needed, and gave Ed a good whack when he was a teenager.

To keep the children warm during the winter, I purchased sheet blankets from Montgomery Ward and made what I called a 'Bundle Up'. I used three layers per child and cut them to size with moving room. I wanted zippers, but there were none made as long as I needed, so I used snaps. The children slept snug and warm. I had requests from friends to make some for their children, which I did. Years later when we saw such items in the store, Tom said we should have gotten a patent. It was not long before Hap and Dad installed a stoker furnace they found in a house that was being demolished. The furnace heated the entire house including the basement where the children played and Adolph slept. What a wonderful gift that was, and it was so appreciated.

The next thing Hap and Dad said was that we needed to have a well drilled. We knew the well we had was drying up. The owner of the drilling company came out to the farm, walked around and told us that there was no water on our farm. He found no low spot, but Tom and Dad (using a witching stick), asked him to drill about 35 feet out from the dining room window. It took a day to set up the drilling equipment. The children and I would watch from the dining room window. The drill kept working deeper and deeper—200 feet, 300 feet, 400 feet, 500 feet. We were asked if we wanted them to keep going and we said "yes." Just before the 800-foot mark and to the surprise of the men, they hit a wonderful vein of water. We were all yelling and dancing around. Only God could have made that possible. It took three more days for the men to finish capping the well and laying the pipes. Since it was close to the house, they dug a cellar-like hole which led to our basement and placed the pump there—how convenient, and how grateful we were to have good drinking water, enough water to bathe each child separately, and to have enough water immediately to do laundry. I planted grass, trees, and flowers in the yard.

We had visits from our close high school chums. There were six couples, and all but one married their high school sweethearts. We would gather once a month for potlucks since we all lived within 70 miles of each other. Sometimes the guys would come our way to hunt. Well, I learned later they came mostly to have the big breakfasts and other meals I fixed.

Tom's dad formed a basketball team through the Amateur Athletic Union. They were called "The Nix Clippers." Dad drew from former high school and college players, so the team ended up on top the first year. Tom played that year but decided it was too much after that.

The surrounding farmers hired Mexican Nationals to work for them, especially in hoeing and caring for the sugar beets. Old railroad boxcars were their homes. I went to call on one family with three children and nearly suffocated from the heat inside that boxcar. I bought some extra ice cube trays and took ice and food we could spare to them every day. The children came running when they saw my car. It was all I could do to help in some small way.

Medical Issues

In March 1953, I was in the doctor's office with Eddy and Susie for their checkups. Dr. Flaxer came to the waiting room and asked if I could assist him with surgery. A man had been severely injured at his job. I pointed to the children, and Dr. Flaxer said the Browns who owned the drug store next door would care for them. Dr. Flaxer knew of my interest in medicine. I donned the gown and gloves and set about assisting him. I was amazed at Dr. Flaxer's quickness and skill. He asked if I would be on call to help him when needed. I explained that we did not have a phone. It would have cost $1,000.00 to run the wire from the one-and-a-half-mile mark. He asked about the neighbors. Before I returned home, I visited the Weimers who lived closest to us. They were more than eager to receive the phone calls. From that time until we moved, I assisted Dr. Flaxer, while kind neighbors and the Browns took care of the children.

There were three times that Tom was the patient. He had been chasing a cat out of the milk house and jammed his hand into a broken window trying to catch the cat. In the process, he severed an artery in his arm. I made a tourniquet with a dishtowel and belt, piled the children into the car and drove to the doctor's office. Adolph went to the Weimer's house to call and let the doctor know we were on our way. Dr. Flaxer said he could not inject a painkiller because he needed to tie the artery and veins together. A painkiller would interfere with the blood flow. Tom had a high tolerance for pain, but that was difficult for him. Dr. Flaxer asked if I was OK. I said no, and added that I understood why doctors did not operate on their own families.

Kenny was six months old when Tom had an emergency appendectomy. He was getting along fine after the surgery when he decided to walk down the hill from the house to visit Adolph and me as we were fixing the fence. On his way down the hill, he slipped and fell. He seemed to be OK until around 8:00 that evening. He was in a great deal of pain. Again, Adolph ran to call the doctor and then stayed with the children. Tom was in such pain that we had difficulty straightening his legs to get an accurate X-ray. Finally, we had the X-ray, which showed there was a blockage. Everything was pressing toward the upper intestines and the heart. We worked with Tom for two hours with no results. I asked if we could call the ambulance and take him to Denver. Dr. Flaxer explained that Tom would die when the ambulance hit the first bump. We tried more painkillers and relaxant drugs, but nothing seemed to help. Tom was in and out of consciousness; three hours had passed. I asked Dr. Flaxer if there was anything else he could do. He asked me to heat water to a boiling point on his hot plate as he lathered his hands with green soap in another container. He explained that the green soap was a vegetable oil soap used as an antiseptic and was known to soften the skin, but he did not know if it would work internally. I cringed as he prepared an enema with that very hot water and lathered green soap. We finished the enema and waited. After 20 minutes there were some results. We repeated the procedure as I prayed that God would allow the soap to do its job. In another 10 minutes, it began to work and the Xray showed that things were beginning to move. In another hour, Tom was conscious. After a pain injection, we were able to move him to the car for the 7-mile trip home. I summoned Adolph to help move Tom to bed. The time was 1:30 a.m. Tom had a slow recovery, and his insides were sore for some time. I fell into bed exhausted but grateful. God had spared Tom's life.

There would be one more emergency for Tom. The tractor radiator was steaming and for some reason, Tom placed his face over the cap as he unscrewed it, burning him. I knew not to put anything on his face, so we took off for the doctor's office. Susie kept asking Daddy if he was OK and did it hurt, and she was so sorry. She was always tuned into others' feelings.

After bringing Tom home, I felt weak and sick. The doctor discovered that my thyroid was low functioning, so I began a lifetime of taking thyroid medication, grateful that nothing more serious showed up. I was, however, in a back brace for six weeks from tossing 100-pound feed sacks from the truck into the barn loft.

Adventures on the Farm

In 1954, the children came running to tell me that Grandpa had arrived with a big box in his pickup. It was a big box all right. He was smiling as he carried it into the house. He, Mom, Hap and Mae had purchased a Philco TV for us. Later, he and Tom put the antenna up on the roof. The children were so excited to have it plugged in. We received two channels, mostly Channel 2 from Denver. We watched a lot of Saturday Night Fights. There was a program from Denver where Pete Smythe was the mayor of a make-believe town called Tincup, Colorado. He had talented people on his program and also liked unusual things. I told Eddy that I would call Pete Smythe and mention the portable old-fashioned wind-up record player we had. Pete said he would be interested to see it, so he booked Eddy and me for a show. Eddy had a great time explaining about the record player, and Pete played a record on it. That was a childhood highlight for Eddy. Then we sang a song as Pete played the piano. There was also a children's program called "Fred and Faye." Each month they had a birthday party and show. Since Kenny's birthday was close, I called. The children and I were invited to be on the show. They had a special place for the mothers and non-birthday children to sit. The birthday children were in a row of chairs behind a small fence-like structure. The party was great fun with hats and noisemakers and cake. Fred had a cloth frog that he threw to the children, and they threw it back to him. When Kenny caught it, his throwback hit Fred in the head.

Tom and Dad added on to the back porch with a stairway entrance to the basement. That was wonderful for everyone, especially when Adolph left for college and Eddy moved to the basement bedroom. He was only 7 years old, but he never complained about being afraid. The fact that he did not have to share a bedroom with his brothers and sister made him happy. The basement made a great play area for the children. They especially loved racing the riding tractor around, rolling cars and balls across the floor, and playing "hide and seek."

Doing laundry one day, I heard a rattlesnake. As I followed the sound of the rattle, I discovered him wrapped around a concealed water pipe with his head stuck out of a surrounding hole just big enough for his head. The rattlers had come in droves after Tom plowed the field across the road. However, we had not seen one for a while. We had become experts at killing them with a shovel or hoe and Smokey did his part, too. After the chores were done, we discussed what we could do to get that snake out of the basement. Tom decided that he would hook a hose up to the exhaust of our big truck and run it between the wall where the rattler was. I took the children to the neighbors and returned to help. After 30 minutes, we did not hear the snake, so we stopped the procedure. Eddy slept upstairs that night. The next morning, Tom was outside and moved a two-by-four out of his way where he had been working on the cultivator. Lying on the ground was a rattler, sound asleep. We decided it had to be that same snake and chopped his head off.

The most puzzling snake we encountered was the copperhead. We were not sure where they came from. They were more dangerous than the rattlesnakes because they never made a sound before making a move. One day, when the children were playing on the front porch, they came running inside to tell me there were snakes underneath the porch. I went to check and counted at least six copperheads looking like they were entwined. I piled the children into the car and took off for the Herb Foos farm just down the hill. It was 11:30 in the morning and Herb had just come in for lunch. I asked if I could borrow his pistol to kill the snakes. Herb gave me the pistol, picked up another gun and accompanied me back. The children stayed with Pauline. It did not take long to kill all the snakes. Herb and I buried them on the roadside.

The years 1956 and 1957 were ushered in with severe drought conditions. The worst year was 1957. The wind blew furiously, piling sand dunes higher than our windows. I ran the vacuum constantly as we gritted the sand between our teeth. It was everywhere. Tom re-seeded the crops three times that year and they continued to dry up or blow out. One day, Tom headed out to check things in the field across the road. I asked him not to go because the visibility was nearly zero. He wrapped his face in a bandana and took off. An hour passed as the children and I waited anxiously for Tom to return, asking God to keep him safe. Forty-five minutes later, he fell through the kitchen door, exhausted and breathing heavily. He had lost his way until he found the fence. Moving hand-over-hand, he made his way to the road and crawled to the house. That year, we were only able to salvage some milo for cow feed. Tom decided to cut all the weeds which we sprinkled heavily with molasses and mixed with the milo. The cows ate that conglomeration and gave milk even though the production dropped. Great curtains of dust continued to penetrate the ground and sky. The wind howled and shrieked its way across the fields and yard. It seemed as if the dust and sand came through the walls of the house. Sometimes, we could make out the sun and its red glow. However, in times of crisis or troubles there is always something to be thankful for. Because of the wonderful water supply in the house, I was able to wet towels and place them across the door threshold and in the windows. After a while, I placed them in the rinse tub and ran them through the wringer of my Maytag washer and started over again. The children's bedroom and the basement were the best places for them to play. All four children were so wonderful and remained unaffected or worried about the storm. Occasionally, one of them would say, "Mommy, it's time to run the sweeper again." The storm finally subsided, and we could see the sky. We pressed our faces against the windows with each cloud we saw, praying for rain. At the dinner table one evening, Tom said, "We have been praying for rain, but our farmer friends have their hay in windrows and rain would not be good for them. God sure has to make a lot of decisions from all the prayer requests He hears." After that, we prayed mostly that God would give us wisdom and keep our family healthy and strong.

Hap and Mae with the four Nix kids

In November 1957, we decided to take six bull calves to the sale in Greeley with the intention of buying a Christmas tree and presents for the children. We even planned on treating ourselves to a hamburger after the sale. We were met with an unbelievable surprise—the calves only brought 50 cents each. One can imagine how dejected we felt as we headed for home! I told Tom we would have a good Christmas. Fences were filled with tumble weeds. Some were very large. I could use a tumble weed for a Christmas tree. I also had tucked $6.00 away which would be enough to purchase one toy for each child. That decorated tumble weed made a pretty Christmas tree, and the children were delighted with their toys. In addition, the grandparents were generous along with the neighbors. The Gardner family, who were friends at church, treated us to a meal the day after Christmas at their restaurant in Brighton. They had fed us there after church several times. Kenny was named in honor of Hap and his middle name was in honor of Lynn Gardner. God did send rain as He showered us with blessings from our family and friends. Mr. Culverwell said he was willing to wait for the mortgage payment until we could get on our feet financially. He was such a dear man.

In 1958, Hap began to have serious trouble with the anemia and was taken to Colorado General Hospital in Denver. We took the children to visit him. He had to take the elevator to the first floor because the children had to stay there, and he was determined to see them. Hap joked and laughed with them. I made two more trips to see him. The second time I was there, Hap told me that he would soon be at the Gate. I spent the afternoon with him. Five days later, we had a bad snowstorm. I had a feeling that I needed to go to the hospital even though I knew the Weimers would let me know if a phone call had come in for me. The dirt roads were bad, and I asked Tom to put the chains on the car tires for me. It was a general storm, and I would need them to drive to Denver. He asked if anyone had called. I told him I would drive the truck to Weimers and check. Weimers were just returning from visiting Herb and Pauline Foos across the road so they would not have been home for a phone call. I called home and Aunt Edna said they had been trying to reach me for an hour and that Mae and Anna were at the hospital. I called Bill and Janey, who lived in Denver. Bill was in his first year of teaching in the Denver area. They said to drop the children off at their home. I drove back home, bundled up the children, put them in the car and took off. All the way I prayed I would reach the hospital in time. I dropped the children off at Bill's and continued on my way. As I entered Hap's room, the doctor said to talk into his left ear. He had suffered a stroke on his right side. I took his hand, bent down and said, "Hap, I am here. Tom and the children send their love, and you know how much I love you. I will be sure Mae is all right. You can go through that Gate now." Hap was waiting for me to get there. God was so good. In a matter of six minutes, Hap passed through the Gate. The children joined us at the funeral. Hap was close to 60, but he lived well, especially while enjoying his grandchildren. People loved Hap because of his generous nature, his acceptance of everyone, his kindness, his optimism, and his laugh. He was a much-loved father and grandfather.

In January of 1958, Susie and Kenny had their tonsils removed at Porter's Hospital in Denver. Hospital rules kept me from staying overnight. I kissed the children goodbye and told them I would return early in the morning. Before I left, I told the head nurse that Kenny needed to be watched since he would most likely get out of bed and go exploring. She looked at me in disbelief. Sure enough, when I returned in the morning, there was a net over and around Kenny's bed to keep him contained. The children made a good recovery.

Hudson Farm Memories

When they were adults, I asked the children to tell me some memories of the Hudson farm. Eddy mentioned Bucky. Kenny would climb over the fence where we kept a few sheep and Bucky, the ram. He would bend over, wiggle his behind, and Bucky would give him a flying boost into the air. Both Eddy and Kenny got into big trouble when they crawled out on to the metal roof of the bull's pen and threw rocks at him. On one occasion when Lora and the children came to visit, Kenny told Joe Joe to stand on the ant pile. Joe Joe came into the house and said, "Aunt Patsy, I've got ants in my pants." Eddy recalled the day he went with Tom and Smokey to return a borrowed piece of machinery to Jim Tuercek. They were greeted by Tuercek's two German shepherds. When Tom was unhooking the one-way from the tractor, the two dogs attacked Smokey. Eddy said, "Dad, Smokey needs help." Tom said, "Just wait a bit." Sure enough, Smokey laid into both dogs and they soon retreated for safety. Susie told about the time she hid Kenny. She and Kenny were playing in the basement while I was hanging out the clothes. When I came in for another load, I did not see Kenny and began to call him. I summoned Tom and he joined in the hunt. Eddy and Susie helped. I asked Smokey to find Kenny and he laid down at the basement door. We had already combed the basement. Finally, Susie said, "I know where he is." Somehow, she had hoisted her two-year-old little brother into the baby buggy. He had fallen asleep, so she covered the buggy with a blanket and pushed it into a corner where it was usually kept. When Susie was grown, she would tell people about it and say, "My mother was sad and glad at the same time. She gave me a talking to and a few swats to remind me what I had done was serious." Kenny's memory was when the cows got out in the middle of the night. Tom and I only had time to pull our boots on. Tom took Smokey and ran around one side of the barn and told me to head the cows off on the other side. It was difficult to see in the dark. As I ran, I sank in manure up to my thighs. It was like quicksand, and I could not move. All I could do was laugh. Tom hollered, "Quit your cackling and head those cows off." My reply was, "I can't move. Help!" Tom got a rope and with effort pulled me out. By this time, some of the cows had scattered, but Smokey was taking most of them back in the barnyard. As we rounded up the strays, the manure was squishing inside my boots and my shorty night gown was stuck to my thighs. When we got back to the house, the children had awakened and were close to tears. Tom put them back to bed because I was in the big wash tub downstairs trying to clean up, which took a long time. I did get a new pair of boots!

The Fort Collins Farm

Dad was on the lookout to improve our situation. In January 1958, he told us of a friend who owned a farm in Fort Collins and wanted to get out from under his mortgage. In the old days, when a person made good deals they called him a "good horse trader." Dad was all about horse trading. His friend, Loyd, not only wanted to get rid of his mortgage but would accept our farm and mortgage as a down payment for his farm. Tom and I were skeptical and asked what the catch was. Dad convinced us that all was on the "up and up." He continued to tell us the farm of 230 acres had water rights for irrigation and was close to town. Dad added, "and that's not all. The lower level of the barn can easily be converted into a milking parlor. The house is big and each child can have their own bedroom." Tom and I could hardly believe what we were hearing! It was music to our ears. Although the deal needed to be closed, we gave thanks to God for His incredible love as I whispered, BY HIS HAND. We also were grateful for Dad who loved us and wanted the best for us.

The Nix farm. From left to right, farmhouse, tenant house, barn.

The farm was located across the railroad tracks and east of the Fort Collins Coloradoan newspaper building. It was bordered by Hospital Road which later became Lemay Avenue, the Poudre River to the northeast and Prospect Road which was on the edge of town to the south. A few of the acres spread over Prospect Road. I was in total shock at the size of the house. I counted at least 40 windows as I walked through. We went back home leaving it all in God's hands. We thought it best not to say anything to the children until contracts had been signed. As the men were checking dimensions for the milking parlor, I drove around to find nearby schools. I saw two schools that were in close proximity to the farm. At this point, Ed was in third grade and Susie attended kindergarten at the Lutheran Church in Hudson.

The Foos and Weimer families attended services at the Lutheran church. They asked if I could teach someone to direct a choir. The church had no director, but a young man who loved music agreed to direct if he could have instruction. The pastor agreed so I began working with Steve. In the beginning, he came to the farm where we discussed history of church music along with conducting lessons. The portable record player came in handy. Later, I suggested that we begin working with the church accompanist. Steve worked hard and said practicing in front of a mirror was the most difficult. The time came when I said he was ready to start a choir. The Foos and Weimer families wanted to pay me, but I declined because those dear folks were such a help to us through the years. A choir was established. I directed the first rehearsal and then Steve took over. I was proud of him. For not having previous musical training, he did well. Our dear friends asked the pastor if I could be recognized at a church service, but he would not allow it because I was not a member. Our friends were upset, but I was not surprised because it was a Missouri Synod Lutheran Church. In later years, when Herb and Hank Foos and our dearest friend, Dave Weimer, passed away I sang at their graveside services.

In February 1958, contracts were signed on both sides. It was official. We would be moving to Fort Collins. It was going to be difficult to leave our church family and our wonderful neighbors whom we had come to love as family. We would miss them all: the Weimer, Foos, Harkis, Tureck, and Cook families, plus so many more surrounding farmers and townspeople. I would miss assisting Dr. Flaxer, who taught me so much and had my admiration. I would miss my association with him. Country doctors had small facilities. They drove miles to treat patients any time of the day or night. Sometimes, I accompanied Dr. Flaxer on his calls. Our family was fortunate to be recipients of Dr. Flaxer's long working hours, skills, and caring heart.

Tom and Dad, along with hired help, spent five days changing the horse stalls into a milking parlor at the Fort Collins farm. They poured concrete, built stanchions that would serve 19 cows at a time, a catch pen, feed troughs, fenced in the barn yard, and shored up the chicken yard fence. They installed a pipeline so the milk would go directly from the cows into a milk tank. The milk tanker backed up to a cutout in the milk house and siphoned the milk from the tank. The children were amazed at the operation.

Adolph, who was studying at Colorado State University, came to help me with the chores. The neighbors watched the children except for a few times when Eddy helped out as the big brother. When one thinks of moving an entire farm, it boggles the mind. No need for that, as neighbors showed up with all their trucks. The machinery, tools and household furniture were moved in the first caravan. The children and I followed in our new-used station wagon. The next and last trip was the cows and the few sheep and pigs we had. Tom had a difficult time luring Smokey into the pickup. He had been a big help in loading the cows, but he did not want to leave the only home he had known. Such a sight to behold as the men unloaded the trucks. The cows let out with a lot of mooing in their new surroundings. Milking was a little late that evening. In the middle of the milking, lightning struck the barn. It frightened the cows so much that they all yanked their heads out of the stanchions, tearing them apart. We ran the cows into the catch pen while Dad and Tom began the task of nailing things back together. Fortunately, some workers at the nearby sawmill came to help. I prepared food and coffee during the next few hours and by midnight the milking was completed. Whoopee! It was a short night! It took two days before the cows were back on a regular schedule. One can imagine that the butter fat content of our milk was considerably lower.

I purchased a used swing set. The yard surrounding the house was large, but it had been neglected. Tom soon found that the land had also be neglected. The topsoil had eroded, and the fields needed leveling before irrigation could take place. We applied right away for GI and FHA loans to remedy the situation. Time was of the essence since crops would need to be planted in four to five weeks. We were blessed with quick approval on our loans. What an amazing sight to see large machinery including bulldozers and trucks hauling in topsoil. I kept the children in the house during all those operations. They did not complain because we had an enclosed sunporch spanning the south side of the house which was their playroom. The room had thirteen windows, but the children only broke two through all the years we lived there. I got busy sanding the floors and washing walls. I knew I would be painting the walls as soon as possible because they were bright green and purple. The woodwork would also need help since the beautiful original wood was painted over.

Spring break was almost over, so I enrolled the children in Harris Elementary School. Eddy was in third grade and Susie was in kindergarten. Both children were ahead of the classwork which spoke well for Hudson Elementary. We could not say the same for Hudson High School. When Adolph was a senior in Hudson, there were not enough class offerings. After some investigating, Tom and I discovered that the high school was not accredited. We visited with the County Superintendent and the State Department of Education asking what could be done. We learned that they had made suggestions to the school board which were not followed. The community got in an uproar. The majority of the farming population had quit school in the eighth grade and wanted nothing to do with the "highfalutin' Department of Education." Hudson High School was listed as a non-accredited school. The State Department of Education suggested that Tom run for the school board. The present school board and president had not changed for some time. Several friends and neighbors also urged Tom to run for the school board. That was quite an experience. The former president and some board members said things that to us were unbelievable. It was our first experience with politics. Tom did not win the election, which was a good thing because God had plans for us to move to Fort Collins. However, we were instrumental in beginning a drive to build a new high school that would encompass Hudson, Keenesburg and the surrounding area. Later, when Weld Central High School was built, we received letters and phone calls thanking us for our efforts. It was surprising that many came from folks who had opposed our recommendations at the time.

The children loved playing in the yard and helped me plant flowers and bushes. Iris bulbs went in along with lilac bushes. They made for a colorful border around three sides of the house and yard. The south side of the house needed some topsoil where I later planted some trees and shrubs. Tom and Dad cemented posts for the clothes lines. I was excited to have six lines. Before clothes were hung every week, the line had to be washed. A bag of clothespins hung at one end. One always hung pants up on two lines by the cuffs after creasing them, shirts and blouses by the tail and socks by twos. Sheets were hung over two lines to speed drying. Clothes were hung in all kinds of weather. In the winter, they sort of freeze dried. They were brought into the house to finish drying. It is difficult to describe the clean-smelling aroma that permeated the house as they dried. They were then sprinkled with water, rolled up and placed in a basket for ironing. In those days we ironed everything. I had a surprise one day while hanging the clothes. A little pigeon came to say hello by lighting on my shoulder. He was a frequent visitor. The children named him Dandy. After a time, he was comfortable enough to light on their hands, but his favorite place was on my shoulder. When I finished hanging clothes, he would fly away. Dandy was with us for several months. We were all sad when he did not appear; we could only imagine that he found a girlfriend he liked better than me.

A Modern Dairy Operation

We decided to join the artificial insemination program for dairy herds through Colorado State University. That meant we could sell our bull which was a relief to all—no more chasing after him. Dr. Pierson, our veterinarian, recommended certain semen for insemination. Tom devised the successful feeding procedure. Keeping track of each cow's contribution was made easy for me by taking part in another program. I sent figures to a huge computer (larger than our house) in Utah. I received a printout every month that showed each cow's assigned number indicating their food intake and production. That way, we were able to cull the non-producers and take them to the sale. Those two programs and Tom's expertise assisted us in building one of the top dairy herds in the state.

After a heifer gives birth, it is a push-pull struggle to get her in the barn for the first time. Sometimes we had to use ropes or a pitchfork. One particular heifer crowded out the other cows in the catch pen on the second day to get in first. The third day, I decided to watch her. As she headed to her stanchion, number 19, she took a lick of grain from each stanchion on her way. I dubbed her Miss Piggy. Like humans, cows have their own unique personalities. The children named one cow Kissy. When the children went near her, she rolled out her big tongue, giving them a slurpy kiss on the cheek. They made a game of trying to get away from her before she rolled out her tongue.

The cows were settling down in their new surroundings, as exhibited by their increased milk production. After the first month, Tom decided I did not need to be at the barn when he started milking. I could wait until he had the machines on the first group of cows. Rather than take his boots off to come into the house, he threw pebbles at our upstairs bedroom window to waken me. I would go to the window and holler, "I'm coming, Romeo!" I would quickly dress, slip on my coveralls, boots and scarf and head for the barn. After milking, we ran the cleaning solution through the pipeline. Then I would clean the other equipment and feed the calves while Tom fed the dairy cows. I would use two fingers to help the new calves suck. Invariably, they would butt the bucket of milk and supplement, drenching me.

From everywhere on the farm, we had a bird's eye view of the foothills and mountain peaks. We never tired of the beautiful Colorado mountains and took the children to visit deserted mining areas when time allowed. We would dig up old bottles and other mementos. In the springtime and summer, we drove the back roads where we came upon undisturbed beautiful fields of wildflowers and wildlife.

We were told the original farmhouse was built in 1869. Around 1907, a large house was built over the original. There were five bedrooms. I used the downstairs room as an office. The two large bedrooms had walk-in closets and large drawers built into the walls. The living room measured 17x30. The dining room became our TV room. The large kitchen had a 10-foot ceiling and was where we fed everyone who came to the farm. There were two bathrooms: one was downstairs with a shower that Tom and the boys used. Susie and I had a large powder room with bath upstairs. The front porch spanned the west side of the house, and the screened-in back porch was large enough for shoes, boots, and coveralls. The top windowpanes were French squares. We busied ourselves painting the windows when we had time. Tom took the easy job of painting the lower panes. It would be a while before we had funds to furnish and continue upgrading the house.

It was good to worship again at the corner of Magnolia and College Avenue. Rev. Harrison had retired and much to our surprise, Sherman Moore was the pastor. He had been one of our pastors during high school in Boulder. We joined the choir, and in the early '60s agreed to teach the junior high Sunday school class and to help sponsor the youth group. Tom said he was not a teacher, but he would keep discipline! One Sunday morning, he walked over to Phil, who was reading a paper. Tom took the paper and challenged Phil to repeat some of the lesson. I could barely contain myself because I knew how brilliant Phil was. Phil repeated the lesson and then added some comments. I had to hold my laughter until the kids left. Tom said, "Me and my big mouth!" Another time Tom told the kids we would match whatever funds they brought in for UNICEF. Lyle gave a big speech to the class about collecting around the neighborhoods and from people at church. I asked Tom why he decided to say that. We were just getting by financially. He said

Outside FCC 1965

they needed a challenge. Two weeks later, the class came to Sunday School with overflowing collection boxes. I gulped as the money was counted. All I could do was write a check and place it with the collection, knowing that we would be overdrawn at the bank. Fortunately, our good friend, Austin Allison, was one of the executives at the bank and held our check until we could make it good. I asked Tom how he enjoyed having "foot-in-mouth disease." That was the last of his brilliant ideas for the class.

Farm Help

In 1959, Dad and Joe were building a house in Littleton, Colorado, for Bob, Mary Jane, and family. Bob was employed at a large dairy there. Pete, a boy in the neighborhood, kept asking them to let him help. Dad told him about the farm and said he would speak to Tom about helping him. Pete's parents thought it was a good idea, so Pete began his five-plus years of helping us in the summer months and during other vacations. We purchased another set of bunk beds for Kenny and David's room. Pete had finished the eighth grade that first summer and told Tom he hated school and was going to quit so he could live with us full time. Tom told Pete that if he quit school, we could not use his help. Pete not only finished high school, but he graduated with his BA from Colorado State

University. He helped out occasionally while at the university and borrowed our pickup for dating. He married Sue who went to the same high school in Littleton, but she and Pete never met until college. Pete later earned his Masters and Doctorate degrees. He taught at the university in Bozeman, Montana, and later worked for the Department of Agriculture in Washington, D.C. His mother always introduced us as Pete's "other parents." Indeed, we felt like he was one of our own.

After Pete left, word of mouth sent other young men and boys to our home who needed various types of assistance. Sometimes our children would bring them home. Occasionally, the juvenile judge would call for short-term stays of youth who had gotten in trouble. Putting them in jail with criminals was not the place for them. God made it possible for us to provide lodging, food, and safety for all who came. Jim was a friend of our son, David. He lived a short distance from the farm and asked if he could help with the chores. Jim had a learning disability that was made worse by a stepfather who told him how stupid he was. Tom and I had words with his stepfather and a visit with his mother. Things worked out for Jim to stay with us for five years until he graduated from high school. All he needed was encouragement and confidence in himself.

I taught lessons to supplement our income on the black upright piano that Hap and Mae had purchased for me. The student I enjoyed the most was our own Susie. She was so bright and gifted. When she was in fifth grade, I suggested she take lessons from someone else to broaden her capabilities. She cried, but after thinking about it, she agreed. Tom and I never tired of listening to Susie play. In 1961 our corn crop production was outstanding. Tom said we would buy a new piano for me as he had extra to sell. We drove to Wells Music Company in Denver to purchase a new piano. I had fun trying many pianos and settled on an Everett studio piano.

There was another house on the farm. We were told it was used to house railroad workers in Fort Collins. Charlie Evans, a previous owner, moved it to the farm. It had not been occupied for years and was filled with different kinds of birds and all their droppings. After Dad and Joe completed building the house in Littleton for the Rinker family, we began the task of cleaning up the smaller house. As walls were torn out and all the bird droppings were cleaned out, we discovered that part of the siding consisted of barn doors nailed together. Builders grabbed anything that would work! It took some time to get the house in shape for occupancy. The first occupants were Mom and Dad after Dad retired in the early sixties. Joe and Lora were living in Greeley, where Joe was working on his master's degree in industrial arts. Joe was a superior craftsman. We were recipients of several lovely signs and plaques he made. One of our favorites greeted visitors: THE NIX DAIRY FARM. Since Joe lived in Greeley, he, Tom, and Dad began construction of a house across our hayfield that became Mom and Dad's home. It was a lovely ranch with a full basement. The old house was used later for hired help. Our first worker to live in the house was Bob, a college student. His wife, Pam, ran to the barn one day thinking Tom was calling for help. She ran into the milking parlor and told Tom she thought he was hurt. Tom said, "Gosh, Pam, I was just trying to yodel. "

It was not often that I got the upper hand on Tom for his mischievousness. One time was when he came to the house for lunch after cultivating corn all morning, he asked, "Patsy, did you know you sewed my fly shut when you patched my coveralls?" He proceeded to say that it was not much fun when he jumped off the tractor to relieve himself and found his fly shut. I was so proud of myself. Even though I was dying with laughter inside, I told him that was too bad, and I would fix my error.

He did not know the truth for a year. The second time was not easy to hide. He went to the farm implement store and took a razzing for the heart patch on the backside of his jeans. Tom threatened to dunk my head in the watering tank, but I escaped.

Life on the Farm Becomes Easier

In 1962, the land, barn and cattle were taken care of with our loan. There was money left, and we received permission to use what was needed to remodel the house. What an exciting time! We hired Rex, a contractor who was a good friend of ours at church. The walls of the living room were covered with maple paneling which included valences for new drapes. It was beautiful. The walls of green and purple soon disappeared as the office and the family room received three coats of paint. Fortunately, the sunporch/playroom only needed one coat. The kitchen required the most attention. The tall ceiling and walls were gray and drab and there were few cupboards. Our 500-gallon water tank also adorned a corner. The men carved out enough space in the small basement cove for the water tank. Beautiful oak cupboards were added, plus a

The farmhouse

new stove, sink, dishwasher and refrigerator. The stove only partially worked and none of us knew how to act with a dishwasher and a sink large enough to accommodate large cooking utensils. We chose a new floor design that was easy to clean. Also, we decided to carpet the family room, office and living room. Upstairs was done with wainscoting of beautiful paneling and freshly painted walls. Susie chose wallpaper with roses for her bedroom, and we papered the large bath with the left-over paper. Eddy and Susie received new bedroom furniture. Kenny and David had new bunkbeds. We gave up our early miscellaneous bed for a queen-size bed. Dad decided to help me wallpaper the stairway. Sometimes, we got more wallpaper and paste on us than on the wall! I always enjoyed working with him. Restoring the woodwork and doors took a lot of effort by Rex and his two men, but it was exciting to see the beautiful original wood, which gave character to the house.

We continued to have water hauled by truck and dropped into a huge cistern close to the house. Climbing down to clean the cistern with chlorine between deliveries required me to rig up a good face mask. I also had a formula of how much chlorine to add to the water so we would not become ill from drinking it. We had well water for the cattle and yard with added irrigation water for the garden. Three years later, we were able to purchase water from the East Larimer County Water District. The pipes were laid across the river from Mulberry and extended to our houses and the barn. That was a real "heyday" for us! I could fill the rinse and bluing tubs for laundry without running out of water. When I took the lid off the water cistern that was to be filled with concrete, there were half a dozen carp swimming around—products of Jim, Kenny, and David's last fishing expedition. We had a dickens of a time catching those fish, even with nets, because the water level was three feet down from the top. We were getting ready to lower one of the boys with a rope when we snagged the last fish.

A private phone line came later. We had been on a four-party line. We were not only close to town, but we began to enjoy ordinary things that city folks had. Dad and Tom poured a cement patio and our friend, Dale Bartlett, built a beautiful brick grill near the clothesline.

Tom's impatience and temper continued as he lay into the boys. One day he said, "It's difficult to be both a dad and a boss." I asked where the "boss" thing came from and stated that he treated Pete and others better than his family. I suggested that he just be Dad and teach the boys. I really struck a nerve. Tom did not speak to me for two weeks. I kept talking to him even though he ignored me. I gave him a peck on the cheek since we had promised to kiss each other every morning and every evening. Later, Tom became so angry that he shook his fist in my face. I reached out, lowered his arm and got very close to his face. I told him if that ever happened again, the children and I would be gone and he could run the farm by himself. He knew I meant it! I asked God again what I needed to do, and He said, "be patient and thankful." That seemed very difficult until that still, small voice I had come to trust impressed upon me that God wanted my thanks ahead of everything. I was thankful for my resilient, gifted children, my friends, our church and home. I thanked God that Tom was such a hard worker and for the times he played with the boys. I thanked God that Tom went to church every Sunday with our family and took an active part. I thanked God that humor and playfulness shone through more often than his fits of anger. Tom remarked more than once that he did not know how God could love him. I told him God loved all of us just the way we are. Several times I said, "God loves you, Tom, just the way you are." There are times God answers prayers when they have barely left our lips. Other times, He delays. I continued praying for Tom to be delivered from the anger that held him bondage.

The Kids Keep Busy and Keep Us Busy

We had joined and carried our insurance with Farm Bureau before we left the Hudson farm. It was good to attend meetings with other farm families. We both served on the Farm Bureau legislative committee for several years. Farm Bureau began to schedule a music contest for children. Tom asked what I had planned for our children. The first time, our four children sang and were given a ribbon. Then it was announced that the performance winning first place the next year would compete for district and state honors. I taught the children "Side by Side" with a soft shoe dance. They won the local and district contest. They were quite the performers. At the state contest, David got a little too close to Kenny when they had a kick-turn with the dance. Kenny fell into Susie and Susie fell into Ed. We had talked about mistakes and how to go on. I was at the piano. The children looked at me and with one hand I motioned them to get up. They got up amidst the audience's laughter and carried on. I wanted to laugh, too! I was proud of them as they accepted first place. We have laughed about it throughout the years. All four children had beautiful voices, and we sang a lot. Tom joined us one Sunday as we sang for a special worship service. David also won Stars of

Tomorrow when he was in the sixth grade. He sang "Seventy-Six Trombones" and stood on his tiptoes when he hit a high note.

Like other parents, we were both kept busy supporting our children by becoming active in the Parent-Teacher Associations, 4-H projects, athletics, Brownies, Scouts (Tom was the Cub Scout Master at Harris Elementary School) and other programs. Sometimes, I would be at one school on a given night and Tom at the other. When the boys played baseball, it could get a little wild. Three games, one right after the other. Tom would usually make it about halfway through David's game. I would pack sandwiches, dessert, and fix a gallon of Kool-Aid which we usually ate after Kenny's game before moving on to Ed's game. They also played city-sponsored football. David was hit hard during one game and came out holding his wrist, trying to hold back the tears. Tom and I went over to check him out. For some reason, Tom had not developed much empathy for others' pain, possibly because he was so tough. Tom told David to get back in the game. I told Tom I thought David had a badly sprained wrist. After the game was over, I took David to the doctor. His wrist was broken! The boys excelled at wrestling. Their coaches remarked about the Nix boys' farm strength. Ed held the record for the most pull ups at junior high that was not broken for some time, and he made it to the wrestling quarterfinals at State. Ed also invented a wrestling hold called "The Nix Tipper" which other wrestlers rarely broke and led to pins most of the time. The district athletic director jokingly called it "The Nix Cow Catcher." Kenny told his junior high coach that his little brother in sixth grade could beat the seventh graders. Sure enough, David beat the older boys. The coach asked David's teacher to let him out of class 10 minutes early so he could come to the junior high for wrestling practice. George Wolf, who was an executive for elementary schools at that time, told Coach that it was an interruption for the elementary schedule. Not to be outdone, Coach had the bus pull over to wait for David after school. There was no rule that prevented an elementary student from participating in junior high sports. However, the district later developed such a rule. When David was a senior, he was State Champion in his weight class. He also won the National Championship in college. That was exciting! Kenny had the most finesse as a wrestler, but his wrestling came to an end in high school when the doctor discovered a back problem for which he recommended surgery. Kenny had a huge blood vessel interfering with spinal movement. When it was removed, it weakened the vertebrae which prompted the doctors to do a six-inch fusion. Throughout Kenny's life, he has had four other back surgeries. He continually deals with lots of pain. Kenny was hit by a car, twice. When he was five, he broke loose from Eddy's hand, darted out into the street and was struck. At age seven, he was taking a potted plant across the street to his grandmother after church and was hit knocking his front teeth out and causing many bruises. He rarely smiled because he was embarrassed by the metal teeth he wore for some time. Besides the previous physical problems Kenny suffered, another appeared when he was ten. We were visiting Joe and Lora in Arizona. On one of the few weekend vacations we had, David became ill with a respiratory infection. Joe and Lora's doctor made a house call. We asked the doctor to examine a lump in the front part of Kenny's neck. Our doctor had said it was just a condition that little boys sometimes had, and we should not worry. However, Kenny was running fevers and had difficulty swallowing. After examining Kenny, the doctor told us to change family physicians when we got home. At home we took Kenny to a new doctor in town who diagnosed a thyroglossal duct cyst that occurred from unexpected changes in the womb before birth. It was caused by leftover tissue of the thyroid gland forming a knot-like growth   The doctor sent us to a surgeon in town who made the same diagnosis and told us it was blocking Kenny's airway and would eventually choke him. The surgery was successful. After eating bland foods and ice cream, Kenny made a good recovery.

Susie played a lot of softball as an adult and spent time on the mountain ski slopes. She became proficient on the piano, was an excellent flutist, and learned to play the organ.

During junior high and high school, the children were members of choirs and bands. Kenny played trombone and David played the trumpet. Ed took private trumpet lessons. Later, his interest was in the electric guitar. We purchased a Fender guitar on which he became proficient. His interest grew to a point of organizing a dance combo of five members. The boys would practice at the farm. Since none of them had a driver's license at that point, Tom and I hauled them, their instruments and equipment back and forth to their gigs.

Work on the farm is a family affair. Each child had chores to do. Susie helped me in the house and in the huge garden. Her favorite place to be in the summer was on the roof outside her bedroom, sunbathing. I remember calling Susie to come help and she would reply, "But mother, I am sunbathing." My response was that she could continue sunbathing while she helped. The boys had their chores as well. Because Ed was the oldest, more was expected of him and he was very responsible. One responsibility was to keep tabs on Kenny and David to see that they were completing their jobs. The pigs and chickens needed to be fed.

Old Pal, our horse, also needed to be fed. Dad bought Pal at the sale. She had been a cattle horse. When the veterinarian mouthed her, he said she was 32 years old. All four children would ride on her at the same time. When Pal got tired or had enough of the kids, she came to the house and just stood there. If the children gave her a kick, she put her head down which told them she was really through. Off they jumped while Pal wandered down to her stall. We never locked Pal's stall as she had the run of the farm. Even at her age, we had her bred and she dropped a beautiful colt. Unfortunately, the colt got into the river one day and drowned. Dad and Tom found Pal standing at the river's edge. She was crying real tears. Four years later, Pal slipped and fell into the grain trough upside down. Tom and David tried to get her upright and were unsuccessful. The veterinarian came but could not save her, so he helped her pass. The entire family cried that day.

Ed, Kenny and David took turns helping to scoop the manure out of the milk house. Tom and I would tease each other about being president and vice president of the Sooper Dooper Pooper Scoopers. Tom suggested Kenny and David should take care of the calves. I hesitated because I knew they would not notice if the calves were catching a cold or other health issues. Sure enough, their job lasted two weeks. I was back taking care of the baby calves. The boys and Susie would help with harvesting the garden. After I canned and froze enough food for us to have during the winter, we would give the excess away, especially to needy families. Ned, who was the manager of Beaver's Grocery on Mulberry, would ask me to bring in any leftovers for him to sell. Usually, I had beans, squash and cucumbers for him.

Adult Activities Are Important Too

In 1962, I was asked to be Director of Music at church. There was an adult choir, and I enjoyed adding a Cherub Choir and Youth Choir. Reverend Mell, our pastor at the time, asked Tom and me to start a Sunday School class and monthly Sunday evening gatherings for young parents. On Sunday evenings, baby/child/youth activities were arranged. The group would be called "Hearthstone." We also planned family gatherings. I can still see the smiling faces of the Woodards, Sullivans, Smiths, Clapps, Schmehls, Herveys, Beers, Bartletts, and Farmers, and I remember how we all were blessed with close friendships and a desire to grow spiritually.

Tom and I were invited to sing in the Community Chorus directed by Kathryn Bauder. I would finally meet the outstanding teacher I substituted for in 1947 at Fort Collins High School. I was so grateful that the music staff at CSU had given me the opportunity to teach there for six weeks when I was a sophomore. Kathryn was a superb director. I happened to mention at church choir rehearsal that I would give a lot to study with her. Later in the week, Myron and Leota Hayward came to the farm. As we visited, they said they would like to pay for my lessons with Kathryn. They said, "Patsy, we know you will pass on to others whatever you learn." I whispered thanks to God and expressed my thanks to the Haywards. In 15 months, I was able to pay for my lessons. I not only learned choral and vocal techniques from Kathryn, but she helped me overcome the difficulty I had with my voice for years. I enjoyed our weekly lessons and conversations about spiritual matters. Kathryn joined our family for dinner many times throughout the years. She was delighted to hear our children offer grace and ask God to bless her. Heart problems placed Kathryn in the hospital a few years later. During our last conversation, she asked me to give her love and hugs to my family. One of the school district's elementary schools was named for her.

Family Visits Were the Best

We had many family gatherings at the farm that included my brother and his family, Bob and Mary Jane's family, and Joe and Lora's family. Several times, the entire Nix clan came for a week's visit. The twelve cousins engaged in a lot of play and, of course, did things they never told us about. Roxie, Gay, Lora and Judy loved to play with the upstairs old-fashioned roller shades—the kind that pulled down and when let go made a racket and wrapped around at the window top. The girls and Susie also loved getting into my makeup. Susie would always say she never instigated it! The seven boys—Eddy, Kenny, David, Dennis, Joe, John and Jack—got into lots of mischief. They would run across the flume in the river, throw rocks, shoot BB guns, and try to catch mice in the horse feed. One time, they decided to have a dry cow pie fight and drew up sides. Kenny grabbed one that was on the "fresh" side. As he tossed it, Roxie stood up and it went splat in her face. She came to the house and took her glasses off which caused Mary Jane and me to burst out laughing. The only place not covered with manure was around her eyes. When Ed grew

My brother Bill and family: Pam, Billy, Danny, Janey, Barry, and Patrick

Tom's sister Mary Jane with Bob, Roxie, Gay, Dennis, and Lora

tired of the younger boys, he retreated to his room to work on model cars. We would always arrange for the children to see at least one movie. One time, we packed a lunch and told them they could stay and see the movie twice so the adults could have a little quiet and play bridge. The children loved to be at the barn when the veterinarian came to do artificial insemination. Most of them did not understand what was going on but they loved the long plastic gloves the veterinarian gave them. Roxie took hers to show and tell for her third-grade class. She held it up and said that her Uncle Tom did not have a bull anymore because he bred the cows himself. Her teacher could hardly wait to tell Mary Jane. The adults visited, threw horseshoes, played volleyball or cards, helped with the chores, and fixed huge, delicious meals. We just had enough paper plates for lunch one noon and no one wanted to go to the grocery store. Dad hung the paper plates on the clothesline and cleaned them with the hose. We enjoyed all of the family visits. Mary Jane, Bob and family came more often since their drive time was only an hour. Tom was wanting to attend the Christian Men's Conference in Estes Park, so Bob volunteered to help with the milking that weekend which was so appreciated. Bill, Janey and family came whenever they could carve time from their busy lives. Pam, Billy, Danny, Barry, and Pat enjoyed watching Tom milk and helped feed the animals. Barry spent two months with us when Janey was in the hospital and rehab center from a brain aneurysm. He and David shared rooms and had wrestling matches. It was a devastating day when I told Barry that his mother was in heaven. We all missed Janey a lot. Bill later married Joyce who had three children. We loved being aunt and uncle to Joel, Julie, and Laurie.

Tom's brother Joe with Joe Jr., John, Judy, Lora and Jack

I loved watching and listening to Kenny, Susie, and David at play. At least twice a week they held a church service. It contained a few words, a song, and communion. At times their words were wise or just funny, perhaps something they heard at church or Sunday School that they would put their own twist on. They took a large piece of homemade bread and asked if they could have a glass of grape juice. After they took communion, they offered an "Amen." They played tag and loved their swings. My doctor's name was Bonham. They called him Dr. Bottom and made up a game. As two children were swinging, the other tried to hit them on the bottom saying, "Dr. Bottom, you're out." We brought the feather mattress that was on the basement bed at the Hudson farm with us. Kenny and David held wrestling matches on it. Some evenings, Tom would wrestle with them. There were times that Ed would join in with all three boys attacking their dad. They would say "we give up, Dad," so Tom would stop, only to have them jump on him again. When the boys were older and more skilled, Tom said, "Only one of you at a time from now on!" Some evenings, Kenny and David would take turns "shaving" their dad without a razor while Susie and I brushed each other's hair.

Susie rarely frowned. Usually, she was laughing and her blue eyes sparkled. We visited a lot as she offered to help me with household chores and putting out ingredients for baking. Susie was excited when I made mother and daughter dresses which we often wore, and we would play dolls or make believe. We had a few teas with chocolate icing spread between graham crackers. She kept tabs on little brother, David. Susie was very observant. I often asked what she was thinking. In our church, classes were held for fourth graders to prepare them for baptism. Susie had just started third grade when she told me she wanted to be baptized. I said, "Tell me what you understand about baptism." Her reply was, "I have Jesus in my heart, and He knows I am ready." There was no doubt that Susie was ready for her baptism in the spring of 1962. Eddy, Kenny and David were all baptized during their fourth-grade years. Those were precious moments for Tom and me. The most important thing we could do as parents was expose them to Jesus and His love. As children, they loved the bedtime Bible stories. They also learned from attending Sunday school and church. When they were little, children were supposed to sit perfectly still and not talk during church service with no coloring books or toys. How boring for them, but we know they absorbed some good things. Dr. Ritter, one of our church elders, would play hide and seek with the children. He told them the baptistry was a good place to hide. It did not take the children long to find out if they jumped up and down, the metal part of the baptistry would let out a long popping gong. One can imagine what that was like while meetings were going on in the church basement.

My Career in Music Education Begins

In the fall of 1962, I enrolled at CSU to complete my BA degree (I had quit college 12 years earlier after Ed was born). Most of my classes were during the day when the children were in school. I asked to do my student teaching at Lesher Junior High School because it was close to the farm. Ed was in one of my classes since he was an eighth grader. He acted up in class one day and I said, "Edward, pay attention to the business at hand." That night he said, "Mom, please don't call me Edward in class." My comment was, "OK, as long as you behave." I graduated the summer of 1963 with a degree in K-12 Music Education with a minor in English, and applied for a position in the school district. There was an opening for a traveling elementary music teacher. I interviewed with Don Webber, head of personnel, and told him he probably would not want to hire me as I answered his question about my priorities. I told him God was first, family second and then teaching, but that I would be a teacher who always put students first. His comment was that he would not recommend me if I had said anything different. (Later, Don became an outstanding superintendent whom I respected and enjoyed working with from 1973-1984 when he retired.) After my interview, I talked with the person in charge of curriculum. He commented about my teaching abilities but expressed reservations about a woman who had four children and was still helping on the farm. I referred him back to my credentials and experience and asked that he judge me on those. In five days, I received a letter stating that I had been hired, and my starting salary would be $4,600.00 for the year. The first three years, I taught at Bennett, Laurel, Mountain View and Washington elementary schools plus two mountain schools, Poudre Canyon and Stove Prairie.

Christmas time was very busy! The teacher at Poudre Canyon always had a cup of hot tea ready for me which was appreciated, especially in the winter. Stove Prairie had two rooms. I loved joining the children at recess and lunch, walking on stilts or playing ball. One day I mentioned that I would like a spruce and aspen tree on my farm. Later, the children presented me with both. They had taken a collection and one of the fathers had purchased the trees. Those trees were a source of enjoyment and a remembrance of those dear children. I felt as blessed as Chippy. Chippy was a chipmunk who frequented the school. He loved peanut butter, so the children made sure they always had a peanut butter sandwich for him. He played like a kitten, chasing a string across the room. It was a sad day when he did not make a showing. However, the children had Mrs. Whitefoot, a large cat who spent every day at school. The children were allowed to pet her when she jumped on their desks as long as they continued to do their work.

The first year I taught, my supervisor, Faith Denton, asked if I had thought of getting my master's degree. I told her that was "in the future." She suggested I begin soon because she would be retiring in a few years, and her position of Elementary Music Supervisor would be open, adding that there were certainly no guarantees. I discussed it with Tom, and we decided to have a family discussion. At dinner, we told the children what would be expected from all of us if I returned to school in the summer. The children said, "That's great. Go for it, Mom. We'll do our part." It was difficult for me because CSU did not offer a master's degree in music education and supervision. I would need to enroll at UNC in Greeley. Mom and Dad were very supportive and said they would help. Al Dzingle was the college help on the farm at the time. He and his wife, Arlene, lived in the tenant house. Those were busy and trying times for everyone, as I went to summer classes three days a week. There were nights I never went to bed, especially if the children had activities or wanted to see a movie. On several occasions, Tom would come downstairs and say, "That's enough. Come to bed."

With all the support and everyone working together, I graduated in the summer of 1966 with my master's degree in music education and supervision. Mae came to spend the weekend with us, as she did periodically, and attended the graduation ceremony. She told me how proud she was and that Hap would be busting his buttons. I could hear Hap saying, "Way to go, little girl." Mae was experiencing high blood pressure. Tom and I encouraged her to sell the house with the big yard and move to an apartment. She moved to an apartment a few blocks away from her home. The doctor told her to drink a beer every night, but since she did not like beer, she had bourbon and 7Up. When we visited Mae, she would always say, "Come on Tom and join me in a drink." Mae introduced Tom to what became his special cocktail after the children left home. Our family and friends knew Tom's favorite drink was bourbon and 7Up, which he enjoyed every night. The bourbon had to be Evan Williams. According to Tom, that brand of bourbon tasted as good as Jack Daniels and did not cost as much. We did not know how to thank our children for hanging in during the summers I worked on my degree. After hugs and expressing appreciation, we took them to a special dinner, gave bonuses for their work and arranged for Susie to take a trip with the Harwells and their two girls. Tom and the boys called Susie "Cookie" because she prepared lunch for them three days a week. I was so grateful for the sacrifices Ed, Susie, Ken, David, Tom, Mom, and Dad made.

Unknown to me, Tom and his parents had arranged for us to go on a trip to celebrate my graduation. In the past ten years, we had only one weekend vacation away from the farm. Our hired help, Skip Avril, Dad, and our boys would take care of the work. Mrs. Bee would come to fix meals again, and the Tague family would keep the children company. Ellen, Harriet, and Carol Tague also sat with the children during church so Tom could sing in the choir. Ellen's husband had passed away and later, her son, Jerry. Such heartache for her. God made it possible for us to assist Ellen and the girls in numerous ways throughout the years, just as we received so much help from church friends, family, and neighbors. We usually delighted in giving anonymously, but it was different for Tagues and a few other folks.

The trip Tom arranged was a visit to Harwells, our close friends who lived in Iowa, and then on to South Dakota to visit Mount Rushmore and then to Wyoming to visit Yellowstone National Park and watch Old Faithful. We had a wonderful time. It proved to be like a second honeymoon, and it also gave us time for much needed conversation. Tom asked me how I could put up with the terrible things he said to me and how he took out his frustrations on the boys. He stated that he was a good-for-nothing and that I seemed so close to God. I told Tom, "God does not make good-for-nothings. I am no different or better than you or anyone else and need to work on my own thoughts and actions. I was blessed because God allowed me to listen to the Holy Spirit at a very young age. I trusted Him and reached for His hand. I reminded Tom of the day God spoke to him about attending church with Eddy and me instead of working. Also, the day he heard God speak through Eddy's song, and we prayed that he would not take God's name in vain. Tears flowed as we prayed together. We did have a deep love and knew each other's hearts. While visiting the Harwells in Des Moines, Iowa, we toured the John Deere factory and spent two days at the State Fair. At each booth, I signed up for prizes, knowing that it was rare for me to win anything. As we revisited the booths, I was given an envelope and inside was a paid trip with a week's lodging for the family in Bella Vista, Arkansas. At Christmas, we traveled to Bella Vista and enjoyed visiting the Ozarks. It was our family's first week-long vacation which we all enjoyed. Tom and I agreed to listen to a sales pitch for the development of Bella Vista, a gorgeous area that later became a beautiful city with several lakes and golf courses. Tom and I vacationed in Bella Vista eight years later and built a home there, thinking of retirement. However, as we visited during the different seasons, the humidity and pollens did not agree with my allergies, later diagnosed as asthma. We sold our lovely home and another one we had purchased as an investment, knowing that there really was no place like Fort Collins, Colorado.

There were three teachers who applied for the Elementary Music Supervisor's position, including me. Mr. Boltz, who was the superintendent at the time, visited to observe our teaching and to talk with each principal in the schools where we taught. I presented several letters of recommendation to the superintendent. One of those letters was from Faith, the Elementary Music Supervisor who encouraged me to get my master's degree. After a two-week wait, Mr. Boltz and Don Webber called me to tell me I had been chosen for the position. The family celebrated by going out to dinner. When I told the children that with more responsibility I would be getting a pay raise, they asked if we would be eating out more often.

I met with the director of curriculum who asked what my first goal would be. I told him to place a music teacher in every elementary school and provide a music room for them. I asked school maintenance to build a large cart on wheels for each elementary music teacher that would hold books, autoharps, a record player, and other teaching items. We were still teaching in dresses while wearing heels and were on our feet all day traveling from room to room over tile-covered concrete, pushing a piano. A student from each class pushed the cart to the next room. In my position, I taught half time, provided in-service (teacher training), offered support, did observations and evaluations, along with team and demonstration teaching. I submitted requests for new equipment with justification, encouraged principals to find money in their budget for teachers to attend the Colorado Music Educators Association (CMEA) state conference every year, and arranged for student presentations to the school board.

I was anxious for the school board to know that music education was more than singing, and how it supported all of education, which led to building confidence and team building among the students, as well as how music touched the spiritual side of us. I also visited with the principals explaining the importance of the music program along with what the children were learning. They visited classes and recognized if a teacher was keeping order but did not have the musical knowledge to judge the curriculum.

It was not long before the principals and district personnel department asked if I would interview new teacher candidates. I was delighted and prayed that God would send teachers who loved students regardless of their color, religion, or background and possessed the appropriate teaching skills or were coachable.

In three years, with the cooperation of the principals and the director of curriculum, each elementary school had their own music teacher with a music room. A song I learned in Sunday School kept echoing in my ear: "Jesus loves the little children. All the little children of the world. Red and yellow, black and white, they are precious in His sight. Jesus loves the little children of the world." And, we, the teachers, were trusted with their minds and hearts five days a week.

The Kids Are Growing Up

Eddy remained our inquisitive, talkative, dependable son. At age six, he took my new Filter Queen vacuum apart. I asked what he was doing, and he replied, "Don't worry Mommy, I can put it back together." He had laid out the pieces in sequence and knew exactly where each one went. When he finished, it worked perfectly. I told Tom that Eddy might become an engineer.

Susie was a bit clumsy and walked like Tom. When I mentioned it, Tom asked, "What's wrong with my walk?" I said, "Nothing. I love your walk, but it is not fit for a little girl who is slightly clumsy" I asked Susie if she would like to try ballet lessons, and she agreed. Susie looked so cute in her ballet costume and did very well. But I could see it was not her favorite thing to do. I asked if she would be interested in knowing how I learned to walk tall and straight. She said, "Yes", so we began to practice. During Girl Reserves (an extracurricular activity in in high school), we had practiced walking like ladies with good posture. Susie began placing one foot in front of the other while balancing a book on her head. She thought it was fun, for which I was grateful. We laughed a lot when she graduated to walking down the stairs. I was so proud of her and often remarked how beautiful she looked as she walked to the car after school with her head up, back straight, wearing a smile. Susie and I enjoyed each other's company and could visit for long periods of time. Years later, her husband, Jim, and I were driving to Ridgeway, Colorado, for a family gathering. When we arrived, Jim said, "I can't believe how you two women could spend over five hours visiting. "

In fourth grade, Kenny was still having a rough time adjusting to school. His hyperactivity and impulsiveness were getting in the way of listening and following through with his assignments. He was also accident-prone. I asked Tom to let up on disciplining him while I set up conferences with his teacher and the principal. After the conference, we decided to make an appointment at the mental health clinic. As Tom and I talked with the doctor, I explained that Kenny was born with physical problems, and I still questioned if the medication I was given while carrying him contributed to his behavior. We made four appointments for Kenny. Unfortunately, the doctor and psychiatrist told us what a nice little boy he was and suggested that Kenny would probably outgrow his behavior. I thought I should be able to help Kenny more. We had family counseling, which seemed to help everyone except Kenny. He clearly did not have an accurate picture of how his behavior affected himself and others. We sought every kind of help available. I told Tom there had to be something seriously wrong that no one could detect. I spent time talking with Kenny, pointing out his behavior, which sometimes he denied. One night at his bedside, I said, "If you were the parent trying to help your son's behavior problem, what would you do?" He said, "I really don't know. I try, Mom, but I just can't help it. Sometimes I get blamed for things I do not do." We discovered there were times this was true at school and at home.

There were times Kenny would lag behind Susie and David on the way home from school. I discovered he was stopping at the rest home on the corner of Lemay and Elizabeth to visit a dear friend, Mrs. Longman, and other residents. He would listen to their stories and hug them. Mrs. Longman said that God would bless him for his kindness and compassionate heart. That side of his personality was a blessing.

Dad came in the house one day and asked why we did not do something about Kenny's behavior. I told him teachers, principals, our pastor, and we had tried everything to help him. Also, Tom was beginning to understand that harsh physical punishment did not work. Dad went back outside, kicked Kenny, knocking him down and said, "I could kill you for causing my son such embarrassment." I was so angry and sad to think a grandfather could treat his grandson that way. My admiration of Dad hit a low, and I gleaned more understanding of Tom's anger issues.

Kenny played practical jokes on people, including a serious one was when he was in junior high school. The armored car pulled up to the school. When the driver came out of the school, Kenny jumped out from behind a bush and yelled, "stick'em up." The driver whirled around with his gun pointed at Kenny. Luckily, he quickly realized that Kenny was a child with no weapon. Kenny attended military school in Salina, Kansas, during his junior year in high school. Tom and I visited him every three weeks. David and I drove down for the military ball, which was an enjoyable weekend. Although that year was rocky, Kenny finished with decent grades. He experienced successes during his senior year at Fort Collins High School and later while attending school at the Arizona Automotive Institute, where he was class president. He came home and assisted in giving speeches and knocking on doors to convince the public to support building additions at Aims College in Greeley. He received letters of appreciation and a trophy for his efforts. We were very proud of him. He decided to head to El Paso, Texas, and stayed with Bob, Mary Jane and family for a few months. He and his cousin, Dennis, were good buddies. Ken got a job and moved to his own apartment. Before long he got mixed up with the wrong crowd and lapsed into his old behavior.

Later, he was diagnosed as being bipolar and having ADHD. No one knew about those mental issues when Kenny was growing up. It would be several years of continued prayers and loving him unconditionally before the triumph over drugs and alcohol took place.

David was an easy child to care for, and he loved having Susie fuss over him. He came into the house one day with a huge bumblebee in his hand saying, "Look at this friendly bee, Mommy." He enjoyed being outdoors with the animals. When he started kindergarten, he told me he would rather be home working with Dad. He repeated his desire for two weeks and finally realized he had to be at school. When David was in fifth grade, his teacher called and said she needed to talk with me, so I went to Harris Elementary after school. She began the conversation by saying, "Now, Mrs. Nix, I know we all talk differently at home. David copied the wrong problem down during a math race at the board, and said, 'Oh crap!' Not appropriate language." I found out Mrs. S was quite naïve and did not understand little boys. She had no children and was from the South, which gave me a better understanding of her. I told her as a parent, we cannot always control what our children say, but that indeed, I would talk to David. At dinner that night we talked about not using farm talk at school. We cleaned crap out of the milk house, the barn yard, and asked the children to wipe the crap off their shoes before coming into the house. I often heard Tom say, "Oh crap!" Unfortunately, David and other little boys did not fare well in Mrs. S's class. I asked that Dave be transferred to the other fifth grade class, but there was no room. It was a bad half year for him. David was creative and later composed several songs, accompanying himself on the guitar.

Kenny and David decided to take a little trip one winter. I had sent them to their rooms for misbehaving. During that time, I went down near the barn to check on the calves. When I returned, Kenny and David were not in their rooms. I opened the front door and noticed their tracks in a light snow that was falling. I could see them walking down the lane, so I grabbed their coats and drove slowly behind them in the car. They each had a stick over their shoulders with bags tied around it—their food for the journey. When I asked where they were going, they said to Grandma and Grandpa's in Arizona. I remarked it would be warm there and that I had brought their coats. I said, "I hope you have a nice trip." I began to back the car up when they cried, "Wait!" and got in the car. They decided that home was the best choice.

When it snowed, the undisturbed fields looked so beautiful, and that scene meant fun for the children. Tom pulled the toboggan behind the tractor giving them quite a ride over the fields. Eddy sat in front as they held on tight to each other. It took a long while to remove all those wet clothes, and Eddy would often have icicles on his face. They looked forward to the cookies and hot chocolate I had prepared for them. Stormy weather presented obstacles getting the chores done, and it took longer to clean the cows' teats. Since Tom was allergic to chlorine, we used a sterilization product called iodophor. As each cow was stripped before placing the milker on, the barn cats patiently waited for their milk. Some liked to have Tom squirt it into

Tom pulls the kids on a toboggan.

their mouths. Another chore during or after a storm involved Tom clearing the one-half mile dirt road with the blade and tractor. Because our farm was at a dead end, the school bus would not pick the children up if the road was not cleared.

Eddy, Kenny, and David loved playing checkers with Grandpa at his house, especially during the winter months. Dad took the boys on a fishing trip to Seven Lakes area near Walden, Colorado, in the spring, and they brought home lots of fish. Tom and I took the family to Red Feather Lakes, Colorado, on Saturdays, when we could go between milking, to fish and picnic. David always got car sick and had to sit in the front seat. The other children thought he was faking until he threw up. Mom, Susie and I attended musicals and movies together. Dad, Mom, Tom and I enjoyed a lot of bridge games through the years.

Farm Pets

Puffer was our big yellow Angora tomcat who came with the farm. If a contest had been held, he would have been voted the champion ratter. He loved to hunt rats along the river and bring his catch to the house for us to brag about him. One of those times, Kenny grabbed the rat and began to chase Susie and her friend, Chris, around the yard. The girls were screaming at the top of their lungs and decided to jump in the car where they would be safe. They sat there secure until Kenny saw that a window was down, so he threw the rat in the front seat where they were sitting. They popped out of the car, ran into the house screaming and headed for the bathroom to wash the rat stink off. We never knew what happened to Puffer. He just did not show up one day.

Our faithful Smokey patrolled the perimeter of our farm every morning, just like he had done at the Hudson farm. It was his way of being sure that we were safe, and no other animal or human was intruding on his territory. Still protecting the children, he knocked our neighbor down one day and stood over him. Kenny was yelling with delight as Mr. Shaw pushed him in the wheelbarrow, and Smokey thought Kenny was being hurt. The Shaws rented our tenant house. We had informed them that no dogs would be accepted because of Smokey. On the last trip they brought their big dog, Buster. We insisted they keep Buster in their large fenced-in yard. Smokey was thirteen and had begun to show signs of arthritis. One day, Buster got out and attacked Smokey, biting him on the shoulder. The bite abscessed so I took Smokey to the vet hospital at CSU. I left him there so the abscess could be drained and treated. When I went to pick

Smokey and me 1951

Smokey up, the veterinarians remarked about his intelligence. They had never treated a dog who understood everything they asked him to do. He was so happy to see me and went to say thank you to the two who had treated him. Buster never got out of the yard again! Smokey also put up with the bum lambs we raised. Whenever ewes would not accept their babies, I would wrap them in towels and place them in the oven on the lowest heat. They were bottle fed and cuddled until they were old enough to join the flock. Occasionally, one would end up palling around with Smokey or running into the back porch when the door was opened. We helped the runt piglets in the same way. The runt was pushed and crowded out of the way to suck the hind teat which did not always produce enough milk. That's where the saying, "sucking the hind teat" originated. Since the time Smokey was a puppy, he preferred to be outside. However, when arthritis got the best of him, he did come into our screened-in back porch. After a while, he inched his way across the threshold to the kitchen. We all gladly stepped over him, speaking to him or patting his head. He did go outside for short periods, sauntering down to the haystack and checking things out. After he made his rounds, he came back inside. One thing Smokey did not like was the John Deere tractor. When the compression release petcocks sounded off, Smokey bit at the front tires. We all decided the noise hurt his ears. Biting those tires would be his undoing. In 1966, Smokey was sixteen. He was outside when Ed started the "Johnny Popper" after he filled the gas tank. As was Smokey's habit, he bit at the tractor tire but could not move out of the way fast enough. As Ed turned the wheel, Smokey was thrown and fell, injuring his back. I took him to the vet hospital. After they examined Smokey, they said he could be patched up with a long hospital stay but with the injury and severe arthritis, he would still be in pain. They handed me a paper to sign allowing them to euthanize him, saying Smokey would feel no pain. I had a difficult time signing the paper but knew it was kinder to follow through with the doc's suggestion than for Smokey to live in pain and not be able to move. I gave Smokey a big hug and told him goodbye. I spent time thanking him for being our faithful friend in every way. I cried all the way home and managed to fix lunch. Tom's dad was eating with us that day. After grace was said, none of us could eat. We spent the time crying, remembering and sharing all of Smokey's helpful and brave feats, especially how he protected us from harm.

We did not have good luck with dogs after Smokey died. We did have three puppies from Smokey and a friend's collie. We gave two of them to farmer friends and kept Skipper. The name fit him because he would not stay home. The other puppies turned out to be good farm dogs. When we had enough of chasing after Skipper, we gave him to a friend who lived in town. I was in Woolworth's one day, turned around and there was Skipper, running through the store with his new owner after him. Later, we came home with two small dogs from Arizona after visiting Tom's brother, Joe. Their names were Duchess and Curly. Duchess was like a porpoise in the corn field. She ran up the rows, jumping high above the stalks. Duchess and Curly would chase after the racoons, but if the racoons turned on them, they made a beeline for the house. Curly had a litter of pups which the children enjoyed until we found homes for them. The children would sneak Duchess and Curly into bed. When I asked if the dogs were in bed with them, they said no, but soon the wagging tails would move the covers. Duchess darted in front of the tractor and was killed. Tom and I were attending a farm sale and the owner's dog, Bill, began to follow us around. The owners said they could not take Bill where they were moving and asked if we would take him. He was a wonderful farm dog. However, he and Curly began to chase the neighbor's sheep with rogue dogs that ran along the river. Sadly, we had to have them put down along with our next dog, Queenie, who also began to run with the pack. We told the children, "No more dogs." About three months later, David went home from school with the Voss children. The family had Dalmatian puppies. David called and told us he was holding a puppy in his arms and that she loved him and could he bring her home. Tom and I finally agreed, so David brought Pebbles home. She proved to be a wonderful kids' dog. The children dressed her up in sweatshirts, socks, hats, and glasses. She enjoyed it as much as they did. When she was three years old, Pebbles was crossing the road from the house to where Tom was mowing hay. Our hired man's wife was speeding down the road, struck Pebbles, killing her. We said again, "No more dogs. We can't take this anymore."

We got Bambam the cat after Puffer disappeared. Kenny and David taught her to slide down the stairway banister and turn a flip. Then she would run to the living room and do another flip or two. We would clap for her. Whenever we had company, the boys asked if Bambam could show her tricks. She enjoyed the attention so much that she would sit and wait for the applause. I made capes for the boys. They never tired of playing Zorro with their friends on the stairs. Bambam ran up and down the stairs with them.

When David was in the seventh grade, he came home with a black puppy in his arms. I asked where he got the puppy, and he said she hung around school and Coach Weitzel let him put her in his office. He ended with, "Mom, she is a very valuable dog." I recognized that she was quite ill, so we took her to the veterinarian who told us she had distemper and would probably die. David had tears in his eyes. I asked Jack, the veterinarian, for penicillin and we took the puppy home. For two days and nights I gave her penicillin with aspirin every two hours, warmed towels for her bed and hand fed her. On the third day she began to perk up and ate a little bread crumbled up in milk. David could hardly wait to play with her. We named her Beauty. She was all black and appeared to be a cross between a border collie and lab. Beauty was a real character. She greeted us every time we got out of the car, and if we ignored her in the least, she stood in front of us and talked to us by showing her teeth and making her dog voice go up and down. Beauty had a good, long life.

When Tom and I moved from the farm into a condo where there were no yards, the people who rented our large farmhouse continued to care for her. The other children had left home, and David was in college in Arizona. I drove out to the farm every week to visit Beauty but realized she would not adjust to her new owners if I continued. Beauty later moved with them to a different city.

Submarines and Cars

Tom taught our boys how to weld. It was fun watching the boys donning their goggles to weld small items. Kenny and his friend, Ernie, decided to make a submarine out of old oil barrels. David wanted to help but did not have the interest to continue. Kenny and Ernie spent a month building their submarine complete with an escape hatch. David hung around watching. The day came when the submarine was ready to be launched. The boys asked me to fix their lunch as they were planning to eat while resting on the bottom of the large pond that was part of a deeper lake. Tom hooked the submarine up with a chain to the tractor, and we all helped to push it into the pond. The boys climbed in, hooked the latch, and down she went. I asked Tom how long we needed to wait before rescuing Kenny and Ernie. It wasn't long before we saw bubbles and two heads bouncing around. Their escape hatch really did work. Goodbye, submarine!

Tom was always eager to show the boys how to drive their vehicles. When Ed was fifteen, we purchased a road-ready Vespa scooter for him. Ed was proud to receive his driver's license to drive on the streets. Tom said, "Let me show you how to drive this scooter." He got on the scooter, was riding it around near the barn yard, decided to rev it up, and crashed into the fence. Ed was not too pleased with the scratches on his new scooter! Ed and three of his friends were at a building on the CSU campus one night when one of the boys decided that breaking the windows out would be fun. Ed said, "My mom and dad would just die if I did something like that." One of the boys replied, "Do you always do what your mommy and daddy say?" Ed said, "I try to," hopped on his scooter and headed home. He said he was glad to have his scooter!

That night after Tom's wreck on the scooter, he insisted on carrying the watermelon from the barn to the house because Pete might drop it. He was lecturing Pete about how to carry it when it slipped out of his hands. I was watching everything unfold. Tom looked at Pete and said, "We might as well eat some," so they sat on the ground and began eating. I hollered out the back door and told them to leave some for the rest of us.

A Busy Place

Our farm was a busy place, like "Grand Central Station." Since we were close to town, the children's friends, mostly latchkey kids, would drop by, knock on the door and ask if dinner was ready. I often prepared dinner for five or six extra people. There was a special area near the river that was perfect for Boy and Girl Scouts, and 4-H groups to hold meetings and weekend campouts. Our barn loft was a gathering place for square dancers, youth groups, and basketball. Tom put a basket up at each end. The boys made a circle in the middle with the initials NBL—the Nix Barn League. Hayrides were organized in the fall for different groups.

When I discovered the second graders in the school district studied "The Farm," I asked if busing could be arranged for visits to the farm. I was delighted when approval was given. All second graders had an opportunity to visit our farm. When they arrived, Tom would take them to our pit silo explaining how the grain was harvested and packed in the pit ready for the cows' consumption. The next stop was the milking parlor, where we explained the milking procedure and pointed out the pipeline that carried the milk to a 3,000-gallon tank, where it was cooled and awaited pick up by the milk tanker. Some of the children had never seen a cow up close. Their eyes widened as Tom explained the cow's anatomy. The four parts of the cow's stomach was always of interest, as was chewing their cud. The children loved seeing the pigs, chickens, and sheep, and Old Pal, our horse. So many of them had never been close to animals. We took them to an area where lots of birds filled the trees and for a short walk along the river sharing about nature, the fox, pheasants, deer, and other wildlife found on our farm. They heard about the importance of the river that provided irrigation water for the crops. It was an exciting, fun time of learning for the students.

We tore the tall, brick silo down because of safety issues and the men began work on digging the pit silo. Later, we hired men to enlarge the silo. While digging, their equipment hit a grave. The skeleton was standing straight up and still had his hat on. We called the Sheriff, who called the anthropology department at CSU. They discovered that two persons had been buried in the grave but only one skeleton was complete enough to be studied. The bone features indicated that the skeleton was probably that of an American Indian, 5'6" to 5'7" tall with arthritis of the spine. His death happened somewhere around the turn of the century. He was buried along the narrow road that ran adjacent to the railroad leading to the farm from what later became Prospect Road. Some thought it was one of the first wagon trails that led into the area.

More Adventures on the Farm

During our time on the farm, we had two fires. I had sent David and his friend, Charles, to clean the chicken house. They were taking a long time, so I went to check on them. They said they were just talking instead of working. That night around midnight, I was awakened with flashing lights. Employees at the hospital had seen flames and called the fire department. We hurried down to find chickens running around, some with feathers burned off. We had to kill some of the chickens right away. We gathered others and put them in a room at the barn. Poor things. The next morning, I killed the remaining chickens and prepared them for the freezer. Susie always looked away when I wrung their necks. I preferred that method over using the axe. We were fortunate that the chicken house was isolated from other buildings. David and Charles had been playing with matches and thought they had stomped out a smoldering area.

Another fire was caused by the hired man's five-year-old playing with matches near the stacked hay which was near the barn. When his mother saw flames, she panicked and tried to reach her husband who was in class at CSU instead of calling the fire department right away. Tom was working in the lower field. It was getting dark when I was driving down the lane after work and saw the lapping flames. It looked like the buildings were on fire. The cows had been herded to the south side of the barn. The fire truck ran out of water, but every employee of Cook's Lumber Yard from across the railroad tracks was there with their equipment, spreading the fire out and digging ditches to prevent it from reaching the barn, propane tank and tenant house. How fortunate and blessed we were by those men, including the firemen who worked several hours to get the fire out and deal with the smoldering ashes. We offered thanks to God that our livestock and buildings were saved and that no one was injured. The hay was destroyed, which meant Tom was on the phone to ranchers in Wyoming trying to find hay for sale to replace what we had lost. Fortunately, our insurance covered the cost of replacement.

In 1965, Ed spent quite a bit of time building a car. He purchased a 1931 Ford chassis from friend, Bruce Kuster. It had a 1950 Oldsmobile V8 engine with four 2-barrel carburetors. Ed put a single 4-barrel carburetor along with a timing chain in it and the car ran. Tom and I marveled at how Ed took every piece he worked with, cleaning it thoroughly, and sometimes spit cleaning each one. It was like watching an artist at work.

When the car was running well, Mom came down from their home across the field. Ed said, "Hey, Grandma, how about going for a ride?" Mom was always a good sport. I can still see her today. There was no floorboard yet, so Mom hoisted her legs and feet onto the dashboard and away they went! I'm reminded of the time Mom decided to ride Susie's new bike. She told us no one ever forgets how to ride a bike. However, I doubt that she ever rode on gravel! Sure enough, down she went after riding about ten feet. I had grabbed the camera beforehand, and we have still/action pictures of the event. She was unscathed. Mom made the children laugh when she would take out her teeth and say, "Look what the good Lord has done for me!" At times, she reminded us of her mom, the hilarious Grandma Purdy. Once when we were eating dinner at Mom and Dad's, we finished the meal, ready for dessert. Mom pulled the oven door down and said, "Oh I forgot the damn beans." We still laugh about it. Mom was a devout Christian, never missing her daily devotions or church service. It was good for the children to know she was human. Mom was very hard of hearing. We thought that was why she always gunned the car engine each time she started it. Not so! Mom was taking Ed and visiting cousins to the swimming pool. At the stop light on Riverside and Mulberry, a young smarty pulled up beside them. He looked at Mom and gunned his engine. Mom said, "That little brat thinks he is going to beat me." When the light turned green, Ed held on as Mom stomped on the gas and left the young man in the dust. Mom was an excellent piano player. She would play the piano every week at the Lemay Nursing Center located a short distance from the farm. She would say, "Those old people like my music." She was older than most of the residents! Mom missed her daily task of gathering the eggs in her apron after the chicken house burned down.

Ed had four other hot engine cars. The Corvette got him in trouble on the road. A few years later, he traded the 1963 Corvette for a 1956 Nomad. He put fuel injection on it which made it a road burner. We caught Kenny sneaking it out at night to race it. Ed got in trouble driving the Corvette and had to sweep the jail on a few weekends. I enjoyed a trip to Denver behind the wheel of the Nomad. It was sort of strange to drive because the steering wheel was half the size of a regular one. Kenny and David kept asking me to "giver 'er the gas." We were on I-25. I checked the traffic. I saw no one in front or in back of me, so I pushed it to the floorboard and away we flew for about two miles. I said, "OK boys, that's enough." Ken wanted me to be sure to include this in my story!

Every day on the farm, I stood in awe of the sunrises and sunsets. God unfolded each dawn with newness and ended the day with breathless beauty. Standing in the corn field, one could almost hear the corn grow. After Tom's work of planting, cultivating, and irrigating, the corn, oats, and alfalfa produced good yields. One year, our corn grew so tall that Tom and I stood on top of the tractor, and it still waved above our heads. We have pictures! One fall, the weather prevented us from getting into the fields. It snowed heavily causing us to wait a week. I remember driving the truck, creeping along in fourth gear while Tom operated the corn cutter. I saw him push the corn down into the cutter. I stopped the truck and asked him to be careful since we knew of farmers getting their gloves caught, losing a hand or fingers.

I remember a remark I made at the National Stock Show Rodeo when I was a junior in high school. I said I hoped none of my children ever decided to ride bulls in a rodeo. Some of David's friends invited him to watch them practice roping at the CSU Arena when he was in high school. He came home and said he liked to watch the bronc and bull riders and wanted to try it. When Dad heard about it, he rigged up a barrel with ropes for David to practice. Dad would pull the ropes different ways, trying to make David fall off. Later, he graduated to the real thing. When Dave was experienced enough to enter rodeos, we watched, holding our breaths each time. At a rodeo in Estes Park, Dave rode a saddle bronc. He got hung up in the wrap and when he wiggled loose from that, he became hung up in the stirrup. He hung upside down with his head bobbing around. The horse's kicking hooves came very close to his head. That night I asked Dave for a promise that he would ride the bare backs instead of the saddle broncs. He promised and made good on it, but he still rode the bulls. A short time before his high school graduation, he was riding at Cheyenne

Frontier Days. The bull threw his head back, striking Dave in the face. I don't know how he stayed on to ride. Fort Collins High School colors are purple and gold. As Dave walked across the stage at Moby Gym to receive his high school diploma, laughter broke out from those who could clearly see him. The purple robe accentuated his two purple and black eyes. The rodeo cowboys are outstanding athletes. They have to be in great condition to ride. After working a 40-hour- a- week job, the cowboys drove all night or all day or caught a flight to make the next rodeo. At a rodeo in Burlington, David fell on his head and neck after being bucked off by a bull. The rodeo clowns ran the bull into the pen. One clown ran over to Dave and said, "Dave, I am a brother in Christ, and I ask right now that the Lord heal you of any injuries." I went to Burlington to pick Dave up and took him to the doctor at home. The doctor had X-Rays taken. He told us Dave had broken his neck but by some miracle, it had healed. We were overjoyed and thanked God for His mercy, healing, and love. The family gave thanks at dinner for Dave's healing and sang a Praise Song! Tom and I were hoping that would be Dave's last rodeo, but after recuperating, he was back on the road. We were not too fond of the lifestyle among some who drank a lot. Dave continued rodeoing until he was 35. That year, he was National Champion in a rodeo sponsored by Coors in El Paso, Texas. I remember telling him that his bones and muscles would ache and hurt a lot as he aged. By the time he reached his 60s, he indeed was suffering from all the injuries and beatings his body took. He said, "Mom, you were right, but I would do it all over again!" He did not need to tell me that. I already knew.

Ed and Ken delighted in scaring Susie and me. I was working in the laundry room, after cleaning black widow spiders from the furnace room and in another area close to the house. Ed had purchased a large spider connected to a small tube with a pump. That thing jumped on me. I proceeded to stomp on it. Ed said, "Gee, Mom, you didn't have to kill it. Now I can't use it anymore." Ken had to go bigger and purchased a tarantula. Susie and I were in the bathroom when Ken opened the door a crack and made it jump. I had just stepped out of the tub and began beating it with the towel while Susie went screaming to the window.

Later, I saw an advertisement on the TV about losing weight. I had gained eight pounds. Even though I got plenty of exercise with all types of chores, including running up and down the stairs, I had only lost two pounds. I purchased this TV item, which was a rubberized suit that had a blow-up mechanism. The idea was to put it on, blow it up and then exercise which was to cause sweating. I stepped into it, zipped it up and blew it up so much that I looked like a sumo wrestler. I was moving around the upstairs hallway as the suit made a swishing, sucking sound. Hearing the sounds, Kenny called from downstairs, wanting to know if I was alright. I said, "fine." About that time, I lost my balance and rolled over into a corner. I hollered a faint "help." Kenny came upstairs and was laughing so hard he could not help me until he gained his composure enough to pull the plug. I took a real family ribbing at dinner that night. Of course, I was laughing along with them. I was glad no one else saw me!

Tuffy Mullison, a friend of ours who was a football coach, stopped by for a visit. He had just begun to teach exercising using isometrics which are intense contractions of muscles against each other. When I heard about the benefits, I asked Tuffy to teach me. He said he would show me if I would teach him how to play the guitar. I agreed. I have continued isometrics to this day and attribute strength in my arms and legs, and particularly, the core of my body to isometrics. I also began to lift cans of food at Tuffy's suggestion until regular weights for women were available.

Adventures in Education

I made a point to invite each new teacher I hired to the farm for dinners, especially new graduates. One teacher needed additional encouragement because she moved to Fort Collins with her little daughter while her husband remained in Kansas until he could find employment in Fort Collins. I prayed daily that I would be an inspiration for God to teachers and students. Interesting things came up during those years.

I received calls from classroom teachers at an elementary school telling me the new music teacher was not wearing a bra. I went to observe Pat's teaching and asked her to drop by my office after school. I told her of the calls and asked how I could help. She assured me she did wear bras, but they were old. A recent college graduate, she could not afford new ones. I asked if she would allow me to help, so we went shopping.

Another teacher, Suz, wore miniskirts and was on the chubby side. In teaching music to elementary students, teachers would often walk up and down the aisles between desks and bend over to listen to individual students sing. I talked with Suz later and asked if she could do me a favor. She said, "sure." The favor was for her to go home, bend over in front of the mirror and look back at her reflection. She called me and said, "Oh my God, Patsy, I never dreamed what was visible." One time Sally called me at midnight to say she was afraid of her boyfriend who went outside behind the house to do drugs with friends. I suggested she pack some clothes and necessities and walk to the nearby store that was open all night. I picked her up and she stayed with us until she moved into an apartment with two girlfriends.

Jeanie taught elementary music. She had been having an affair with a married man. The man's wife came to my office. Through tears, she asked if I would tell Jeanie to break it off. I felt sorry for her as her husband was known for his wanderings. I did talk with Jeanie, asking if she knew the married man she was seeing had been involved in several affairs. We talked a long time and she agreed to assess the situation. I asked if I could pray with her and she said, "please do." I was grateful that her decision was to end the affair. Years later, I met Jeanie at our hotel while attending a National Music Conference in Anaheim, California. (Tom always looked forward to attending the conferences with me. He remarked that nowhere else could he enjoy such wonderful music performances for the registration fee!). Jeanie shared that she was teaching at the high school level and had married the wrestling coach. They had three children. She expressed how happy she was and thanked me for our talks and for keeping her episode confidential. (The teacher names I have used here are fictitious.)

The superintendent called and said he needed help and asked if I would come to his office. When I arrived, there were five ladies sitting around the table. They had moved with their husbands and families from New York. Their husbands were employed at Kodak. They were upset because the music teachers were including some carols in the Christmas program. They were of the Jewish faith. I explained that Hanukkah songs and games were also part of the program. I was happy to tell them that I hired an elementary music teacher of their faith in the fall who said she would show respect to all students and include Christmas carols in her program. I also told them I had been to two workshops held by rabbis, seeking more Jewish songs that had melodies children could sing. I asked for their help. Even though one parent volunteered to find more Jewish celebration songs, I never heard from her again. I sometimes facilitated meetings between music teachers and principals who were at odds over misunderstandings. When some parents claimed the Supreme Court ruled that sacred music could not be sung in public schools, I produced proof that the statement was false.

I have shared just a few examples of happenings that made my life as a music supervisor interesting. Because I was led by God's hand, my door was always open, and I made myself available to help in many situations. I desired for the teachers to be healthy in every way because of their influence on the students. The Bible had a place on my desk. Colleagues stopped by during the years to ask for a Bible verse to help their situations. Depending on the situation, we would pray together, or I would place them on my prayer list. God was so good as I was led to pray with folks on the stairway, in the parking lot, offices, or in the restroom.

Life with Teenagers

In the fall of 1969, I could not believe my first-born was off to college. I teared up as I waved goodbye to Ed. Mark "Ox" Oschner was Ed's roommate in college, all six foot five and 300-plus pounds. On one trip to visit Ed at Southern Colorado State College in Pueblo, we ate at Shakey's Pizza Parlor for dinner, enjoying the piano player as we visited. Ed said we would have strawberry shortcake with ice cream for dessert at home. When we got to his apartment, we found that Ox had eaten the entire half gallon of ice cream. Ed said, "My gosh, Ox, that dessert was for my mom and dad." Ox went to get more ice cream!

Tom and I attended the CSU football and basketball games for 50 years. We were active in the Alumni Association and the Booster Club. Tom served as president of the Booster Club for two years. We sat in the Ram's Horn (a VIP area) for several years while our family sat in the seats we had purchased when Hughes Stadium was built. We were able to attend several out-of-town football games after we moved from the farm. Once, we were invited to fly with the team to Albuquerque, NM. We sat next to the Channel 7 sportscaster. On the way home, the plane lost altitude and dropped over a thousand feet. After the pilot gained control, we breathed a sigh of relief. The sportscaster was as white as a sheet. He made a beeline for the bathroom holding a napkin over his mouth. When he returned to his seat, he told us that flying was part of his job that he did not like.

Ken was fourteen when he became interested in electronics. He purchased a box radio. He could hear people speaking on all channels but had to install a crystal allowing two-way communication. Later, Ken was in a contest and won the same model which he installed in Tom's pickup. Ken placed an antenna on the back of his bike and carried the radio in his front basket. He would call Tom, but most of the time Tom could not figure out how to answer. I took Kenny to the bank so he could borrow funds to purchase a Lafayette H450 radio with a battery pack which was easier to operate with the dial on the front. Tom had replaced the pipeline in the milking parlor, so he and Ken installed a 30-foot pushup pole on top of the farmhouse using the old pipe, securing appropriate wires inside. Ken could talk to people on the Gulf of Mexico. He especially enjoyed conversations with truckers in every state. Ken's call name was "Colorado Koon Hunter." He joined the CB club in Fort Collins where he learned valuable lessons from the adults

Susie and I enjoyed talks at bedtime. Susie's first crush was on a boy named Mark. When Mark told her he did not have time for girls, her 15-year-old heart was crushed. Tears flowed for two evenings while I hugged her. Later she said, "Mom, I don't know why I feel so bad. He really is a dork!" Through the years, Susie called me her best friend, even telling me her girlish infatuations. Music to a mother's heart!

Faith and Church Continue to Be Important

In 1967, our church moved into a new a worship space on the corner of Drake and Stover. Tom and I were both on the building team committee, which was a wonderful experience. Tom became an Elder again and I resigned as Director of Music and Drama. I dearly loved serving God in this way and working with the different choirs, but I would be dragging at Christmastime and other holidays with my supervision and teaching responsibilities in the school district. I wrestled with the decision for some time until God let me know that I would still be a witness for Him and it was okay.

The end of 1968 was the start of over two eventful years in the life of our congregation at First Christian Church. Our pastor began a class on The Life of Christ using a movie, video, and conversation. Christians from other denominations began to join our congregation at First Christian Church for this study. When the study ended, all those who had participated expressed a desire to continue worshiping and praying together. This grew to be an ecumenical prayer group. We first met in homes once a month on Sunday evenings. The group grew so large that our spacious farmhouse could not accommodate it. We began to meet at our church, at Our Savior's Lutheran Church, and at Holy Family Church. Later, the Episcopal church opened its doors. The prayer group prayed for our nation, state, city, the churches, schools, families, and individuals. During the two years we met, we witnessed many miracles, including healings and deliverance of some who experienced different types of bondage. Numerous people confessed Jesus as their Lord and Savior, while others experienced being born again. We were taken with the humility and prayers of a Catholic priest. He never missed a meeting and asked us to pray for him. He had fallen in love. After a year, he moved to a different parish in another town. At the end of the next year, he resigned from the priesthood and married the love of his life. All requests to keep things confidential within that large group were honored. Love and blessings flowed in awesome ways, made possible by our awesome God and His Holy Spirit.

In 1970, a few of the women joined forces to picket a 7-Eleven store. They had placed pornographic magazines near the counter where they could be easily viewed by children. When we carried signs on our designated streets, we received many thumbs up and car horns. The store removed the magazines.

We had our own story to share with the prayer group. It was near the end of 1969 that Tom called my office asking if I could come home for lunch. He stated that he would put TV dinners in the oven. I walked to the door and knew immediately that Tom was different. That morning, he came in from doing the feeding to eat his breakfast. I always left his breakfast consisting of bacon, eggs, and potatoes in the oven. After eating, he brushed his teeth. Tom told me, "When I finished, I was forced to look at myself in the mirror. I tried to look away but could not. At that moment God spoke to me through His Holy Spirit and said, "It is time for you to realize, to really know that you are loved." I heard God loved me at church and the many times you said God loved me, but I would think "Yeah, sure, not a sinner like me. Tears began to flow, and I spoke about all the verbal abuse I laid on you, and the way I ignored you, the way I beat the boys because I could not control anger that welled up inside me. I clearly heard God say that I was forgiven, that he loved me and had a purpose for the new person I would become. All I could think about was how Jesus hung on the cross, dying for my sins. I fell to my knees and cried for a long time. I stood up, exhausted, overwhelmed by God's love with a peace that I cannot describe. Patsy, I was born again! I am so grateful to you, my faithful wife, for your prayers and not giving up on me. I remember Mary Jane saying that you were the only woman in the world who would put up with me. Can you forgive me for all the torment I inflicted upon you?" I told him I had forgiven him all along the way and shared how God led me BY HIS HAND, teaching me to be grateful and patient in all circumstances and to keep trusting Him. We thanked God as we wept in each other's arms. Nothing is impossible for God! He answers our prayers in His way and in His time. Tom later told the children he was sorry. They did not grasp the full significance of his apology right away but soon saw the change in him. When Ed came home from college, he asked what happened to Dad. As Ed stated years later, "We could still see Dad tighten up, wanting to lash out at times, but God took over. Dad's body would soften as he gained control." Tom began to rise a little earlier each morning to spend quiet time with God. We held hands as we prayed together daily, asking for guidance to do God's will and be used by Him. We prayed for protection, healing, and spiritual growth for our children. Our dear friends, Jack and Marilyn, asked if they could have what they noticed in us, and God granted them their own spiritual experiences.

God had made it clear that our ecumenical prayer group was not to become a church but to share with our congregations what we experienced and witnessed. The congregations began to increase in size.

Plenty of Time for Fun Too!

Susie, like her brothers, had many friends who spent time at the farm. One of her favorite things was to join a group that went boating on Long's Pond. During Susie's sophomore year in high school, she got a job in one of the nursing homes near the farm. After a few months, she said she would rather work somewhere else.

Susie was good friends with Pam whose parents owned and operated the Safari, a popular dinner/dance night club for adults in Fort Collins. She and Pam waited tables. Tom and I were frequent customers on the weekends as we loved to whirl around the dance floor, sometimes until 1:00 a.m. When the Charco Broiler grew from a hamburger place to a restaurant, we would drop in there afterward with friends for coffee and a sandwich. If we happened to get home around 3:00

Tom and I always enjoyed dancing

a.m., instead of crawling into bed for a short time, we donned our coveralls and boots to do the milking a little early!

We would also visit the Charco Broiler after the Symphony and Larimer Chorale concerts. Tom would take his hearing aids out and fall asleep during the concerts sometimes, asking why Beethoven and other composers had to repeat the ending three to six times. He accompanied me to school concerts. The music teachers' favorite place to hang out after a concert was a restaurant called "Out of Bounds." The delicious bowls of shrimp went well with any kind of drink! Tom attended with me all of the American Choral and Music Educators' National Conferences held in different major cities across the country, as well as the yearly state conference at The Broadmoor Hotel in Colorado Springs. Many times, Poudre School District choirs, bands, and orchestras were selected to perform at these conferences.

Susie Gives Us our First Grandchild

In 1969, our dear Susie and I went to Dr. Ray, who confirmed that she was pregnant. I told Susie that she would make a wonderful mother, and we would all be part of a beautiful family. As soon as Susie finished high school, she and Steve were married. Maxine Burchfield, a dear friend, made her wedding gown. She looked like a model as Tom escorted her down the aisle. Mom was beyond happy, explaining that God had answered her prayers. She asked for a great-grandchild before she died. Susie and I spent many hours sharing together.

Steve got a job working for a farmer in Sterling. I missed Susie, but we talked on the phone every day as she kept me posted on how she felt and what Steve was doing. On Easter Sunday, 1970, little Gregory Steven was born. We hurried to Sterling where I stayed to help out for over a week. Tom and I asked Steve and Susie if they would like to come home and live in the tenant house. Steve could help with the milking. I knew of a babysitter who would come to the house while Steve and Susie attended classes at the university. What a delight to have our first grandchild so near. Mom and Dad delighted in taking Greg to the church ballgames which Tom coached. They held him during church and Mom could not rock and sing to him enough. Her prayer of having a great-grandchild before she died was fulfilled

In May of 1969, I went to observe the music teacher at Bennett Elementary. After school, I drove up beside the school bus at Bennett Road and Shields. I could not see traffic coming from the north. The school bus driver motioned it was safe to go. As I pulled into the intersection, I was hit by an oncoming car and ended up in the front yard of the Olander home. Thank God, neither I nor the other driver was injured. Of course, I received a ticket to appear in court. Our insurance covered repairs for both cars. We were well acquainted with Judge Tobin. Tom called him and said, "Hey Tobin, Patsy had an accident and will be coming to court. Tom said, "She is a teacher and should know better. Why don't you throw the book at her." I had no idea about his prank. I appeared in court and pled guilty. Judge Tobin said, "Mrs. Nix, please be careful. We need you to continue your wonderful work in the school district. I am only going to charge you half price because you have all you can possibly handle living with that husband of yours." I said, "Yes sir. Thank you very much." Tobin and I were having a difficult time keeping a straight face. One man, waiting for his turn with the judge, was sitting on the end bench. He motioned to me. As I bent down to hear him, he said, "Please touch me so some of that good luck will rub off on me." I could hardly wait to call Tom from my office and tell him what Tobin said. Tom shared what he had told Tobin and burst out laughing. I said, "You, Mr. Ornery, will be taking me to dinner at the most expensive restaurant tonight. By the way, I have something for you from the judge. I handed Tom a summons to appear in court for obstruction of the justice system of Larimer County!

In May, Ed graduated with an associate's degree. We were proud of him and asked if he had any interest in pursuing a degree in engineering. He said not right now. He got a job with John Deere Implements. As always, he enjoyed working on machinery.

The Kids Leave Home

Ed Joins the Army

In October, Ed came home and announced that he was going to join the Army. I got a lump in my throat. He reported for active duty in March of 1970 for basic training at Fort Lewis, Washington. In July he entered the Army Engineering School in Fort Belvoir, Virginia. In the fall, Tom and I wanted to visit him. I talked with my immediate boss and asked if there was any way I could be gone for a week to visit Ed. He said, "When the Silver Burdett Company flew you to New York to critique their new junior high music books, you told me about a music supervisor in the Washington, D.C. area who expressed he would like you to do a workshop for his teachers. Why don't you contact him? That way you can offer a two-day workshop and schedule the rest of the time visiting Ed. The School District will pay for that part of your trip." I had to restrain myself from giving him a hug and embraced God's unbelievable goodness! Tom and I spent two days in D.C. while I gave the workshop for teachers in an all-black school. I loved interacting with them and the students.

The second phase of engineering school was completed in November. Ed had received the second highest grade ever achieved in the engineering school. We shared that with everyone. He was able to be home for Thanksgiving and Christmas. Ed drove his Mercury Comet to the base in Fort Benning, Georgia. He was assigned to the 43rd Engineer Battalion, A Company, where he received Ranger Training. In June, Ed was on his way to Vietnam.

In our ecumenical prayer group, there was a very devout woman who had prophetic gifts. Knowing how concerned we were for Ed, Cora began to pray and told us that God was placing His protective shield around Ed. That comforted us, but Ed was the one whose assignments often placed him in harm's way. We sent letters back and forth until Ed was able to purchase a cassette player. Sending tapes was an improvement over the letters. Ed described living in huge culverts with rats as big as dogs. He taught the ARVN (Army of the Republic of Vietnam) soldiers how to repair equipment that broke down, sometimes without protection, receiving commendations for his service. Sadly, the soldiers he taught could not be trusted, so Ed and his buddies always walked in groups when away from the base. Ed wrote a letter for me to read to our ecumenical prayer group.

A young lady named Marilyn who was majoring in art at the university said she would like to write to our son. (There were several college students who attended the prayer group.) I gave her Ed's address and invited her to have dinner with us that week. We enjoyed Marilyn's company. Ed made E-5 after he had been on several missions and became an aide to the Chaplain. In March of 1972, Ed was part of the Phase Down Release Program which was approved. He boarded a plane for home on April 2. Mortars fell around them as they took off. On April 3, we picked Ed up at Stapleton Airport in Denver. We gave thanks to God for his safe return. Ed was hungry for a steak dinner which was provided.

The men and women who served in Vietnam withstood verbal abuse from U.S. citizens upon their arrival home, causing most of them to dress as civilians. Our divided nation was in turmoil. Antiwar protests emerged mostly on college campuses. Our flag was desecrated and burned, draft cards and women's bras were burned. Draft dodgers escaped to Canada. Buildings were destroyed and burned. Over 250,000 Americans protested in Washington, D.C. asking for troop withdrawal. Those of us who remembered welcoming home soldiers after WWII felt pangs of great sadness. In 1982, the Vietnam Veteran's Memorial was finally unveiled in Washington, D.C. Ed experienced people calling him names and being spit upon. He never wore his uniform again, and put his commendations in the waste basket, which I retrieved. That treatment by his fellow citizens remained with him, along with PTSD. In 2023, he received treatment and recognition, including monetary funds for his service to our country from the Veterans Administration in Cheyenne, Wyoming.

Frank, who was a good friend of Ed's, came to tell us goodbye before he left for Vietnam in 1968. Frank was a Green Beret and often called me mom. I will never forget that day. After our visit and several hugs, Frank turned as he walked out the door saying, "Mom, I have a feeling I won't see you again." Frank gave his life in Vietnam. Tom and I attended Memorial Day activities at Edora Park every year until Tom's illness prevented us from participating, which was two years before he went to be with Jesus. Ed served on the American Legion Honor Guard at both celebrations the city sponsored. We have pictures taken by the Fort Collins Coloradoan of Tom and Ed placing their hands on Frank's name at the Edora Park Memorial containing the names of our fallen soldiers from each war. We also traced our fingers over Frank's name on the traveling Vietnam Veteran's Memorial, remembering his bravery and smiling face.

After Ed got settled, Tom and I asked if he would like to meet Marilyn, and he said, "yes." We arranged to take them to dinner, followed by a Neil Diamond concert. We hoped Ed would not think we were pushing Marilyn at him. After three months of dating, they became engaged with wedding plans for the next year. Marilyn said God told her Ed was the man she would marry. Tom and I joked about accompanying Ed and Marilyn on their first date! We were delighted to think of Marilyn as our daughter-in-law since we already loved her.

Finding Dennis

In 1970, Bob, Mary Jane, and family moved to El Paso, Texas, where Bob had top level responsibilities at a large dairy. The day before they left Littleton, Colorado, teenager Dennis ran away. Mary Jane called to ask if we had seen him. I know they were frantic with worry, but we had not seen Dennis. Approximately two weeks after Dennis ran away, I saw Kenny and David carrying food out of the house. At first, I didn't think much about it because we were always feeding numerous kids, and I thought they were taking snacks. But I decided to follow them to the river where they had a makeshift tree house. Up in the tree was Dennis. Kenny and David had secretly supplied Dennis with food and water. He had been bathing in the river. I called Bob and Mary Jane immediately. Bob flew to Denver and drove a rental car to the farm. One had to know gentle Bob to fully appreciate him. Most fathers would have read him the riot act, but Bob looked at Dennis and firmly asked, "Well, are you ready to come home now?" They left the next morning.

Losing Mom

In February 1972, Tom flew down to visit Mom in the hospital. The doctors thought she had the flu but discovered too late that she was suffering from heart problems. When Tom walked into the room, she reached out with both arms and said, "Tommy, I knew you would come." Tom stayed for two days and returned home. Mom passed away on March 9, 1972. I would miss fixing Mom's hair, the confidential talks we shared, our bridge games, and the sound of the car motor as she revved it up before pulling out of the driveway. I sang for her services in Arizona and at the gravesite in Boulder, CO.

Our Nursing Home Ministry Begins

Tom and I began visiting nursing homes with communion and prayer for individual residents. We would call ahead and ask the attendants to recommend those we would visit. We always had a soft spot for the elderly. I had been thinking for some time about preparing a tape ministry of sermons and music for the homebound in our county, but I did not know how to distribute them or arrange funding for the project. My friend, Ilene, worked for the county visiting the homebound and disadvantaged, so I discussed the issue with her. After checking with her boss, she was granted permission to distribute the tapes and move them from home to home. However, funding was not available. I talked with Don Weber, our school district superintendent, who was supportive and agreed to fund the project by providing the tapes and cassette players. I provided the sermons and music for our communications department who made the tapes. My next problem was to provide enough material. However, I belonged to a group of Christian Educators who met for breakfast twice a month. They each agreed to tape sermons and music every week in the churches they attended. The program lasted several years until churches began to broadcast their services and make other programs available on TV.

Health Issues

In April of 1972, I was planning to observe the music teachers in two mountain schools. As I prepared to leave, the room began to spin, and my heartbeat escalated. I was near the couch in the family room and laid down to rest. Tom came in a short while later and asked what was wrong. By that time, I was experiencing pain in my left arm. Tom picked me up, put me in the car and we left for the doctor's office which was nearby. Dr. W. examined me and said I was having a heart attack. So I was taken around the corner to Poudre Valley Hospital where I remained for 10 days.

On the second day, a patient was brought in who had a mental breakdown while making a presentation in Loveland. At that time, the hospital did not have private areas for those who suffered mental problems. From my bed, I could see the happenings in Wilma's room. I asked the nurse on night duty if I could talk with Wilma and she agreed. I took Wilma's hand and asked if she would like a prayer. She said, "Oh yes." It was as if God placed me there at that time to help Wilma. We prayed often. Wilma told me she remembered what happened. The difficulties at home and pressure at work grew to be too much. The next day, her husband and two children came to see her, but I noticed there were no hugs. They stood at the foot of her bed. I became acquainted with Wilma's husband and children. It was her husband's choice not to work, so Wilma was supporting the family. I mentioned how much hugs from my family meant, and I thought their hugs would help Wilma. I was so pleased to see the family offer hugs from that time on. Wilma would come to my room to visit and was so taken by all the flowers, and I mentioned that to her husband. Wilma's family brought flowers and a plant on their next visit. After they left, Wilma came running to my room and said, "My flowers came, my flowers came!"

There were no heart specialists in Fort Collins, so I was attended by our family doctors and an internist. My doctors gave me orders to quit running around the hospital. I told them I only went to my neighbor's room. When I was dismissed, I asked Wilma to promise that she would take her medicine and that I would call her every day. In two weeks, Wilma was doing so well that she was able to go home. I thanked God and continued to pray for Wilma and her family. Two years, later, she and her husband came to the farm to thank me. They shared how family counseling had helped them to understand each other. The children were doing well. Wilma worked part time since her husband was employed full time. God is so good.

After my hospital stay in 1972, the internist and my doctors made an appointment with Dr. H., a well-known heart specialist who practiced at St. Joseph's Hospital in Denver. I was placed in a room with three other patients and wrote a poem about it. After a fluoroscopy examination, he told Tom and me that there appeared to be some heart damage and recommended I have a new procedure called an arteriogram. He explained that they were losing 1 out of every 200 patients during the procedure but he highly recommended it. We agreed. After receiving a relaxant, I was strapped in a submarine-like cradle where I could see the thin tube as it moved through my femoral artery to my heart. It was very interesting. Afterward, I was placed in ICU for 24 hours. When I asked for Tom, the nurse said he got sick thinking about what I was going through and they had put him to bed down the hall. He came to see me thirty minutes later.

From the ICU, I was placed in a private room. The next day, Dr. H. stood in the doorway of my room shaking his head. I said, "I do not have damage?" He said, "No, and I cannot explain it." I told him I could explain it and proceeded to tell him that in a matter of 15 minutes, hundreds of people in Fort Collins could be praying and that we had just experienced an answer to prayer. He said, "I still cannot medically explain it because the previous tests indicated heart damage." The doctor said I had been through a lot and my family doctor would keep tabs on me. He would not dismiss me until I had help at home. One of the teachers who came to visit told me about Lou who was trying to find work while her children were in school. I called Lou and was fortunate that she took the job. I told her that Tom took a short nap after lunch every day and would appreciate her waking him after 30 minutes, and to use a broomstick. I explained that Tom always came up swinging when awakened. Lou's sense of humor kept her from telling us to forget it. She not only cleaned, did laundry, etc., but she always had a casserole in the oven for dinner when she left each day. The going rate for housekeepers then was $.75 per hour. We were blessed, as Lou remained our housekeeper for twenty years.

Returning home, I found the kitchen table filled with letters and drawings from students and several casseroles from friends. What a cheery and blessed homecoming! My recovery was slower than I had anticipated. I spent a lot of time with the Lord who convinced me that I did not have to be super mom, wife, teacher, and friend. Tom asked why I had not told him I was feeling ill. The truth was I did not know. I had been on the treadmill for years and could not seem to get off. I was averaging 4 hours of sleep a night because there was laundry, ironing, mending, cooking, chores, work goals, etc., to be done. I decided I caused the problem for not taking care of myself and asked God to forgive me for not taking care of the body He gave me. At the doctor's direction, I began a slow jog down our half mile dirt lane every day. Since supportive walking/running shoes had not been made for women yet, I developed huge calluses on the balls of my feet. I am sure part of the problem was caused earlier by the pointed toe high heel shoes that women wore. The podiatrist shaved the calluses but said they would return. Dr. W. said to walk instead of jog, which was better for the knees. I was so grateful to God for His healing, mercy, and love. I spent hours in scripture, writing poems and prose.

Back at work, my secretary reminded me to slow down. My boss said that I was to only do minimal work for a period of time and gave me an assignment. I was to watch my colleagues at work who usually put in eight-hour days. He added, "No one works as hard as you or moves as fast. Patsy, you meet with teachers before school. You serve on state, school district, and community committees. You attend concerts and programs to support your teachers and the students. You are supportive of your family and care for added people in your home. Please think about what I have said, and slow down!" I knew he was right because I had never given my schedule a thought. I was so goal oriented that I had never noticed the pace at which others worked. On top of everything, my perfectionism prevented me from spending more quality time with my children. Tom said he accepted some responsibility for always being so demanding of me and my time. A close friend shared that Tom was not the only demanding influence in my life. Because others could depend on me, they expected pieces of my time. Another friend put it this way: "People will work a good horse to death." Being a farmer's wife, I fully understood that comment!

God knew I needed lots of help to overcome former habits. "As always, I felt led BY HIS HAND. I spent hours in the scriptures and talking with Him. I was so grateful for His healing, mercy, and love. *Philippians 4:13* "I can do all things through Christ who strengthens me." (A verse that has carried me through many circumstances and experiences.) *Psalm 37:5* "Commit everything you do to the Lord. Trust Him to help you do it and He will." (A few of the writings and poetry that I penned during my recovery and at other times can be found later in these memoirs.)

We celebrated our 25th anniversary in June 1972 with a party planned by Susie. As always, Tom presented me with a dozen red roses and beautiful sentiments. I wrote a poem for him. The children presented us with beautiful mother and father rings. We so enjoyed our oneness in Jesus. The time we cherished the most was holding hands and praying together every day.

Selling the Dairy Herd and Moving

Tom came in from feeding the cattle on a Saturday morning and told me that God had been working on his heart to get out of the dairy business because of my health. Also, none of our children were interested in inheriting the dairy business. Through the years, we had offers to sell our land for a golf course, housing development, or other business adventures. Earlier, we sold five acres bordering Prospect Road to Bath Landscape. The five acres were not useful to farm since it was previously the railroad trestle area that led into our farm the back way. The boys parked with their dates there. The children did not know that Tom and I parked there, too, when we wanted to get away! Our primary concern was running our top herd of dairy cows through the sale. Our veterinarian told us of a young farmer in Wray, Colorado, who wanted to purchase some dairy cows and gave us a phone number. We discovered we had known Kenneth and his wife. During their student years at CSU, they sang in the church choir I directed. We did not want to move until David and Jim graduated from high school, so Ken and his wife signed a contract to purchase our entire milking herd plus some of the young heifers the following year. God is good and full of surprises!

We began to search out places to live. It would be difficult to leave our land, wide open spaces, walks along the river, mountain views, and the special place where we raised our children and provided sanctuary for many others. We found a new housing development north of Fort Collins called Adriel Hills. The plans were for a neighborhood of condominiums where streets would have biblical names. There would be a six-hole golf course. Exploration of other developments did not grab our attention. We told our good friends, Jack and Marilyn, about Adriel Hills and they made plans to purchase the show home. We made it known to the realtor and builder that we would be interested in purchasing a condo in a few months and would like one with a mountain view.

Tom was offered a position to supervise the dairy at CSU. We knew what the hours entailed and also found out that if a student did not show up as scheduled, the supervisor stepped in to do their job. Because of that, the job held no appeal. At the suggestion of a friend, Tom began to consider becoming a real estate salesman. In January of 1973, he began studying for his license. Real estate offered new experiences and was not a 24-hour-a-day job.

I called our two teenage sons to sit down in the family room and proceeded to ask about the high phone bill. There was silence. I asked again. I was usually a patient parent, but they knew I was running out of patience. Finally, Kenny said, "You ruined it all, Mom. We are throwing you and Dad a surprise retirement party. The phone calls were to all our former farmer neighbors in Hudson, a few of your high school chums and Fort Collins friends." Unfortunately, the phone bill came three days ahead of a wonderfully planned party. Tom and I did a good job of acting surprised!

I had two months during the summer to practice recuperating and learning to slow down. My mind was always busy, making it difficult! I practiced how to sit down, take a deep breath and rest which was foreign to me. I remember times when Tom would come in the house, and I thought I needed to be busy. So if I was sitting down, I jumped up and busied myself. I certainly caused myself a lot of trouble. God continued to speak to me through His word and I continued to lean on Him and reach for His hand.

I had to admit that I enjoyed the quiet of the house during the summer. I continued to clean the milking equipment and took care of the baby calves. I got caught up and made improvements on bookkeeping for the dairy and our personal items. In our entire married life, Tom never participated in the business side of our partnership. In later years, I remember asking him if he would like to sit down and learn about our financial details in case something happened to me and he would need to take over. He answered with an emphatic "NO" and added, "If something did happen to you, I would rely on our son, Ed, to do it." He enjoyed telling everyone he had to ask me for spending money every week! Every week, he buttered me up for spending money and ended it with a fish kiss.

1973 was an eventful year. David wrestled for Fort Collins High School, and we always attended all of his wrestling matches in and out of town. David came close to losing the privilege of being a wrestler. During the 1972 football season, Fort Collins High School was playing Poudre High School. After half-time, it was customary for the hosting team to run onto the field through a big hoop held by the cheerleaders. David decided to beat the team through the hoop. Cheers went up from the Fort Collins crowd and boos echoed from the Poudre fans. David was asked to leave the stadium! The following Monday, Tom and I were summoned to the Fort Collins principal's office. David was there. The principal was one of my colleagues. The Poudre High administrators were asking that David be punished by declaring him ineligible for wrestling. Tom heavily expressed his opinion. The principal was smiling when we left. We never knew what he told the administrators at Poudre, but David was allowed to continue wrestling. Tom told him, "Good job, son." At the state tournament, David kept winning. During the semi-final match, Tom and I were sitting close, and in our exuberance, rushed out onto the mat where the ref was recognizing Dave as the winner. We were quite embarrassed and decided to sit in the balcony for the finals. It was always exciting to watch our boys wrestle. One never sits still. Yelling through gritted teeth, the body is standing, sitting, tensing, and swaying. We were sitting in the balcony when David won the state championship, and I got so excited that our camera flew over the balcony. Tom and I nearly tripped on the stairs as we made our way down to Dave. He had just beat the wrestler from Loveland whose picture appeared on the program as the one expected to win the title.

We purchased a travel trailer which was pulled behind our car. The first trip was to Crystal Lakes in the mountains. Our friends, Jack and Marilyn accompanied us. We parked near a lake, enjoyed an outdoor barbeque, and played bridge all evening. Tom's legs were too long for the bed. It never occurred to us to try out the beds beforehand. The next morning, Jack, Marilyn, and I walked around the lake while Tom took his shower. We discovered that Tom used all the water, so Jack, Marilyn and I bathed the best we could on the shore of the cold lake. The three of us decided that Tom would carry buckets of water from the lake which were heated on the stove for washing and cooking. We got drinking water from a nearby cabin.

In January of 1973, we sold our milk cows and several heifers. Steve, Susie, and Greg moved into the farmhouse in July. We purchased a condominium in Adriel Hills on Elim Court. It was on the west end overlooking a lake frequented by geese and blue heron. There was a large irrigation ditch that ran between our condo and the lake. Buffalo and horses roamed up and down between our condo and the east side of the lake. Behind our condo was a large greenbelt which would make a great play area for our grandchildren. Our view of the mountain range was wide and long. In addition, there was an indoor-outdoor swimming pool and a six-hole golf course. We were blessed!

Tom was offered another position at CSU. It would be working in research to treat dogs who had developed cancer. He decided to continue to pursue real estate instead. Tom studied every day until he felt prepared to take the real estate test for his license. When finished, he mailed it to Denver. Those who graded the tests were known to be very slow. As time passed, Tom thought he must have made a poor grade. On May 5, 1973, we stopped to check the mailbox. The letter was there. Tom asked me to hurry and open it. I opened it and said, "I'm sorry Tom." He said, "I knew it." My reply was "you only scored a 96." We were on our way to a very joyous occasion. Ed and Marilyn were married that day!

Tom's Real Estate Career

Tom began his real estate career the week of May 8. The office was near the Charco Broiler Restaurant on East Mulberry which was across the river from our farm. Ten days later, Tom came home and made the comment that he did not realize how some women threw themselves at men. I said, "Welcome to a different world." Tom enjoyed being a realtor and the broker said he was a natural. I was not surprised because Tom was intelligent, a man of integrity and kindness who liked being around people. His outgoing personality was an added plus. Toward the end of May, Tom made his first sale. The check passed from his hand to mine for deposit into our account.

Tom got his feet wet by selling farms, residential, and commercial properties. We read books on the history of Larimer County that documented water rights from early settlement days. For our farm crops, we drew water from the Emigh Lateral, Arthur Ditch, and Horsetooth Reservoir water from the Poudre River through the Chafee Ditch. Tom also served on the city and county water boards. His knowledge was vast. It was not long before he became the "go-to person" about water rights. Lawyers and other realtors sought his expertise. Years later, a graduate student from the University of Northern Colorado was assigned to gather information from Tom about early to present-day water rights. The interview lasted for three days. The final report is housed in the Documents section of the UNC Library. I assisted Tom with typing any information he needed and also with contracts. On weekends, Tom asked me to accompany him when listing and showing properties. Sometimes, I would sit with him at an open house. I learned a lot about the real estate business. After a few years, as the Tom's realty firm expanded, it looked like I would need to upgrade the computer and purchase a different modem. However, one of Tom's realty colleagues offered to co-partner with him and do the work I had been doing.

We had a graduation party for David and Jim. We said goodbye to Jim as he took off to join his biological father in Kansas. While working in a plant, Jim was burned with hot melted ore. After he recovered, he appeared on our doorstep. Although his burns had healed, he did not look well, and I suggested he see a doctor. He declined, but David convinced him to go and accompanied him to the appointment. Jim needed emergency surgery where a large portion of his colon was removed. Our family was a frequent visitor to the hospital. We were so happy on the day Jim came home. Eventually, he moved to Denver and began working at the Denver Mint.

After some discussion, Dave decided to attend Mesa Community College in Arizona on a scholarship, where Tom's brother was the wrestling coach. Joe was an outstanding coach, but he and David's personalities clashed. Dave enrolled at CSU for his sophomore year. Toward the end of his junior year, Dave told us we were wasting our money on him. He was interested in farming.

A Marriage Crisis

The second week in June, Tom came home and changed his clothes to take care of the cattle. Tom stood in the kitchen doorway as I was making preparations for dinner. He usually was ready with some teasing remark but was rather quiet. I said, "Is something bothering you?" He asked if I thought a person could be in love with two people at the same time. I said, "Why do you ask?" (Tom and I shared everything with each other as promised on our wedding night.) Tom proceeded to tell me about a lady realtor from a neighboring community who had come to the office. When their eyes met while being introduced, fireworks went off. He described that she was beautiful and told him she had been Mrs. Colorado in the late 1950s, which greatly impressed him. We will call her "Irene." David came home so our conversation ceased. Tom and David went out to tend the cattle and I returned to preparing dinner. Neither of us said anything that evening. As was Tom's custom, he fell asleep in the recliner while David and I watched TV, and he went to bed ahead of everyone. Morning did not lend time for discussion. We had our morning prayer together, as usual, that always ended with, "May what we do and say be pleasing to you, O God." As I drove to my office, I remembered a sermon I recently heard that stressed the need to be on guard, especially when things seemed to be going well. *1 Peter 5:8* says, "Be self-controlled and alert. Your enemy, the devil, prowls around like a roaring lion looking for someone to devour." He especially liked to attack Christians. I said, "God, I am not doing very well right now. Tom is vulnerable in his new worldly surroundings. When he was born again, You said there was a purpose for him in the new person he had become. He is being attacked. Right now, he is stumbling. Please rescue him and please help me." God said, "Trust me." *Proverbs 3:5* came to mind: "Trust in the Lord with all your heart and lean not unto you own understanding." At 10 a.m., Tom called to remind me about our luncheon date. I arranged to pick him up at noon. As was my custom, I parked at the realty office and went in to greet everyone. Tom was talking with Irene. We were introduced. Irene certainly was a beautiful woman and appeared to be near my age. She was tall and her makeup was impeccable. Every flowing hair was in place. She knew how to own the room and was focused on Tom. When Tom and I were seated for lunch in the nearby restaurant, I asked, "Did you plan for me to meet Irene today?" He said, "No, I did not know she would be there." I said, "From my observation, she plans to be there often. When Irene and I were introduced, I felt insignificant and like I was intruding." Tom looked shocked, expressed his love for me and said he would never want to hurt me. Under my breath, I asked the Holy Spirit for the right words. I spoke of Irene's beauty and added that no doubt she has turned the heads of many men. (Irene was married and had two sons.) I said, "From what I have observed, Tom, you are in the position of encouraging or discouraging Irene's presence. Please be careful with the choice you make." I wanted to say much, much more, but the Holy Spirit stopped me. He brought to mind the day I shared with Tom how much I enjoyed conversation with a colleague. This colleague was kind and considerate during a time when Tom was overboard with verbal abuse. The gentleman was pressing me to have lunch with him. I had observed the damage that could come from the so-called harmless luncheon dates, so I distanced myself from him and thanked God for His counsel. The Holy Spirit now prompted me to steer our conversation toward our move, which would take place next month. We embraced for a long time before Tom left the car. I told him I trusted him.

I was prompted to make an appointment with our pastor. Because our families were close-knit, I hesitated, but knew the situation needed more prayer power, and I would never discuss the happenings with anyone except our pastor and his wife. Our pastor greeted me with a hug and asked me to sit down. I told him I came to ask for a prayer of prevention. He smiled and said, "No one has ever asked me for a prayer of prevention." I explained the circumstances and said, "Jesus knew we needed prayers of prevention, especially in the prayer He taught us: "Lead us not into temptation but deliver us from evil." We had a discussion of other prevention petitions in the Bible. I also asked for prayers that Tom would not be influenced by an office colleague who was engaged in an extramarital affair. I asked for prayers that I would keep my eyes on Jesus and not on the circumstances. Our pastor's prayer was comforting and powerful. Tom and I continued our daily prayers together.

When two weeks passed, Tom shared he had told his dad about Irene. Dad said, "Tom, you have the most wonderful wife in the world. Don't screw it up! Are you prepared and willing to give up the love and respect of your wonderful wife and family?" Tom told me those words jarred him. He said he had really been trying to battle his thoughts. When he heard Dad's words, he repented and asked for God's forgiveness. Tom said, "Patsy, you are the love of my life, and my best friend. Please forgive me." I expressed my love and forgiveness and thanked Tom for his forgiveness when my words and actions were not those of a loving wife. We praised God for the gift of deliverance through Jesus and the words He gave Dad. None of us are free from sin, and it all begins in the mind. We held on to *Philippians 4:13,* "I can do all things through Christ who strengthens me." Tom relied on our prayers and guidance from the Holy Spirit when he talked with Irene. He told her of his love and devotion for me and how much his family meant to him. He said, "Irene, Jesus loves you. The only kind of love I can offer you is like the love Jesus has for you."

As I write this, Tom has been with Jesus for three years. I know Tom would want me to share this part of the story, because when I told him I planned to write my memoirs, he told me to "tell it all, the good, the bad, and the ugly." It is a story about being tempted, remaining steadfast and trusting God when we are attacked by Satan. It is about triumph and giving glory to God. I continue to lift up our prayers to God for our children and grandchildren. Tom and I prayed through the years that our children, grandchildren, and great-grandchildren realize that temptation lurks around every corner, and it is easy to be caught up with self and desires of the flesh. We prayed for them to know that there is indescribable joy in married oneness that God intends for us. We desired for them to know how praying together, every day, for family and each other's needs and shortcomings creates a strong marriage bond. We prayed for our children and grandchildren to be grateful, every day, for Jesus who suffered and died for our sins. We prayed that they rely on the Holy Spirit for guidance. We prayed for them to remember they can depend on our ever-present, ever-loving, forgiving, faithful God for help in times of need and trouble. When we prayed, it was not a blanket prayer for family. We lifted each name, individually. Tom was able to speak each name until three weeks before he passed into the arms of Jesus.

Tom became totally dedicated to please God through countless types of service in the church, in Fort Collins, and wider communities. It was his desire to share the love of Jesus with everyone.

Tom's colleagues were urging him to join them for after-hour drinks. We made a promise that we would never have drinks with colleagues after work unless we were together. We enjoyed FAC gatherings from both of our offices and some of the schools.

Dad married Aunt Jo, Mom's sister, in 1973. Some of the family were not too pleased at first, but it soon became evident that it was a good marriage for both. We delighted in the visits we had with them.

Moving Off the Farm

We moved to 1721 Elim Court in Adriel Hills on July 27, 1973. We enjoyed furniture shopping for our new home. Our favorite purchase was the grandfather clock that would be placed on the first landing of the stairway.

In September, Tom bought me a new car. Shopping for vehicles was great fun, and Tom was a wheeler-dealer like his dad! I did need a different car, but never dreamed I would become an owner of a 1973 Sedan Deville Cadillac.

Susie and Steve presented us with our second grandchild. Jacob Russell was born on October 9, 1973. It was such fun having a newborn again. I spent a few days with the family to help out. Afterward, I would pop in during lunch hour or on the weekends to play with Greg and cuddle with Jake. Since Tom was still farming part of our farm and caring for cattle, Greg was his shadow, always wanting to help Papo. He knew which wrenches to hand Papo when he was repairing machinery, and he loved to ride on the tractor. Jake liked to play in boxes. It was not unusual to find him in a box or the waste basket. Jake suffered from food allergies. At age two he would bow his little head before eating and ask God to let the food do good and not hurt him.

Earlier, in late July, Tom had expressed that he had not done enough to show his love and appreciation, so he was taking me to Hawaii for Christmas. We planned a trip that would include a week's stay on Oahu and two-night stays on Maui, Kauai, and both coasts of Hawaii. I had mixed emotions on missing out on spending Christmas Eve and Day with the family, but I was excited about the two of us spending time together on the islands. Christmases on the farm were joyful and full of activities. We decorated inside and out. The trees and shrubs glistened with lights. Our evergreen tree in the living room touched the ceiling. There was a bench on each side of the fireplace adorned with the nativity scene and huge red bows hung on the stairway. We welcomed guests for Christmas Eve and Christmas dinner, especially those who were alone. This was a standing invitation—always. The Christmas Story from Luke was read by Tom or the children. This year, we planned an early Christmas celebration in our new home. The celebration would include a Christmas Day birthday party for Ed and Alicia. The time came for Tom and me to leave for Hawaii. Vicky, a teacher I had hired to teach elementary music for the Poudre School District, had moved to Oahu the year before. She had many plans for us that included: visits to the Polynesian Center with marvelous dancers and good food; snorkeling in the waters on Sunset Beach; watching whales; nightclub shows; a visit to the Arizona Memorial where so many servicemen died when the Japanese bombed Pearl Harbor. We visited several other sites, did a lot of shopping, and the week was up before we knew it. We hopped on a small plane that took us to Kawaii, the Garden Island. It was so beautiful and peaceful with gorgeous plants, flowers and waterfalls. After our two days on Kawaii, the plane took us to the big island of Hawaii. We landed on the Kona Coast. The accommodations were the best yet, and the luau was fabulous. Standing on the rim of the Kilauea Volcano and looking down into the crater was quite an experience. (Since 2007, visitors have not been allowed on the rim.) On eruption, the volcano can spew 2 billion gallons of lava. The oceanfront was heavy with volcanic rock. Our next stop was Hilo, the other side of the big island. Tom and I looked forward to visiting museums on our trips. The one on Hilo was incomplete because of the 1960 Tsunami. Many historical items had been destroyed. On Maui, we stayed at the Kaanapali Hotel on the beach. We spent New Year's Eve eating and dancing. We were so blessed to have that time together. We played a lot of rummy on the way home. I usually beat Tom, and he said there was no way I could be that good—so it must be the luck of the Irish! When we arrived home, it was fun sharing and delivering gifts to the family.

The Mid-1970s

Susie was secretary for Range RV Sales. She called and was excited for us to come see a fifth wheel that had just rolled off the production line in Denver. It was a Riviera. It did not take us long to arrange for purchase. We traded in our trailer and also purchased a 1973 Cheyenne Chevy pickup. We paid $7,000 for the deal. The fifth-wheel was more spacious than the trailer and had lots of cabinet and closet space. We were surprised to see a roomy, sunken bathroom. Two beds were upstairs, and the kitchen area would sleep three people in queen and twin-size beds. We were thrilled with the air cooler. We began making plans for our first trip. Our close friends, Jack and Marilyn, helped us christen the fifth wheel with champagne on a mountain excursion. That began many years of traveling with Jack and Marilyn.

Our boys surprised Tom for his next birthday with a new box and chrome bumper on the 1973 Chevy pickup.

In the fall of 1974, our nephew, John (Joe and Lora's son), came to stay with us. Our son, Ken, had been welcomed into Mary Jane and Bob's home in Texas, and our niece, Roxie (Mary Jane and Bob's daughter), had lived with Joe and Lora in Arizona. The children thought the hospitality of those three Nix siblings and their spouses was special and unique!

From 1974-1978, David was busy with custom farming, including the crops on our farm. We also had 150 pair of cattle (mothers and babies) that David and Tom moved to different pastures. Tom carried coveralls and boots in his vehicle so he could help with the work and the cattle. He took David's lunch to him whenever he was not busy with real estate business.

On November 2, 1975, our third grandchild made his appearance. Ed and Marilyn named him Thomas Edward Nix IV. Tom was pleased because that name has been in the family for generations. Tommy was premature, but he was strong. However, at three months of age, he became very ill with respiratory problems. Ed, Marilyn, Tom and I, along with other family members and friends prayed for that precious baby. Tommy made it through the night which was a good sign. We gave thanks as Tommy improved each day. He would be in the hospital one more time at 17 months of age with an oxygen tent over his bed. When I visited, I sang to him. On one occasion, I was singing, "If you're happy and you know it, clap your hands." He stood up and began jumping up and down on the bed. He soon went home. From that time on, Tommy thrived, and grew to be a healthy, strong man.

Susie had been in counsel with our pastor who advised her to separate from Steve, so Steve left. Susie and the boys moved into the farmhouse in 1975. We were praying for both of them, hoping everything would work out. David and John moved to the farmhouse to stay with Susie and the boys. Frances, a lovely young woman, lived in the house across the hay field that had previously been Mom and Dad's home. She and John were married in January of 1976 in Danforth Chapel at Colorado State University. We loved planning and hosting their wedding reception in the farmhouse.

My Coaching Career

In 1976, Susie asked if I would coach a women's softball team. She was willing to gather the women. I suggested that Mary, the school district's Elementary Physical Education Coordinator, and Lynn, an art teacher friend of mine, would make good players. I told Susie I would pay the fees if she would enroll us in the city league. First, I needed to have the OK from my boss, the director of curriculum. I told him that it would require my being at practice once or twice a week by 3:30 p.m. His comment was, "Everyone is acquainted with the extra time you spend for the district, so it is OK." I was excited! Not only to be involved in athletics again, but that my daughter asked me to coach the team.

Tom was already coaching the church baseball team. He was an excellent coach and a few top players in Fort Collins joined our church so they could be on the team. The baseball team began their tenth year. First Christian was playing First National Bank for the city championship. The score was tied, and our guys were up at bat in the last inning with two outs. Darrell came sliding into home plate and was called out. Well, there was an uproar and foot stomping from our fans, but the ump would not reverse the call. I was yelling that the ball was stuck in the backstop. After Tom and the players tried to talk with the ump, Tom threw his glove down and walked away. First National Bank's catcher never had the ball in his glove when he tagged Darrell. He had missed the tag. The ball really was stuck in the fence, but the First National Bank Team was declared the winner. The ump was a teacher in the school district. The next time I saw him, he said, "Don't say it, Patsy." The theme from the TV detective show called *Friday* was in my head. As I walked away, I sang, "dum, dum, Da Ump." He said, "I heard that!"

I loved coaching the women and according to them I was tough. We practiced hard while I timed base running. They were huffing and puffing for the first two weeks until I handed the stopwatch to the catcher while I ran the bases. They decided to get the lead out! I did have strict rules about being on time for practice and games. I announced there would be a show of respect for each other and no swearing at any time. Also, that it was my job to argue with the umpire, if needed. Val and Jen, who were sisters, played first and third. Both were tall with great stretches and their throws were accurate. They liked to play on each other's nerves, so I benched them from time to time for cool-downs. Karen was one of the best catchers I ever observed in women's softball or baseball. Once she was late for a game so was benched for two innings. She said, "But Patsy, you should know better than anyone what it is like when the pigs get out [on the farm]" I did understand, but I explained if rules are not followed someone would be late and expect to play for a lesser excuse. Susie was excellent at short stop and kept the chatter going. Mary, Lynn, and Patty had throwing arms that were unbelievable as fielders and were three of our heaviest hitters. Mary and Jean alternated pitcher and center field positions. Ruth was the best at third and Janie played second base. The four substitutes didn't let any grass grow under their feet, so we were a strong team. We won the city championship and also cleaned up at district. I ended up having emergency surgery before the state championship game. I had such confidence in Tom that I asked if he would coach the girls in that game. He hesitated but finally agreed. I warned him about Jen and Val and told him to bench one of them if they got into each other's face. I had permission from the umpire to watch the game from behind the fence in the car. I was propped up with pillows and used my binoculars. Right as rain, Jen and Val got into it. Val was credited with an error and Jen would not let up. Tom was not quick enough to pull them out. Then Jen missed a throw allowing the opposing team to score the winning run. When Tom got to the car, I thanked him and asked why he was slow in benching the girls. He said, "Golly, I did not know what to do with those emotional women." I had to smile, but felt sorry for the team. Susie and the team asked me to coach again next season. I explained to them how much I loved coaching and getting to know such a fine group of talented women. However, my administrative position had increased to a ten-and-a-half-month job. Since I was now the K-12 Music Coordinator, I needed to be fair and appreciative to the community that paid my salary. We had a fun picnic party to end the summer.

Tom and I had an opportunity to attend a seminar at Oral Roberts University in Tulsa, Oklahoma. Oral Roberts and his wife, Evelyn, were gracious hosts from whom we learned so much more about the power of prayer, the baptism in the Holy Spirit, bringing God into the whole of our lives and feasting on God's Word. Oral asked us to stay in the Spirit as we shared with other Christians on returning home. He closed the seminar with these words and prayer: "Humanity has built a civilization based upon man's mind and partially his body, but without the spirit and soul. One of our greatest wrongs is to fail to love all our people, all of our races, and all of our differences. We want to intellectually run our own lives, but God can integrate us spiritually, physically and mentally. Repent from your mind overruling the way God created you." His prayer: "It is so good to talk with you, God, Creator of All. Thank you for coming to us in the dimension of Father, Son and Holy Spirit. It is so good to know you are at the point of our need this very moment. Thank you for enlightenment that comes to our understanding while studying your Word. Thank you for the redeeming power of Jesus. Thank you for the miracles you have performed this week. And now, may each person here know healing in heart, mind, emotions, and body while the Holy Spirit is at work within them. Through Jesus Christ, our Lord, Amen and Amen." Oral Roberts always offered two Amens! We were excited to share what we had learned with our brothers and sisters in Christ. God also opened the way for us to share with unbelievers. We were grateful that our pastors at First Christian Church continued to provide seminars, workshops, speakers, and Bible studies for our spiritual growth. We immersed ourselves in reading books by Dennis and Rita Bennett, Terry Law, Hal Lindsey, Agnes Sanford and others.

Tom became active in the Lion's Club and often transported eyes to Denver for transplant. In visiting with a teacher from LaPorte Elementary, he learned about a blind student who would benefit by having a computer. Tom solicited funds from all three Fort Collins Lions Clubs to purchase a Braille computer. We watched as Annie lightly brushed her fingers over the keyboard with a million-dollar smile on her face.

I was excited about my job promotion. I had already been assisting the secondary music teachers, but now it was official. However, I learned that my salary would not be increased. One of the men in my department was given more responsibility with a nice raise. Tom and I discussed it, and he supported me, as always. Title IX had been enacted into law in 1972. It was about discrimination and imbalances on the basis of sex in education programs receiving federal financial assistance. I made an appointment with my boss to tell him he could have my job. I told him it appeared that since I had been doing the job voluntarily for 10 years I could continue without compensation. He asked me to sit down, took out a notebook and began running his fingers over some figures. He looked up and said, "We can afford to raise your salary." He mentioned an amount. I said, "If you want to match what other school districts are paying their music coordinators, it should be $1,500 more." My boss hesitated but expressed appreciation and added the $1,500. I encouraged women colleagues to stand up for what was right. Some were too shy or afraid to ask. It would take years before the contributions of women in the workplace were rewarded with equal pay.

Ed Martin, president of one of the Fort Collins Lions Clubs, asked me to give a music program. I told Ed I would secure a high school group. He said, "No, Patsy. Tom said we should ask you to perform and added that he was your manager and bodyguard!" Colorado's Bicentennial was in 1976. I called my friend, Faith, a sister in Christ, to ask if she would be interested in performing a program to celebrate the Bicentennial. Faith was an outstanding pianist and accompanist who I had worked with for other performances. If I was a little hoarse or had a cold, she could transpose a piece of music, on the spot, to a different key. Our program featured songs of the Westward Movement, early settlers, and music from the 20's to the present. Patriotic and sacred songs anchored the program, and I did some soft-shoe dancing. We were booked for 20 performances throughout the state during the year. The largest audience was the National Convention of Germans from Russia. I sang several songs in German for that one. Tom, my best supporter and cheerleader, never missed a performance. After the Bicentennial year, Faith and I performed different programs in Fort Collins. My favorite offering was to praise God through my music in worship services.

Tom and I continued our communion service on Sundays for those in nursing homes or the hospital. There were times we prayed for the nurses as they received communion with the patients. We asked God every day to use us and deepen our spiritual understanding. We attended and co-taught Bible studies and Sunday School classes. Our church had training sessions and seminars on Christian Counseling and Inner Health as well as Guidelines for Soul Healing Prayer every week. After five months of attending classes, reading and praying, we had met over 20 requirements to become counselors. The program encouraged counselors to work in pairs which was perfect for us. We were blessed in the counseling sessions as the Holy Spirit's healing touch led people to Wholeness. We continued in this ministry for 10 years and called on the training to help guide others through the years. We prayed each day that our marriage would be a witness for others.

My Work as K-12 Music Education and Vocal Coordinator

After becoming the K-12 Music Coordinator, I found weaknesses in the Junior High Music Program. I began holding in-services, providing needed support for the teachers. I visited with each junior high principal explaining that new and challenging music was needed along with new textbooks for general music classes. I had use of some funds at the district level but needed their help. After two and a half years, there was updated and interesting music for students. God had sent outstanding teachers who loved teaching junior high school students.

Our school district was divided into three sections: North, Central and South. Three people performed their duties as assistant superintendents but were called executive principals. This was a wise decision because the public could not say we had too many superintendents whenever a vote was taken to raise the mill levy. During those times, Tom and I helped organize rallies which were great fun. We also signed up to give speeches to community organizations. The community has been great to support students, teachers and administrators in the Poudre School District throughout the years. The three executive principals held the purse strings for each of their areas. I was thoroughly prepared each time I requested funds for the music program. The requests ranged from textbooks and materials to pianos, instruments and later, band uniforms. When the execs saw me coming, they would say, "Now, what do you want?" Later, I told them if they would turn the funds over to me, I would not have to bug them so much. And to my surprise, they did! I worked with the Director of Finance who sometimes was able to find extra dollars in the budget for the music program.

The secondary teachers and I began to plan what we called "Cluster Concerts" for the district areas: North, Central and South. There would be performances from the high schools, junior highs, and elementary schools. The three concerts were well attended, which gave teachers, principals, administrators, and the community a larger picture of the music program. I had funds to pay well-known choral conductors to direct the high school groups. When the State Department of Education asked for goals and objectives for all education programs, the music staff led the way in our district. Because God answered prayers to send excellent teachers and the dedication of each teacher to do their best for students, as well as support from principals, administrators, and the community, the Poudre School District music program was selected to receive the Exemplary Music Program Award, one of two in the nation. A special Choir Night performance by the junior high schools helped to build the program as one recognized throughout the state. The teachers had worked hard to reach that status.

I was invited to serve on the Governor's Fine Arts Taskforce for two years. Three other music coordinators from other school districts and four community people who supported the Arts were also invited. Three years later, I became a member of the State Teacher Tenure Review Committee. I certainly learned a lot about legislative process and procedures.

My friend, Sylvia Maxey, the District Art Coordinator, and I began to make plans for a presentation to the school board, the superintendent and his staff to begin a Gifted Program. The principals were already on board. It was approved. As it grew, the district hired a coordinator for the program.

I enrolled in workshops that taught about Bloom's Taxonomy which is a model to classify educational objectives in cognitive, affective, and sensory domains. For teachers, Bloom's Taxonomy offers ways to classify and organize what students are learning. Students are challenged to understand, apply, analyze, evaluate, and create. I have always been a proponent of teaching how one subject relates to another, maximizing the potential of individual learners. Otherwise, unrelated subjects are organized as individual blocks in students' brains. As I shared Bloom's Taxonomy with my immediate boss, he asked if I would give a presentation to the principals. After the presentation, the executive principal of the North Area asked if I would give workshops for elementary classroom teachers. I thoroughly enjoyed working with the classroom teachers.

I used the same learning objectives along with music therapy for the mentally and emotionally challenged children in our district. At the time, the emotionally challenged students were taught together at Box Elder School. I learned of each child's needs by working with the psychologists. Those students loved talking about their feelings through music or by playing their stories on the piano. The piano sounds ranged from gentle to very angry. I was overjoyed when the psychologists reported the music therapy was making a difference in student expression and behavior. Our mentally challenged students were housed in their own classroom within elementary buildings. I gained permission from parents, the principal and teacher in an elementary building where I taught some classes to work with and videotape the students. After two months, I requested that certain students be mainstreamed into regular music classes. It was great to see their excitement, improvement, and the way they interacted with other students. Those that remained in their own group were learning to recognize letters and all but one learned to spell their names. I used Orff instruments (wooden and metal xylophones), along with drums and triangles to assist them. Even though our administrators saw the video which supported use of the instruments, it would be two years before I had enough funds to purchase the Orff instruments for each elementary school. I held music therapy in-service for the elementary music teachers. We were offering music therapy six years before it was part of the curriculum in universities.

I continued to attend classes and workshops to advance my understanding of student learning. Most interesting and challenging were sessions of application brain research to student learning and retention. I served on the Asian Studies Committee, the junior high building team, graduation requirements committee and as president of the Poudre R-1 School Executives. I later represented the group by being a board member of the Colorado Association of School Executives.

30 Years of Marriage: Time to Explore the World

On June 22, 1977, the children hosted a family dinner with a few invited friends for our 30th wedding anniversary. Tommy tried to keep up with Greg and Jake. Such a delight! Tom and I had celebrated earlier with a dinner out where we were given free drinks and cake. Tom wrote this on his card: "Patsy, you are my life. When you are happy, I am happy. When you are sad, I am sad, also. When you are sick, I feel bad, too. I feel hurt when someone hurts you. I share your joys and your troubles. I am proud of your successes. Thank you so very much for 30 years of growing together, and I look forward to the coming years. I love you and I always will. I praise God for your companionship and love." Tom repeated these beautiful words to me several times over the years. I wrote this for Tom: "Tom, you are my Love and Best Friend. For thirty years you have been by my side through thick and thin. We have stood together through good times and bad, and held each other when happy or sad. I am proud of you, wonderful man of my heart. You've been

Our 30th anniversary

trustworthy, honest, loving, funny and mischievous, right from the start. I thank God for you and love you with all of my heart!"

In July we headed out in our fifth wheel with Jack and Marilyn. We were bound for Washington and a tour of Alaska. We stopped at Pete and Irene Burfening's home in Bellevue, Washington. Pete had arranged for us to leave our fifth wheel in storage while we toured Alaska. Two friends, Reid and Erma from Fort Collins, met us at the airport. We flew to Fairbanks and visited Mount McKinley National Park (now Denali). We were fortunate to see the top of the mountain since it usually had cloud cover. The caribou and bald eagles were plentiful along with other wildlife. A truly wonderful experience. We spent five days in Anchorage. We were on the top floor of a hotel when a minor earthquake hit. The building swayed for some time while we held on to our drinks. From there we boarded a bus which drove onto a train. The train dropped us off and we got on a yacht that took us to Valdez where work was being done on the Alaskan Oil Pipeline. From there we traveled by bus to White Horse, Canada. The next day we left by train that rolled over the mountains and down into Skagway. We boarded the Sun Princess ship that cruised around the Portage Glacier area. When huge mounds of ice broke off the glacier into the sea, it sounded like a bomb. We saw seals on icebergs giving birth to babies. After a day's visit to Sitka, the first capital of Alaska, the ship took us to Vancouver. Traveling on a cruise ship was delightful. We were invited to eat at the Captain's table two different nights. We entered into every activity offered on the ship. We were grateful to visit America's last frontier.

After we picked up our fifth wheel from storage, we headed for Ilwaco, Washington. Tom, Jack, Marilyn and I had reservations to deep sea fish. We walked on to a small fishing boat at 4:30 a.m., joining six other people and the captain. Sack lunches had been prepared for us. Before we reached the five-mile mark, we saw a gorgeous sunrise over the ocean. It was breathtaking! Being used to trout fishing, we jerked our lines at the first bite, losing the salmon. We learned that you let out the line and pull it in, over and over to wear the fish down. I hollered for Tom's help when I had a big one on the line. He said I needed to land it myself. That salmon gave me a battle for over 20 minutes. I was worn out but delighted that I caught the largest salmon that day. We docked and the salmon were weighed for processing. We chose to exchange our catch for canned, smoked salmon, since we had no way of keeping it fresh. The four of us continued on our trip to visit Redwood National Park. The beautiful towering trees took our breath away. Tom and I took two other trips during the next few years to ocean fish at Ilwaco, Washington, adding visits to high school friends along the West Coast.

Throughout the 70s, 80s, and 90s, we enjoyed attending National Music Conferences in ten different states. We attended National and International Lion's Conventions held in five states, Canada, and Japan. I learned enough Japanese so I could communicate with taxi drivers where our Colorado group wanted to go and phrases that were helpful in restaurants and shopping areas. In 1945, the USS Lexington Aircraft Carrier served in the occupation of Japan. We were allowed to visit the area in Tokyo Bay where the Lexington had docked, which pleased Tom, since that was the ship he was stationed on in 1945. Tom told of how the incendiary bombs had destroyed most of Tokyo and how backward the country was, using visible street troughs for toilets. The Japanese credited General Douglas McArthur for the modern, busy city it became. Leaving Japan, we toured

Hong Kong, Singapore, and Thailand. How wonderful to have the opportunity to visit and become acquainted with people of other cultures and to visit historical sites.

Our visit to San Juan, Puerto Rico, was a pleasure as we traveled inward to the rain forest. We saw such beauty and many different colored birds. While there, we boarded a small plane which flew close to the ocean and over the USS Eisenhower on our way to St. Thomas, a very busy island with good food and bargain shopping. Although I would enjoy describing in detail the experiences, scenery and wonderful people we enjoyed on all our trips, that would take another book.

Tom and I decided to experience the other side of real estate by building homes. We secured a construction loan and purchased twenty-seven lots east of Rocky Mountain High School in 1977. Our contractor was a friend whom we trusted. The high-quality homes we built offered the latest building and decorative upgrades with a ten-year protection plan. We were at the sites often, checking on everything. Word traveled fast and the houses sold quickly. We built tri-levels and ranch-style homes with full basements. They sold for top prices ranging from $48,950 to $51,950. We prayed about the last home on Wagon Wheel Drive. Susie and the boys were renting a small home at the time. We would offer the last house to them. Susie was overcome with joy while Greg and Jake kept running up and down the stairs claiming first dibs on the bedrooms. We enjoyed our adventure in building homes but decided not to continue. The reason? Most of the profits went to the IRS.

We saw my brother, Joyce, and the kids about every three months. As the children grew older, Bill and Joyce would spend periodic weekends with us. We planned a fishing trip to Flaming Gorge. I was driving near Wheatland, Wyoming, when a right front tire blew out. It made the truck and fifth wheel sway, but I was able to control the situation and bring us to a stop. It took all the strength I had. Tom said, "Patsy, you handled that like a man. Great job!" I managed a whispered thank you, and we both thanked God for our safety and were grateful for no oncoming traffic. My brother, Joyce, and their two youngest boys, Patrick and Joel, were behind us, pulling their boat. They said we had no idea how much the fifth wheel was swaying side to side while they prayed for it not to tip over. The temperature was over a hundred when Tom changed the tire. I threw two blankets under him so he would not be burned by the hot pavement. Bill held the jack so it would not slip. We reached our destination and enjoyed the lake and the many fish we caught.

Mae would visit us about four times a year. When she gave up driving, I went to pick her up in Boulder. She delighted being with the grandchildren and great-grandchildren. She would always remark how much Hap would enjoy them. The children patiently waited for her to open the tins of molasses and peanut butter cookies. Of course, Mae and Tom enjoyed their favorite evening drink of bourbon and seven!

In 1978, we welcomed Jim Blaha into the family. He and Susie were married in November. That same year, we backed David in the purchase of a farm near Kersey, CO. The old couple who owned it were so dear, but the house was rundown. We lost track of how many buckets of cockroaches were swept up. The house required fumigation. Our entire family spent

Mae with Tom and me and our 4 children

weekends helping Dave install windows, and replace cabinets, rotted wood, water pipes and flooring. The walls required two coats of paint. When the project was complete, David had a nice, comfortable home. His idea was to invest in Cargill Units to raise pigs. Mountain Plains Production Credit would loan the money for the units and the purchase of pigs.

In 1979, David called and said, "Dad, I need your help." We did not know David had been drinking. We took him to rehab, and Tom stayed at the Kersey Farm to take care of the pigs. He said those two weeks were the loneliest he ever had. We talked daily as I was working and taking care of things at home. I did join Tom on the weekends. We played lots of rummy!

David met Lynn while singing at Cowboy Church during a rodeo in 1981. She was a beautiful barrel racer. They were married in 1982 and worked as partners on the farm. Lynn and Dave enjoyed wearing hard hats when the oil company began pumping natural gas on the farm property. The oil company laid the pipes to furnish the house with natural gas. A good deal!

The 1980s

In 1980 Dad suffered a stroke in Arizona where he and Aunt Jo lived. He was taken to the Veterans' Hospital in Grand Junction. Tom and I flew there to visit him. The stroke affected his speech center, which was very difficult for Dad who loved to visit and tell stories. Dad and the Nix boys never met a stranger and would strike up many conversations while the women patiently waited.

Ed and Marilyn presented us with our fourth grandchild. Matt was born on September 17. He was also premature. Treatment for preemies had improved since Tommy was born so Matt did much better. When we told Dad about Matt, he wrote, "Good. One more great!" He was proud of the letter he received from Dave. Tom visited Dad again near the end of the month. Aunt Jo gave Dad the news that he had another great-grandchild. He shook his head and smiled hearing that Joshua James was born on the first day of October.

Dad passed away on October 6, a month before his 84th birthday. His presence in the family was greatly missed. Ed, Ken, and Dave recalled some special memories: Grandpa liked to spend time on the farm and help with everything except the milking. Grandpa always liked to hum an old hymn while working. He also sang "Ka Ka Ka Katie" a lot. We never heard him say a cuss word. If he hit his thumb with a hammer, he would say "Boy that smarts and it will feel better when it stops hurting." We would walk together in our swim trunks carrying towels to the lake. One day, a billy goat jumped on the haystack. From the stack he jumped on the hood of our big truck. Grandpa was so mad he punched the goat in the jaw, sending him through the air. We never knew where the goat came from, but after he recovered, he wandered away. Grandpa never left the dinner table without expressing thanks to Mom or Grandma. He lost his false teeth in the hayfield. Grandpa and our mom papered themselves while trying to hang wallpaper above the stairway. He taught us how to fish, shoot and break horses while he spun stories about his youth.

We now had five grandsons: Greg, Jake, Tommy, Matt, and Josh. How blessed and grateful we were to see them often. Josh developed some breathing problems and allergies as a little tyke. Susie called us several times to lay hands on him and pray when he was in distress. He had serious sinus surgery when he was eleven. Josh is now a big, strapping man, and remains careful with food choices.

First Nix family reunion, 1984

The 1980s continued to be busy with packed opportunities to serve the Lord, to travel, enjoy our grandchildren, attend family gatherings, and face unexpected happenings. We enjoyed the Nix family reunions every three years. Tom, Mary Jane and Joe took turns hosting. The first one was held at a ranch Dad and Joe purchased near Gardner, Colorado in 1984. The large house had been the area post office at one time. Lora and I cleaned rat droppings and excrement throughout the house and burned anything that was left behind.

It reminded me of some renters we had after moving from the farm. We trusted people and never dreamed we would encounter the "landlord blues." The first renters were very nice people. When they left our lovely farmhouse, we discovered large bucket-size burns on the countertops. The lady worked with hot leather. Her husband overhauled his motorcycle on the living room carpet and their cats tore the drapes. Another family who rented our tenant house left junk and personal debris throughout, which called for fumigation. Two young college men who rented the trailer left and padlocked the door. Even though they were gone, we had to wait seven days before entering the trailer because of renters' legal rights. When the padlock was cut, we opened the door and were met with a stench that nearly knocked us over. Dog poop was everywhere. The trailer had to be destroyed. Our expectations of renters changed. With our lawyer, we drew up a very tight lease. The next renters of the farmhouse proved to be of another cut. We will call the man "Lee" who was involved with drugs. The couple renting the tenant house called to tell us that Lee was intending to leave and take furniture from upstairs that belonged to Ken. They noticed he had a gun. Tom said he was going to talk with him. I asked if he should call the sheriff, and Tom said, "No, it would most likely start a gun fight." We prayed together, asking the Lord's direction and protection. Tom would not allow me to go with him. I remained in prayer until I knew Tom was safe. When he got to the farm, he encountered Lee. My brave husband stood up to Lee and told him he knew about the gun and said, "You don't want to deal with me, Lee. If you are not out of here by morning, you will have to face the authorities." Tom walked away with his back to Lee. As Ken said, "Dad was above and beyond brave." When Tom got home, we thanked God for His protective shield. A few months later, we heard Lee was picked up for an expired out-of-state license plate which led police to find out that he was wanted in Texas. We were told he was sent to prison. After that episode, we asked for character references. How sad that some people could not be trusted. We rented out the barn and horse stalls to Ron, a college professor who took over management of the rentals. It was well worth the 10% of rent money received that we paid Ron for dealing with repairs and rent collection. We remained friends with Ron and his family through the years.

We exchanged visits with Bob and Mary Jane throughout the years. Mary Jane and I had such fun together, especially shopping in Juarez, Mexico. We purchased dresses alike and paraded in front of Bob and Tom with choreographed singing. The four of us crossed the border to eat the authentic, delicious Mexican food. We enjoyed our nephew, Dennis, and nieces, Roxie, Gay, and Lora. When Bob and Mary Jane visited us, we took trips to the mountains, visited friends in Boulder, ate out, and played lots of bridge. Their last visit was in 1987. As we drove home from the movies, Bob asked, "Patsy, would you do me a favor and sing for my funeral?" I said, "of course, but what if I go before you?" He said, "Don't ask me to sing for your funeral." We all laughed. Little did we know that dear Bob would pass away in November of 1988 from a heart attack a short time after he retired. I sang "His Eye Is on the Sparrow" and "How Great Thou Art" for his service. Mary Jane remained active with church activities and teaching nursing classes. Before long, she applied to serve on one of the Mercy Ships for a year where she shared her excellent nursing skills. She later moved to Montrose where she enjoyed an apartment in her daughter, Gay, and husband Rich's home. We always looked forward to Mary Jane's bi-annual visits. She also attended some national music conferences with us.

We exchanged visits with Joe and Lora, enjoying the state of Arizona. They lived in Queen Valley on a golf course. The four of us played golf and bridge often. We watched John Wayne movies in the evening (Joe's favorite movie star!). Visits with Joe and Lora's children—Joe, Judy, John and Jack—were delightful. We always looked forward to attending services at the little church in Queen Valley. Joe and Lora joined us in our fifth wheel for ten days as we explored San Diego and parts of Mexico. Throughout the years, Lora and I would stay up after the family went to bed, sharing and laughing while we ate jelly on soda crackers. We had been close friends since junior high school.

In 1984, Jack and Marilyn joined us when we exchanged our timeshare for one in Myrtle Beach, South Carolina. We had a beautiful condo on the beach not too far from the challenging, picturesque golf course which we played on twice while we were there. As we were driving to South Carolina, we visited many historic sites. While there, Ed and Marilyn called to tell us our sixth grandchild arrived. Alicia, like her dad, was born on Christmas Day. We loved our little boys, but were delighted to have a girl, especially since Marilyn had miscarried earlier. Because Alicia was a preemie, she was taken to the Children's Hospital in Denver. By the time we arrived home from South Carolina, she had been brought back to Poudre Valley Hospital. I went every day to rock and sing to her. She was doing great with the exception that she had not learned to suck. After she went home, I popped in during the noon hour or after work to cuddle her and spend time with Tommy and Matt. I could not get enough of our six precious grandchildren.

Adding Instrumental Program to My Job Responsibilities

During the year, our superintendent who had been in his position for two years, called a meeting of his staff and the subject coordinators where he announced the administrative budget had to be cut and some coordinators would be sent back to full-time teaching. My colleague, Glenn, had coordinated the instrumental program. His name was among those who would teach full-time. The Superintendent announced that I would be in charge of the instrumental program along with the K-12 Music Education and Vocal responsibilities. What a way to inform people of a change! I visited with the superintendent afterward and told him I felt his approach was unprofessional. His comment was, "Well, everyone has a job." I enjoyed working with the instrumental teachers as we set about writing goals and objectives in keeping with the State Accountability Law. They were lagging behind and grumbled some but completed the job.

In the 1980s, Ed spent a year working for a project administered by the Department of Defense. When that was complete, he became lead mechanic for Range RV Sales and Service. Later, he started his own automotive business in North Fort Collins where he employed two mechanics. When he and the family moved to a home on Swallow Road in Fort Collins, he discovered the block was zoned for business. He closed the automotive shop and began repairing cars from the garage of his home. I sent all of the single women music teachers to Ed for car repair. Because of his integrity and honesty, I knew he would never overcharge anyone. Ed also received his teaching certificate from CSU and taught automotive classes for veterans at Front Range Community College. Later, as a member of the Outreach Team for our church, Ed kept the church vehicles in top running condition. Marilyn worked for a photographer and later managed the Boy Scout store in Greeley. We appreciated her excellent artistic talent and were recipients of wonderful paintings that adorn our home.

Ken graduated from the Arizona Automotive Institute and worked for Frontier Tractor Equipment Company, Case Dealership, and repaired cars on the side. We never knew how he accomplished that type of work, having had three back surgeries. Ken married Ann in 1987 and adopted her two young children, Johnathan and Jennifer. It became evident that Ann was only interested in having the children adopted. She soon left and took the children to California. We were concerned for Johnathan and Jennifer because Ann's fuse was short, and she lashed out at them. Ken told her to never touch them again or he would report her for child cruelty. Ken received custody of Johnathan when he was six because Ann beat him around the face and was reported to the authorities by the school principal. Both children had also been abused by Ann's boyfriends. Jennifer was sent to Child Help USA, a national organization dedicated to eradicating child abuse and neglect. She would remain there for an indefinite time. Tom and I drove to California to visit Jennifer and were pleased to see the care she was receiving. Two years later, Ken gave permission for Jennifer to be adopted since he was unable to care for both children. We visited her a few times and were pleased with the stable home situation. Johnathan thrived with the love of Ken and our family until Ken married Cheryl in 1990. He did not want to share his dad. Cheryl and Ken presented us with two wonderful grandchildren: Cody and Casey. Johnathan tried to injure the babies, so Ken arranged for him to be placed in another home where he would receive therapy. Johnathan joined the Army when he was eighteen and received distinguished awards as he fulfilled his position as a Ranger. He married Jenn and little Thomas Michael was born in 2007. Since they lived in Arizona, we were able to see them as we spent two months a year in Casa Grande in our fifth wheel. Johnathan began having difficulties and left his wife and baby. Later, he moved to Wisconsin to be near Ken and enrolled in the university. Tom encouraged Johnathan to attend the American Legion where he could receive help for his PTSD. He thought he could handle his problem. In 2017, six months shy of receiving his bachelor's degree, Johnathan got into trouble and left. We have not heard from him since. Johnathan's sister Jennifer was doing very well in high school, but during her senior year gave into drugs. She contacted us a few times and then dropped out of sight. Ken has not been successful in finding them. Johnathan and Jennifer never recovered from the abuse they suffered at the hands of their mother and her boyfriends. Our family continues to pray for them. Perhaps someday, we will hear from them.

In 1984, Lynn, Dave's wife, left him. Dave followed Lynn to Arizona, wanting to know why she left. I do not think Lynn knew why. She portrayed a certain amount of unrest as she shared pent-up ill feelings toward her adoptive parents because they would not help to find her biological parents. About that same time, Susie decided that her marriage was not healthy. Before Lynn left, she and Susie invited me to lunch. I asked if they had thought about the ramifications of their decisions on family and themselves. My main concern was Greg, Jake, and Josh. I spoke about how nursing and reliving past hurts leads to bad choices and regrets, that their worth and value was in God, who heals brokenness. I suggested they wait and seek counseling. Tom and I gave tearful support and prayers for Dave, Jim, and the boys. We included Susie and Lynn in our prayers, especially our dear Susie as we recognized she was dealing with depression. We knew Susie's roots in the Lord ran deep and asked God, every day, for restoration. Sometime later, Susie asked to speak to our church congregation. As she stood facing everyone, she expressed remorse for her past actions and asked for forgiveness. To confess one's sins publicly takes courage. Susie began seeing a counselor whose name was Kate. Susie shared her concerns and progress, which I kept in my heart. She and I knew that God's forgiveness, love, and strength, along with counseling sessions with Kate saved her life. Later, Susie became a dedicated witness for God. She became anchored in Jesus through storms of the past and future.

Losing Mae

In the spring of 1984 on one of our visits to Mae in Boulder, Tom and I found she was ill. Mae explained that after going to the bathroom the evening before, she had trouble finding her way back to the bedroom. As we talked, I suggested three options: I would stay with her, call for home-nursing care, or she could go to her sister Anna's home. Always thinking about others, she spoke about how I had job responsibilities and a husband, so she chose to be taken to Anna's. Mae had suffered a stroke. At her direction, Tom and I gathered up clothing, important papers, favorite jewelry and her knitting. Mae had knitted throws for years that she donated to the hospital. She also gave one to us and each of her grandchildren. When we were preparing to leave Anna's, Mae told us to take her furniture for Ken. She knew Ken was living with bare essentials in the trailer at the farm, and the other children were not in need. Ed and I visited Mae during the next two weeks. I called Anna the third week to tell her I was on my way to Boulder. She was preparing to call me, as Mae was failing and had not responded to Anna or her brother, Ray, who had come from Arizona. When I arrived at her bedside, I took her hand, bent down and said, "Mae, I am here. It is alright to go. Jesus is waiting for you." She opened her eyes, smiled, and drew her last breath. Mae was 93 years old. At her family service in Fort Collins, the children told of her gentle nature and how they looked forward to her peanut butter and molasses cookies and also how much she enjoyed the great-grandchildren. Grandma Mae had a giving nature and never said an unkind word about anyone. Tom spoke of her strength and reliance on God. I recalled stories she told of teaching in a one-room schoolhouse in Coal Creek Canyon, Colorado. She lived in a cabin over a mile from the school, so she traveled by horse and buggy in all kinds of weather, every day, to build a fire in the potbelly stove and prepare to teach the children. I spoke of how encouraging and supportive Mae was to me. I was Hap and Mae's foster daughter for five years, but they treated me as their own in every way. God truly blessed me the day they became my parents, and I was proud to recognize them as my mom and dad.

In 1985, Mountain Plains Production Credit was bought out by a different loan company. We were shocked to receive a letter from the new company calling our loan which included our farm and the Kersey Farm. This was a devastating blow to us and the other farmers who had large loans with Production Credit. The only way farmers made a living was with loans. For instance, each time we thought we were getting ahead, a tractor tire would blow, a piece of machinery would break down, a prize milk cow would die, or weather conditions would force delays in harvesting the crops. We asked for an extended time but were only granted three months. I drew out the $150,000 that had accumulated in my retirement fund. We cashed in our Water PiK stocks which would have contributed greatly to our retirement. We took a loss on sale of the pigs and Cargill units along with some water rights. Our dear friends, Cal and Lois Johnson, suggested we sell them a partnership in our Fort Collins farm. The economy took a dive in the 80s. The real estate market hit bottom, along with many businesses. We thanked God, our refuge and rock, who always took care of us through good times and bleak times. Aside from our contract with Cal and Lois, we secured a bank loan to make the final payment. We rented the Kersey farm to a nice couple who proved to be responsible.

In 1986, Tom and I attended the twenty-fifth wedding anniversary of our dear friends, Adolph and Beatrice Martinez in Fountain, Colorado. We parked our fifth wheel in their yard for the weekend. While Tom and I were dancing, I slipped on a piece of food someone had dropped on the floor. I hit the floor with a bang, landing on my bottom, but was not hurt. We arrived home on Sunday night. On Monday morning I began to have severe abdominal pains. X-rays showed I had lesions in the colon which the doctor said were malignant 99% of the time. Tom took me to the hospital where I would be prepped for surgery the next day. Tom and the children gathered in my room the night before. Susie said she would never forget how I looked at each person and said, "Let there be no negative thoughts. Pray for the doctors and thank God for His healing power." When I awakened, the surgeon and our family physician apologized for taking more of my transverse colon than was needed. They found two tumors and experience told them I had a malignancy. The pathology report indicated the tumors were benign. I mumbled, "Thank you, God and for praying friends." The doctors spoke in unison, "It's a miracle!" One of my friends said, "God is not finished with you yet!" The surgery took its toll, and I developed pneumonia, so my hospital stay was extended.

We hired help to provide care for me during the day, including grocery shopping and housecleaning. That was a blessing! Tom decided to fix dinner one evening. He put two chicken breasts in the oven. As I inquired about the chicken a half hour later, Tom said he still could not penetrate it with a fork. I asked him to help me to the kitchen. He had not removed the plastic wrap! Another time he decided to have dinner ready when I arrived from work. I opened the door to rolling smoke and could see Tom fanning the dish towel around. He said, "I have watched you fix hamburgers in the oven, and I don't know what went wrong." Instead of using the broiler or baking pan, he grabbed a cookie sheet. Grease had poured though the hanging hole onto the hot elements. After the chicken episode, he swore he would never cook again. From that time forward, the only thing he cooked was oatmeal in the microwave.

A Memorable Trip to China

Dr. Stonaker, one of Tom's college professors, invited us to travel with the Good Will People to People Program to China. The tour would include discussions and exchanging ideas with university agriculture professors and students in Shanghai, Beijing, and other provinces. It would also include visitations to farms. The last part of the trip would be to Inner Mongolia where we would have two days on our own. I talked with the school district superintendent, Dr. Hansen, about the feasibility of establishing a sister school in China. He was excited and stated that the district would pay a portion of my expenses if it could be accomplished. The Poudre High School principal was highly interested. Dr. Stonaker located the headmaster of a large school in the vicinity of Hohhot. I corresponded with Miss Wang. She and her colleagues were very interested in establishing a sister school in the United States. My doctors would not give the OK for me to take the trip until I could walk two miles without resting. It was tough, but I made it. I was also to drink plenty of water. Throughout our trip, Tom carried a flask of water on his belt for me. Through correspondence, Miss Wang arranged a time for Tom and me to visit the school. We were warned that the Chinese government sometimes rearranged the schedule. However, our tour went off without a hitch. In Beijing, we stayed at the Chinese Embassy and were treated royally. We traveled by air and rail. When we reached Hohhot, we stayed in a lovely hotel. I counted 50 smokestacks from the windows of our room. The cities were built around the factories and nuclear plants which were in full force in the winter, requiring everyone to wear masks. Fortunately, we were there in nice weather. Miss Wang and Mr. Zhu, head of the math department, met our tour group and took us to the home of the music and art teacher. We gave gifts of ballpoint pens and pictures of Colorado and Fort Collins including Poudre High School. Peng was our interpreter. After meeting the Yu family, we were introduced to two secretaries of the Communist Party. They were sitting on the couch with their arms folded and managed a lukewarm greeting. We included them in our conversation during lunch and shared how wonderfully we had been treated during our tour. After lunch, the secretaries left. Peng told us we passed their inspection! Mrs. Yu kept hugging me, saying she loved my hair. We were taken to the three-story school, where students entertained us with song and beautiful dances. The students were housed in dorms. Miss Wang told us that the brightest students were brought in from the grasslands to be educated. They did not see their parents for months. We were taken to the grasslands where the Mongolian men raced horses and held wrestling matches for our entertainment. The same men joined in a graceful dance for us that evening. The next morning, we visited the elementary school. The primary children were in music class, and we were amazed at the skill of a second grader who played the accordion. I was asked to teach the kindergarten and first graders a song. I chose "Eency Weency Spider" with the motions. I loved the way they giggled and clapped after learning the song. They bowed and blew kisses. Children everywhere in the world are the same, and oh, so precious! Every encounter we had with the Chinese people was positive. They were gracious and hospitable. At noon, we entered the home of the Ideru family. Even though they were observing a Muslim holiday, they prepared lunch for us. We considered that an honor. Miss Zang was proud that the school was being enlarged and told how studious the students were. We were surprised at the humor shown by the adults. Comparing the size of their feet with Tom's, they dubbed him Mr. Bigfoot. Of course, that was right down Tom's alley as he kept them in stitches. Our last outing was to visit a shrine. Mr. Zhu took Tom's hand to lead him up the winding stairs because he was the oldest in the group. A college student, whose name translated to "Jenny" in our language, took my hand. I was prompted by the Holy Spirit to quietly ask if she was a Christian, and she nodded yes. When we reached the top, a few male college students came close to me and then would back up. I realized they wanted to touch my hair, so I pointed to my head and nodded yes. Each one ran his fingers over my hair. My blond hair was quite a contrast to the black hair of the Chinese. Jenny asked if we could stay for the weekend. Two thousand Chinese were to be baptized downriver in a secluded place. That would have been a wonderful experience, but it was time to join our tour group.

We met other Christians but were careful with our conversation. Our tour included visits to historical sites, outdoor markets, a short walk on The Great Wall, and several shopping areas where we watched many artists at work. We also stood across the street watching the mass of military protection around Tiananmen Square. At the universities, we were treated to banquets as the professors and students had many questions about American farming techniques. We recognized as we visited farms and a dairy that the Chinese were relying heavily on information received from our agriculturalists to improve their farming techniques. We learned that human feces were used to fertilize many crops. Yen, one of the university students, asked Tom for our address. He also told us, in a whisper, that the young people of China were getting fed up with the government and they had hopes for a protest. He and Tom corresponded several times, and I was in contact with Miss Yang. The Chinese Government was slow in approving a sister school idea. Miss Yang and I were discussing plans for her and Mr. Zhu to visit our school district. She reiterated that the wheels of her government would move very slowly in agreeing to her proposal. However, in 1989, the uprising occurred in Tiananmen Square. We never heard from our friends again. We surmised that Yen may have been killed during the uprising or sent to the work farms. There was no further response to my letters written to Miss Yang. We are sure the Chinese Government shut down any correspondence between us. We were left with fond memories of the students and our wonderful Chinese friends.

Dave managed a large feedlot, sold pharmaceutical medicines for pets, and then began his lifelong career in car sales. He was the top salesman at Southwest Dodge and Emigh Dodge in Denver. David earned the award as top salesman in the zone which included five states and was the only salesman to have 100% customer satisfaction. He was a born salesman, known for his honesty and integrity. He was kind and made every attempt to make it possible for folks who were down and out to purchase a car or a van. I never heard him criticize others. Dave became general Manager of Mr. Robert's Auto Sales in Denver. In 1987, attractive Deb caught David's eye as she drove into the dealership. We welcomed Deb into the family in 1988. Deb had a four-year-old daughter, Jordan, whom Dave accepted as his own, and we were delighted to have her as our granddaughter. In the same year, Dave and Deb became parents to

Dave and Deb on their wedding day

Anna Mae. Dave, Deb, and the girls moved to a farm near Kersey shortly after Anna was born. Both Dave and Deb commuted to their jobs in Denver

Grandchildren Antics

Tina offered to babysit for Dave and Deb, so she and Tiana (our first great-grandchild) drove from Keenesburg five days a week to take care of Anna. We loved having Anna and Tiana visit as they grew. Sometimes, they would stay at our house together. What a delight to listen to them playing Barbies, selling real estate, cooking dinner, singing, and enjoying all the other fancies that grabbed little girls. On one occasion, they were jumping from one single bed to the other in the downstairs bedroom. They never told us which one flew against the folding wood closet doors that broke off the hinges. I scolded them and Grandpa told them he would take them home if they did not settle down. We loved their notes. Anna's: *"Dear Grandma and Grandpa, I am really truly sorry. We should never have done that. I am sorry about breaking the closet door. I am truly sorry and love you a lot. It will never happen again. I love you a lot! Love forever, Anna Mae.* Tiana's note: *Dear Mamo and Papo, Anna and I are very sorry and we will never do it again. We will do any chore you ask us to do. I love you two very, very, very much and hope you're not too mad at me. Please forgive me. Love always and forever, Tiana.* Anna, our granddaughter, and Tiana, our great-granddaughter, were close in age. We hugged them and told them we were not mad and would love them forever.

Their notes reminded me of one I received from grandson Jake. Ed had made a beautiful cedar gun rack complete with a drawer for storing shells. Since we did not display our guns, I used the shelf for antiques. On the shelf was an old horn the children loved to honk. Jake was messing around and hit the gun rack, knocking the antiques down. The air went out of the horn. I am guessing he stepped on it. This was Jake's note: *"Dear Grandma, I am so very sorry I broke the horn. I don't know how it happened. Please don't be too mad because I have already suffered excruciating pain! Love, Jake."* We fixed the horn and gave it to Jake when he became an adult.) Another time, Greg was spending the night and asked if he could bring a friend. The boys were around eleven years old. They grabbed the feather pillows from the bedroom for a fight. As I entered the family room, feathers were flying everywhere. It looked like a snowstorm. Straight-faced, I announced the fight was over. Greg looked at his friend and said, "My grandma is a teacher, and she means it!!" He thought he would get brownie points for that. Quite a while later, the boys announced the family room was ready for inspection. They flew up the stairs for dinner saying it was hard work to clean up all those feathers. Josh was often asked where he got his blond hair. He said, "At Target." Josh learned to knit when he was six. I told him not many boys knew how to knit, and I thought it was great. When Tommy stayed with us, he talked about everything God made as we studied the formation of cumulus clouds trying to identify animals and other figures. He also spread jelly on the kitchen wall while I was doing laundry. When I came upstairs, he proudly said, "Look what I did, Grandma." Matt was more interested in exploring and learning how things worked. He liked to examine everything and was highly goal oriented. Sweet Alicia, always wore a smile, loved her stuffed animals and was excited about life. Whenever we played games with the grandchildren, we let them win and lose at checkers. I don't remember ever beating Alicia in a board game. She was too smart for us!

In 1987, my good friend and colleague, Sylvia, retired. She had been the school district art coordinator for 35 years. Sarah, who was the administrative assistant to the superintendent, and I were best friends. Colleagues in the administration building referred to the three of us as the "female Musketeers." For several years, Sylvia and I spent most of our noon hours walking while we munched on carrot and celery sticks with a piece of fruit. The last five years before her retirement, we jumped in the car and drove the mile to exercise at Curves. Sylvia and I traveled in her van to the Four Corners Arts Festival. We enjoyed seeing the fine Indian artists at work as well as attending sessions on art and music education. Sylvia had a retirement home built in Crystal Lakes, Colorado. Tom and I were frequent weekend visitors, as we parked our fifth wheel in her yard. One summer, Sylvia had surgery to remove a cancerous bladder. I spent time caring for her as she became adjusted to using a urostomy. Our entire family was fond of Sylvia, as she spent many Christmas Eves with us. She later moved back to Fort Collins to The Worthington, a senior independent living facility. Periodically, Tom and I would pick her up for a trip to the liquor store to purchase her favorite scotch! Sarah and I also continued with our friendship throughout the years. She gave the best parties! Unfortunately, a few years after her retirement, she developed macular degeneration. We had many lunches together. I asked each restaurant for a colored plate since it was easier for her to see the food. Later, Sarah developed cancer. I was a frequent visitor to the hospital and later to the care center where she died. Years earlier, Sylvia asked if I would sing at her funeral. It was an honor to fulfill her wishes.

During the year, we and our partners sold a portion of our farm to Cowan Concrete for mining gravel. The first time Tom put a plow to our land, he said, "There certainly is a lot of gravel which will take lots of water for the crops." Fortunately, we had plentiful water rights. With Tom's hard work and expertise, we experienced bumper crops except for three years, when we either had drought conditions or too much rain. Concerned about the wildlife, our contract with Cowan Concrete included leaving the land with a stocked lake surrounded by scrubs, bushes, and grass to welcome the birds, pheasant, fox, deer, and other animals. The area borders Timberline Road and is called "Kingfisher Point Natural Area. "

A School District Controversy

The year 1988 also ushered in an unexpected happening in our school district. The school board president encouraged the board to hire a man to conduct a workshop for administrators, program coordinators, and representatives from Poudre Education Association (PEA). We will call him Mr. T. We had never experienced a workshop presenter who had eight people with him who only sat and watched the participants. As one of my colleagues said, "This is weird." Classified employees came to my office saying, "It feels like a dark cloud is hanging over the administration building." The second day of the workshop, memories took me back to the brainwashing meeting that God directed me to leave when I was in high school. The third day Mr. T expressed that he would like to take our brightest students and educate them using the old Harmony School Building. He also shared about the prominent people who were supporting him. As far as we knew, none had connections with education. Mr. T and his group were not trained in education. Everything seemed to embrace secular humanism. Our superintendent, who was very concerned, explained that the school board had not gone through the proper procedures in scheduling the workshop. Our school board president announced he wanted our district to win the Nobel Prize. The workshop created turmoil. On a Sunday morning during Communion, the Holy Spirit spoke to me. I was to share the happenings with our congregation. I quietly headed up front to speak to our pastor. After a brief explanation, he said he would call on me at the end of the service. I explained the situation and told the congregation I would have a petition available next Sunday that would be against turning our brightest children over to Mr. T and his entourage. I met with our Christian teachers group and they prepared to do the same in their places of worship and neighborhoods. Everyone in the administration building signed the petition except a few of my colleagues who said I would be fired. I told them I was standing on the truth with God's guidance. Our superintendent gave the numerous petitions, with an overwhelming number of signatures, to the school board president. I visited with the school board president, explaining my actions had nothing to do with him as a person, but with protecting our students. The school board decided to forgo the request of Mr. T. There were articles in the paper about the situation, especially after our pastor's wife, a teacher, and I asked to organize a workshop on secular humanism, which the pastor and church leaders endorsed. The workshop drew a large number of educators and community members including the reporter covering the story. These are quotes that appeared in the Fort Collins Coloradoan newspaper:

No matter the good intentions of the school board president, there were errors in judgment.

The seminar was not previewed which is district procedure. It was a rush job.

Mr. T did not charge his usual fee, but district money was used to transport his children from Utah, where the school board president contacted Mr. T, to California.

The superintendent told the board last week, 'We've got to move on now. There are deadlines to meet.'

Now is the time for the school board to give us tangible, meat-and-potatoes direction.

Let us leave behind the Nobel Prize. There is no Nobel Prize for education.

Just as it is time for the district to move away from concentrating its energy on an unavailable Nobel Prize, it is time to move away from the Mr. T affair. He is not the central issue in excellence in education.

Excellence will be the standard and goal for the Poudre R-1 School District. Let's hear what the board has to say—every member—about excellence. "

Watching Our Grandchildren Grow Up

Susie and Bill Bennett were married in 1988. Bill served in the Army as a helicopter commander. We missed Bill, Susie, Jake, and Josh during the holidays as Bill was stationed in Mannheim, Germany, for his next three-year hitch. (Susie asked me for something of mine to take with her. She chose jewelry and a throw for the couch.) In Mannheim, Jake was a freshman, doing great on the football and wrestling teams. Josh was a happy second grader. Greg, Susie's oldest, lived with us.

He began his freshman year at CSU, where he joined the track team. Greg was dependable and goal-oriented, which would serve him well in the future.

One of our true blessings was to watch our six grandchildren grow up. We were delighted to watch them at baseball, concerts, school programs, scouts, and the myriad activities they chose. We loved watching them play in the greenbelt area behind our condo, or having fun in the swimming pool. We taught Greg and Jake to play golf. They, along with Josh, were frequent visitors to our home, which delighted us. Tommy had an interest in music. Matt sold 60 poinsettias for a Cub Scout project in elementary school. I think they ran out of prizes for him. Inquisitive Alicia was four on Christmas Day, loving gymnastics. She was a wonderful conversationalist. We delighted in each child's interests and achievements which continued daily and yearly. I enjoyed the lunches with Tommy, Matt and Alicia each year before school started. Tommy visited about school and his music activities. Matt was interested in finishing lunch so we could visit the flea markets. Alicia just liked to visit about everything. Our lunches lasted two hours.

In 1989, Greg graduated from high school. Greg had a busy schedule attending Colorado State University. He was on the track team and had a job. During his junior year, he was offered a full-time job at Ranchway Feed Mills with a considerable salary. After a discussion with Tom, he decided to take the job which proved to be a steppingstone for future employment. Most of the time, Tom and Greg arrived home before me, and there were evenings I headed back to attend a concert at one of our schools. I suggested that the men fix dinner one night a week. Greg's favorite offering was mac and cheese. Tom opened a can of pork & beans with sliced hot dogs. However, most of the time, we ate out for Tom's turn!

Church Changes

In 1988, we began attending the First Christian Church in Loveland, where our friend, Jim Adams, was the pastor. We were sorrowful about happenings in the Fort Collins church. Tom and I served in various capacities throughout the years and were crushed when we realized we needed to leave. Our pastor and his wife asked us to stay, but we knew things would not improve.

We were openly welcomed at the Loveland church and soon were serving as Elders and choir members. I was asked to lead the personnel committee to help solve a long-standing employee problem, and to teach an adult Sunday School class on the Twelve Spiritual Steps. Tom and I continued our nursing home ministry and serving in the community in various ways. We prayed each morning for wisdom to serve God while maintaining a healthy respect for each person we encountered. Everyone deserves to be loved, valued and accepted. I especially wanted that for each student I taught and every teacher I supervised.

Our Senior Years

The 1990s — Time of Transitions

In 1990, the Globokers, who rented the Kersey farm, asked if we would consider selling. Tom drew up a contract. We were still making payments and owed $60,000 on the farm. We did not profit much on the sale, but we were glad to be free from making monthly payments to the former owners. We never did recover financially, but as always, God took care of us, making it possible for us to travel to the CSU/Oregon bowl game in California; Branson, Missouri; Hilton Head, South Carolina; and to visit Bill, Susie, Jake, and Josh in Germany.

Retirement from the School District

In 1990, when I was in my 27th year with Poudre School District, I began thinking of retiring, even though the music staff asked me to stay. I still loved working with students and teachers. Because I had received merit pay for four years, I was at the top of the salary scale for coordinator positions. Checking with my friend, Ken, who was in charge of the finance department, I discovered I would stay at the same salary for the next year, with minimum raises for the following two. That and the fact that we wanted to visit our family in Germany, helped me make the decision to retire. I had spent five years substitute teaching for music, English, and business classes before teaching full-time, so I enjoyed being part of Poudre School District for 32 years. I had two wonderful retirement parties and many gifts. One party was organized by the music staff and the other by colleagues and secretaries in the administration building. Principals from various schools took care of serving goodies. My secretary, Becky Harper, organized the party and presented me with comments and pictures in a large book. I had four secretaries throughout the years, but Becky, my dear friend, was by far the most gifted and outstanding. Five of the music staff teachers, Barb, Neal, Sharon, Linda, and Karen, performed a hilarious musical skit with slides. I still read through the script occasionally when I want a good laugh and to recall thousands of students, dedicated educators, parents and the community I worked with during my career.

After retirement, I joined a senior tap-dancing troupe. We had fun performing in the community, and I became the assistant instructor. My tapping began to take the paint off the garage floor, so Tom purchased a huge piece of plyboard for me. It felt good to tap dance again, and it was very good exercise.

In January of 1991, Bill reported for Desert Storm, commanding a helicopter division. We talked on the phone with Susie every day, praying for Bill's safety. Fortunately, the conflict ended on February 28. We were grateful to God that Bill was not injured. His helicopter division dubbed him the "best scud ducker." A scud was a missile.

A Memorable Trip to Europe

In 1991, we invited Mary Jane to join us on our trip to Germany. On May 20, Greg took us to the airport after we completed last-minute errands. Back problems plagued me on so many trips. Muscle relaxants helped me endure this one. It was so good to see Bill, Susie, Jake, and Josh. Their apartment in Mannheim was small but comfortable and decorated with taste. The first day, we went to school with Susie. She was in charge of the student council where they were holding elections that day. When she stepped to the podium, the students immediately quieted down. Afterward, several students crowded around her and told me she was the best teacher ever. We met the principal and several staff members. School would be out for summer vacation in a few days, and Bill was available to be our tour guide.

We took off on our first trip to Heidelberg, where we visited a castle built in 964. Most people looked at us with interest because all seven of us were in Susie's large station wagon. The next day we were in Luxembourg. It was Memorial Day, and the cemetery was absolutely gorgeous. The music brought tears to our eyes as we passed grave after grave of American soldiers who were buried there. As we walked the streets in Luxembourg, countless people asked if we were Americans, and they could not thank us enough for liberating them in WWII. I will only mention the places we visited without elaborating too much. I kept a journal, so family members can read in detail about our trip.

We visited Brussels, Belgium, and then on to Bruegge where we boarded the ferry to England. Susie had exchanged their timeshare for a home on a lovely estate that overlooked a lake. The house had four bedrooms, two baths with an extra toilet—just perfect for all of us. We visited Nottingham, an industrial city, and later made the long drive to London. We were fortunate to see the changing of the guard at Buckingham Palace, which occurred every 48 hours. We saw the parliament, other government buildings, the London Bridge, and then drove to Liverpool. We visited the Liverpool Beatles Museum. We stopped at the Army base to shop at the PX. Then, it was back to the ferry and the town of Bruegge.

We drove to Antwerp and on to Amsterdam. A highlight was to visit Anne Frank's house and other castles. One thing we learned is that some Europeans did not believe in deodorant which made for unpleasant odors, especially in crowded conditions. Back at the base in Mannheim, we had eight loads of laundry. We attended a revival at the chapel where 50 people accepted Jesus Christ as Savior. It was also great to watch Jake and Josh at their ball practices and games. June 7 was a special time for Josh and all of us. Josh answered several questions the pastor asked, and then he was baptized. Susie and Bill invited several friends for a potluck including families from the former East Germany. When the Berlin Wall was taken down, they were anxious to try out their new-found freedom. Back in the station wagon, we left for Austria. Everywhere we visited, our attention turned to the people, museums, the many castles, cathedrals, beautiful countryside, and the spectacular Austrian Alps.

Austria was especially gorgeous, and people were friendly and hospitable. We exchanged our timeshare for a condo in Alpenland that accommodated us. I mentioned earlier that we spent time at Dachau. At home during the war, we had seen newsreels of tortured innocent Jews, but nothing compared to what we saw at Dachau and in the museum. After liberation, many of our soldiers had vomited when they saw the huge trenches that held dead bodies. There were 23 Nazi concentration camps designed like Dachau with the ovens, showers where people were gassed, torture chambers, and experimental operating rooms. We thought it would be good for all people to visit a Nazi concentration camp to never forget the inhumane treatment of innocent people. As we exited through the chapel area, we wept.

From Dachau, we drove on to Munich and found ourselves in the middle of a festival. The place was jammed. Bands were playing and clocks were chiming. There was dancing in the streets and the Hauf Brau House was filled with people drinking huge mugs of beer. The food was delicious. We could not get our fill of the wonderful German food.

On June 10, we left for Salzburg. Mozart's home and museum was especially interesting for me. The catacombs where Christians hid to worship in the first to fourth centuries was unbelievable. They dug out the mountainside for chapels. We visited the cemetery where the Von Trapp family hid from the German Army. During our trips, we played card games like bridge, shanghai, spades and hearts.

The next stop was Oberammergau where the Passion Play is performed. The people in the city asked God to protect them when a plague hit and promised to honor Him in this way. Something smelled familiar to us as we passed a cow barn in the middle of town!

Back in Mannheim, we began to prepare for our trip home. Bill and Susie would follow later for a short vacation as they prepared for their move to Savannah, Georgia, where Bill would be stationed. On June 19, Greg met us at the Denver airport. Three days later, we met Jake and Josh at the airport who came to stay with us for the summer. Jake spent his senior year at Fort Collins High School, staying with his dad and family. Jake received several football awards. Dr. Pike, team physician, said Jake was a cross between Mickey Mouse and a man-eating shark! We enjoyed the football games and looked forward to watching Jake play baseball. Josh had sinus surgery which helped take care of the many infections he had since he was a little tyke.

On arriving home from Europe, we had a busy time preparing for Ken and Cheryl's wedding. They were married in our backyard under the trees. The reception was held at Sundance Steak House. The evening ended with country western dancing. We were happy to welcome Donnie and Ande, Cheryl's daughters, as our grandchildren. Ken and Cheryl began a business in Wisconsin, selling and installing satellites, TVs, and phones.

My tap dancing was put on hold while I had intense therapy for a herniated disc. During recovery, I did consultant work for the school district, auditioned junior high students for honor choir, and enjoyed P.E.O. meetings. After four months, I returned to tapping—very carefully. I enjoyed helping out for three months at Pat's Hallmark, owned by our friends, Pat and Lee Hendrie. Later, the owner of the Bible Book Store asked if I would help with the year-end inventory. I dealt mostly with cassettes, cataloging almost a thousand recordings. They paid well. Instead of a check, I chose store credit.

Marilyn Goodrich called to tell us Jack had suffered a heart attack, and the medics revived him after 15 minutes. However, it left Jack with damage to his brain, and he was soon in a care center with dementia. I asked the manager if he was interested in receiving music therapy for the patients, and he jumped at the chance. There were 20 patients at the time, and I loved working with them. Jack was still able to strum his guitar and sing a couple of songs. As time went on, it was difficult to witness our dear friend's decline. We enjoyed a close friendship with him and Marilyn for 60 years. Jack passed away the next year. We missed our dear friend! I continued with music therapy for the patients for another year.

Starting a New Church

We finished our time as elders at First Christian Church in Loveland and became members of the Project Advisory Committee, which was working toward establishing a new Disciples of Christ church in Fort Collins. How exciting for us to be among the founding members of Heart of the Rockies Christian Church! In June of 1992, Jeff Wright became our pastor/developer. He and his wife, Janet, were very dear to us through the years as they ministered to our family and church flock. Even in retirement, their thoughtfulness and care continue to be a blessing. The church's first social meeting was held in our home at 1486 Front Nine Drive. Jeff presided over a dedication of our new home. Our church met in different locations until we had our first worship service in our new building in December of 1999. Tom and I delighted in serving God through different ministries at Heart of the Rockies Christian Church, working alongside Jeff, staff members and others in the congregation. There is so much that goes into a new church start-up. Jeff compiled a history of Heart of the Rockies— Our Best Years are Still Ahead of Us: *A History of Twenty Years of Life and Ministry 1993-2013*. It is filled with dates and stories describing every detail of the church's journey. In 2013, Melissa St. Clair became our associate pastor and in 2015 when Jeff retired, Melissa became our senior pastor. She has blessed us with her leadership, caring, talents, and quick wit. She became adjusted to Tom's mischievous ways very quickly. Only Tom could voice remarks during a sermon and get away with it! In the summer of 2024, Melissa resigned to take a position leading the denomination's Center for Faith and Giving. I am looking forward to welcoming a new senior pastor at Heart of the Rockies.

Freedom Bowl Mishap

In December 1992, we loaded the fifth wheel and took off for the Freedom Bowl game in California, where Colorado State was playing Oregon University. During the first quarter, Tom went to the pickup for his cap. The game was exciting and we won in the last 30 seconds. After the game, I stopped to purchase sweatshirts for Susie and Marilyn. Tom had said he would meet me at the pickup. When I arrived at the pickup, Tom was not there. The people who parked next to us handed me the keys. In Tom's haste to return to the game after retrieving his cap, he had left them in the door. I waited and waited. I went back to the stadium and asked ushers to check the restrooms. They were all so kind, but they did not find Tom. I saw an ambulance drive in and went to check if Tom was their passenger. He was not. I sighed deeply and asked God to watch over him—wherever he was. It was getting dark. A policeman on a motorcycle came by. I asked if he had seen Tom. He took a turn around the stadium and came back without Tom. By this time, there was only one other vehicle parked on our side of the stadium and it was dark. A car came near and stopped. It was our friends Oval Jaynes, Athletic Director at CSU, and his wife, Priscilla. Tom jumped out of the back seat of their car and grabbed me. He said, "I could not find you and thought the truck had been stolen and you had been kidnapped. We have been looking all over for you." Tom had turned the wrong way and exited the opposite side of the stadium, which is why he didn't see the truck. We were planning to attend the victory party at the hotel. Oval and Priscilla insisted that we share their suite that night. Since we were camped over an hour away, we accepted. We brushed our teeth with a washcloth and slept in our underwear. We were exhausted after our ordeal and the party, but we took time to thank God for our safety and offer appreciation to Oval and Priscilla for their hospitality. Later, it all became a laughing matter.

Our Southridge Home

In 1992, we purchased a lot to have a patio home built in the Southridge development. Tom, Greg, and I planned to move to our new home at 1486 Front Nine Drive on August 5th. We thought selling our home in Adriel Hills would help our financial situation. That was not to be. Three days before moving, a letter from the IRS arrived saying we would be audited. We were not concerned until we learned the reason. A family member had prepared the information for our CPA from my books over the last few years. We studied it carefully every year, as did our CPA, but no one caught the mistake. There was a huge mistake in transferring figures showing purchases and deductions claimed on the same items. As one might imagine, we owed a hefty amount to the IRS. There was no way we could meet the payments of our new mortgage. As we visited with our CPA and banker, we were advised to take out a reverse mortgage on our home. We made an appointment with a representative from Financial Freedom. After becoming acquainted with the process, we signed up for the reverse mortgage which proved to be a blessing, allowing us to stay in our home and have some cash available. God rescued us again! To this day, the family member does not know about the mistake. We did not ask God to solve a problem that belonged to us. The mistake was ours to bear. We did thank God for forgiving our foolishness in not being more thorough when checking the figures and asked for better judgment in the future. We gave thanks for our new home and wonderful neighbors who welcomed us with open arms.

Health Concerns and Prayers Answered

I had bladder surgery that did not go well. The surgeon did a botched-up job by hitting a nerve and causing problems between my intestines and vaginal wall. In November, I underwent corrective surgery called an "enterocele." By this time, Tina shared our home and was such a tremendous help in taking care of me. The surgeon found a carcinoid tumor on top of my small bowel. After a slow recovery, the surgeon and my family doctor called to say they had met with the tumor board. All agreed that I should go to the Mayo Clinic for tests. An appointment was made, so Tom and I drove to the clinic in Rochester, Minnesota. I was to stay a week for all types of tests. Fortunately, we were welcomed to stay in a P.E.O. sister's home during that time. She and her husband were so hospitable and kind, and we thanked God for them. Tom was patient and encouraging each day as he prayed for God's healing touch. The top surgeon at the clinic informed us that tests revealed I was clear of any malignancy, but I could be sure of another tumor in fifteen years. I learned it takes that long for some tumors to reach a point where they can be detected. There was not much known about carcinoid tumors in the medical field at the time. I was given a paperbound book describing the tumors that could roam around in the body for years before attaching to vital organs. A Chromogranin A blood test was later developed to check for the tumors. For two years, my count was almost off the charts, but bimonthly X-rays were clear. I finally asked my doctor to stop all X-rays, fearing that they could give me cancer. He finally complied and said we would rely on biannual blood tests. It was several years before the readings were below the danger mark.

During that time, I refused to become anxious or fearful and gave thanks as I experienced the depth of God's caring heart. I was reminded of *Romans 15:13*, "May the God of hope fill you with all joy and peace as you trust in Him so that you may overflow with hope by the power of the Holy Spirit." I have never ceased to thank God, daily, for creating my wonderful body and I began to thank each part of my body for functioning the way God intended and for the power of the Holy Spirit in my life. Again, I was blessed by answered prayers of family and friends. As of this writing, I am eleven years past the prediction that I would have another tumor. *Psalm 18:1-2*, "I love you, O Lord, my strength. The Lord is my rock, in whom I take refuge. He is my shield and the horn of my salvation, my stronghold!"

When we arrived back home, Tom and I rose at 5:30 three mornings for a three-mile walk. We so enjoyed that time together and what better way to greet the day enjoying various colors and sounds of God's creation? It rekindled memories of the farm and how the dawn met us with the symphonies of sound—low, rustling, deep, musical, crackling sounds. Greetings by the rooster and mooing cows. And later, the sounds of our children tromping around in the snow, running in the rain, laughing, and arguing. Their calls of "watch me, look what I can do", or tattling on each other. Tom and I had such delight in remembrances. We supported and taught good things to our children, and they knew we loved them. They had a deep faith in God which was of the utmost importance. We also knew we were not present in some of their moments which brought regret. How does the old saying go? "If only we could turn back the clock and live some of those moments again with the knowledge we have today. "

We received the good news that Bill would be stationed at Fort Carson in Colorado Springs after only one year in Georgia. We were excited to have our family back in Colorado.

Jake graduated from Fort Collins High School in 1992. He attended Bethany College in Lindsborg, Kansas, on a football scholarship. Upon graduating from college, he coached football at his Alma Mater and later at the University of Central Arkansas. We were very proud grandparents.

Later that summer, we hosted the Nix family reunion at the Buckhorn Camp & Retreat Center, located west of Fort Collins in the mountains. Our family had grown to over 50. The views were spectacular, and the walking trails headed in several directions. The younger children enjoyed the fishing pond. The cabins were comfortable, and the spacious lodge provided room for meals, crafts, activities and visiting. Our outdoor games were volleyball, softball, races, treasure hunts, and guessing games. As always, we ended with a worship service, praising God in song.

In September, Ken and Cheryl presented us with twin grandbabies, Cody Lynn and Casey Patricia. We could hardly wait to see them and traveled to Wisconsin when the twins were six weeks old. The week went by too fast. Baby Casey began to show signs of a developmentally delayed condition. Some doctors thought she had Rett syndrome (RTT), an extremely rare genetic neurological and developmental disorder that affects the way the brain develops, causing a progressive loss of motor skills and speech. The exact cause is not fully understood and there is no cure. Other doctors could not agree but offered no diagnosis. Ken and Cheryl asked for prayers of family, friends, and our church family. The 700 Club and Joyce Meyer were deeply appreciated. As Casey grew, Ken and Cheryl sought help for her through social services and child help organizations. She had a cute way of greeting, so Ken called her "Squeaky." When Casey heard Ken's voice, she not only let out with her squeak, but smiled as she got on her knees and rocked back and forth until he picked her up.

In December, grandson Tom went to London with his high school band to play in the Royal Albert Hall and to march in the New Year's Day parade. It was also a great opportunity for the students to visit other areas in England.

In January of 1994, I was inducted into the Colorado Music Educators Hall of Fame. Most of my family were present at the induction during the State Music Educator's Conference. I expressed appreciation to my family who had supported me with love and encouragement during my career. I also expressed thanks to the wonderful music staff I supervised, students, administrators and statewide music education colleagues. I did not have the opportunity to express thanks for my appearance in the International Who's Who in Music Education for Distinguished Service, or for being recognized as an Outstanding Music Educator in the United States, since I had no idea how I was afforded these. All I did was thank God for leading me BY HIS HAND.

Tom graduated from Rocky Mountain High School in 1994 and attended Colorado State University on a music scholarship. We were proud of his accomplishments and enjoyed attending music concerts.

The eve of February 14, 1995, the youth of our church sponsored a Valentine dinner and dance for the adults complete with a disc jockey who played all our favorite tunes. After dinner, each couple was asked to write a valentine message for their spouse. Here is what Tom wrote: "Patsy you light up my life. You fulfill every hope and need as a wife that I could possibly have asked for. I thank you for being not only my wife but truly the best friend a man could ever have. I love you and thank you for 37 years of true happiness. Your loving husband, Tom." This was my message: "Tom it did not take long for me to realize I wanted to spend the rest of my life with you. You know my heart so well! You are not only my loving husband but my best friend. I am so grateful for your love and the true partnership we share. I thank God for you every day. I love you, Patsy."

In June, the PEO State Convention was held in Denver. PEO is a Philanthropic Education Organization whose main purpose is to assist women with their education, either college or continuing education. I was on the planning committee and in charge of directing the choir and providing music throughout the convention. After leaving one of the meetings in Denver and blinded by the sun, I entered an intersection on a yellow light and was promptly broadsided by another car; the driver was given a ticket. I called Dave, who was working at Southwest Dodge. He sent a wrecker for the Chevy and gave me a loaner from the dealership. When I arrived home, Dave called and said, "Mom, are you sure you are alright? The Chevy is totaled." I assured him I only had bruises and expressed thanks to God that I and the other driver were saved from serious injury. The following week, Dave drove a bright red Intrepid to Fort Collins and handed me the keys. He had paid for a two-year lease. The Intrepid was a snazzy car, and I enjoyed driving it. A wonderful gift from a thoughtful, loving son.

In December 1995, we drove to Chilton, Wisconsin to spend Christmas with Ken, Cheryl and family. We so enjoyed our visit, and congratulated Donnie and Ande on their achievements in school. The twins were so much fun. Cody was inquisitive and very active. Casey spent a lot of her time watching *Aladdin* and *The Lion King*, a daily favorite! She had a special TV and mostly sat on her knees to watch movies. She always wore a smile!

In August, Joe, Lora, and children hosted the family reunion weekend in the beautiful mountain area near Salida, Colorado. Offspring from Tom, Mary Jane, and Joe numbered in the fifties. We spent time playing all sorts of games, singing, walking, visiting with the adults, reminiscing, and watching the grandchildren have fun. Our reunions always ended with a worship service, hugs, and shouts of "Love you!"

Back home, Tom and I continued our exercise classes for seniors that were held twice a week at CSU at 6 a.m. Arriving early, I walked a mile around the track while Tom pumped iron. Class consisted of cardio and stretching exercises followed by workouts on the bikes and other machines. We made many friends among the group but decided to join Miramont Health Club which was only one-half mile from home. I joined Silver Sneakers while Tom floated among the exercise machines and weights twice a week. We enjoyed eating at Ryan's Sports Grill after exercise and became well acquainted with Ann, our waitress. She shared that her husband, Brian, was blind in one eye, had difficulty seeing out of the other eye and was facing serious surgery. We included him in our prayers. Two weeks later, Ann told us Brian was seated at the bar waiting until she finished her shift. Tom offered to pray for him. Ann checked with Brian who said yes. As Tom laid hands on him and began to pray; the other men put their drinks down and bowed their heads while others became quiet. A few months later, we were told the surgery was successful. God is so good!

At Bible Study, we were asked to write down people who had influenced our walk with Jesus. My list included: my Kindergarten Sunday School teacher who impressed upon me that I need never be afraid because Jesus was always with me; Rev. Brown who taught me to pray for my enemies; and Mrs. Gilstrap who encouraged me to teach the first grade Sunday School class when I was in the ninth grade. Because of that, I was blessed to teach Sunday School for 40 years to youth and adults. Also Geneva Bell, my junior high school Latin and Home Room teacher who showed love and kindness in reaching out to take care of me when I had no place to go; and Marilyn Ferguson, my trustworthy friend and prayer partner. Tom wrote: My mother, who was the spiritual leader of our home. Her great faith inspired me to grow as a Christian; my wife, Patsy, who set the example of what a Christian marriage was all about and taught me the importance of tithing; Marilyn Ferguson who exemplified servanthood in the church.

As Tom and I shared with each other many other names surfaced. Among those names: our children who played church with profound lessons about Jesus and showing kindness toward friends of all nationalities and backgrounds, inviting them home; we were both grateful for numerous saints who had touched our lives and influenced our walk with Christ; we had growing experiences at Boulder Christian Church during childhood and high school, at Brighton Christian Church as very young parents and at Fort Collins Christian Church, Loveland Christian Church and last, at Heart of the Rockies Christian Church. What a blessing to work with and be spiritually fed by the pastors, their wives, congregations, and Saints present and those who went before us. We were challenged and blessed by God as two of the founders of Heart of the Rockies Christian Church with Pastor Jeff, his wife Janet, sons Matt and Nate, and others whom we loved like family.

In 1996 Bill retired from the Army. During the ceremony, he was presented with the Legion of Merit Award which signifies exceptionally meritorious conduct in the performance of outstanding services and achievements. The ceremony was impressive, and we were proud of Bill. Being a civilian was foreign to Bill, and we witnessed times when he would become very angry which we attributed to PTSD and frustration with civilian life. He did find his niche in piloting a Flight for Life Helicopter.

Donnie graduated from high school in June. Donnie and Todd were married two years later in Chilton, Wisconsin. I was privileged to sing for their wedding.

50th Wedding Anniversary Celebration and Trip

In 1997, our children and grandchildren planned a gala event for our 50th Wedding Anniversary with 200 in attendance. We so appreciated our loved ones and friends who helped us celebrate. Susie created the program, which traced our lives that brought tears and much laughter. I marveled at how many details she remembered. Many of them came from our stories. Susie, Ed, Ken, and David each participated in the remembrances. We were humbled as Susie began the program. "We, their children, consider it a privilege and honor to pay tribute to our parents...to their commitment, covenant, trust, and loyalty to each other and above all their faith and love. They never stop praying for us, believing in us, and loving us, even through difficult passages. They have exemplified and truly lived: "Love bears all things, believes all things, hopes all things, endures all things...Love never fails." And that "Faith is the substance of things hoped for and the evidence of things unseen." My brother, Bill, spoke lovingly about how our marriage was an example to others. Our grandchildren, Jake, Josh, Alicia, Donnie, Ande, and Patrick offered sweet words, and grandson, Greg, brought the house down modeling Grandpa's clothes we had given him which, of course, were outdated. David sang a song he had composed and dedicated to me on Mother's Day. Susie and her husband sang a sacred song, "He's More Wonderful." Their rendition was deeply touching. Grandsons Tom and Matt, Ed and Marilyn's sons, played the Boulder High School Fight Song. Several of our high school friends in attendance sang with gusto. Tom and I thanked our children, grandchildren, other family members, and friends for their part in making our upcoming trip possible. Mary Jane, Tom's sister and my maid of honor, and Neva Downing, one of my bridesmaids, spoke and stood beside me. Tom was joined by two of his groomsmen. His brother, Joe, and best friend, Dick Rogers, shared memories. Pastor Jeff offered words about the journey of 50 years of marriage and a beautiful closing prayer.

We traded in our 23-year-old fifth wheel for a new one with slides. Through the years, Ed furnished trucks to pull our trailer and fifth wheel as payback for money we had loaned him. The first truck was a 3/4 ton '89 Ford 250. In 1994, it was a 3/4-ton Chevy, 4-wheel-drive. In 1996, it was a Chevy Crew Cab that pulled our 38-foot fifth wheel with ease. Ed, in his generosity, signed over the pickup to us which we later traded in for Tom's new vehicle.

The first leg of our anniversary trip was a four-day stay with Ken, Cheryl, and family in Hilbert, Wisconsin. Ken was making repairs on the deck where beetles had eaten the wood. They also needed new tile in the bathroom. Tom assisted Ken with the deck repair, and I went to work on the bathroom. Removing the old silicone required a chisel. I grouted the tile and put new silicone around the tub and shower stall. Cody would run from the deck to the bathroom asking questions. He was so interested in the fifth wheel that we lost track of the times he went in and out. He told us it would make a good home for him. Casey was her sweet self as she continued to watch *Aladdin* and *The Lion King* doing a great job as her eye contact and comprehension were improving. We appreciated the prayers offered on her behalf. After a wonderful breakfast prepared by Ken, we pulled out. It was difficult to leave, but we had arranged to pick up Mary Jane at the airport in Buffalo, New York.

We invited Mary Jane to accompany us on the 8,000-mile trip through nineteen states. She and Bob would have been celebrating their 50th anniversary during this time. We always had a great time when Mary Jane traveled with us. She loved to drive. We also enjoyed her visits to us in Fort Collins twice a year from Texas and Montrose, Colorado. After picking up Mary Jane, we camped in Buffalo. A terrific wind blew all night. It was good that we decided to leave as the wind increased, causing damage and power outages in Buffalo. We ran into lots of road construction in Pennsylvania and New York. We toured the grounds at Gettysburg. It was difficult to imagine that 51,000 soldiers died in that battle. Touring the falls at Niagara reminded us of God's majesty. They were awesome while we experienced the roar and spray of water on our rain gear as our boat drew near the falls. We experienced the falls from the Canadian side at night. They were illuminated and very beautiful. We also took the three-mile trip through the locks of the Erie Canal. While we were visiting the Baseball Hall of Fame in Cooperstown, New York, we received a message that our first great-grandchild was born. We were camped in a valley surrounded by trees so our new cell phone would not pick up the call. Susie convinced a telephone operator to break through with the message that Greg and Tina were proud parents of little Tiana, born October 4. Our cell phone was quite large. Tom made me a holster so I could carry it on my belt. During our trip, I would switch the phone from my belt to a large purse.

The beauty we saw around every corner as we traveled the New England states was beyond description. Pictures do not capture the essence of the fall colors. We took a tour of Plymouth and saw the rock, which was small. Studying about the pilgrims as a child, I thought it would be huge. As we boarded the Mayflower II, it was difficult to imagine how it carried 200 people to our shores. We visited the Ocean Spray Cranberry Store. We drove to Cape Cod, stood on the bridge where the Boston Tea Party occurred, and visited Bunker Hill Cemetery. We went on board the USS Constitution. Built in 1797, it is the world's oldest ship still afloat. Then we toured the first cotton mills in Pawtucket, Rhode Island. It was such a privilege to visit the historic places and stand on the ground where America began. We thanked God for our beautiful nation and the freedoms we enjoy. In Maine, we took a boat cruise around Bar Harbor and enjoyed the most delicious lobster dinner—ever! Acadia National Park had trees of many varieties in fall color. The scenery was breath-taking. We called Greg and Tina often to check on little Tiana. Tina had a difficult time but was improving each day. We could hardly wait to see our first great-grandchild! We received calls from Ed with updates about the family.

We found a quaint old-fashioned store in New Hampshire where we purchased more gifts for our family. In Burlington, Vermont we took a ferry to the New York side. Upon our return to the Vermont side, we spent a few hours at the Maritime Museum, where they had a replica of Benedict Arnold's gunboat with small cannons. It was amazing to know that Arnold's fleet of small, crude gunboats threw the British fleet in disarray and contributed to American victory. I can't say much about Arnold after that, as he became a traitor. A wealth of information was found in museums and visitor centers along our way. On our trip, we drove through the Allegheny, Appalachian, Pocono, White, and Catskill mountains. Each had its own beauty. However, we remained partial to the beautiful Colorado Rocky Mountains! We stayed at the Horse Park Campground in Lexington, Kentucky. The statues of Man o' War and Secretariat were very life-like. The International Museum of the Horse was fantastic. On our way home, we stopped in Lindsborg, Kansas, for two days to visit Jake, where he was coaching football. He enjoyed coaching and did a great job! We were grateful for the large cell phone so we could keep tabs on the family as we traveled. No more stopping at payphones along the road.

Back in Colorado, we stayed two days with Bill, Susie, and Josh in Colorado Springs. Arriving in Keenesburg, we could not get enough of holding and kissing our sweet great-granddaughter, Tiana. As we pulled into our driveway in Fort Collins, we thanked God for safety on our wonderful trip, but it was good to be home after traveling for seven weeks. Mary Jane stayed a couple of days before flying home to Montrose. She was a great traveling companion and loads of fun!

In 1998, Tom had both his knees replaced at the same time. He did very well. I told him if his golf game improved, it would be because of his new knees and if it was worse, it would be because of his new knees. Tom became Ministry Assistant at church, and I continued as Director of Music, Drama and Art. Tom told Pastor Jeff that he wanted one dollar a year instead of being a volunteer. His reasoning was that it is difficult to fire a volunteer, and the position did not carry clout! We framed the first dollar bill.

Ed retired from his auto mechanic business and became a realtor. He worked at Realty World Rhoades in the same office as Tom. He later worked for Coldwell Banker. Because of his education and knowledge, he was asked to teach classes on Real Estate Law & Practices, including Water Rights in Colorado for the next ten years. He was granted "Professor Emeritus" standing. Ed became a broker with his own office. On the side, he worked as retail manager for AutoZone and also as commercial sales manager at Car Quest.

In June, we celebrated Greg's graduation. He was promoted to a Technical/Marketing Development Specialist with agricultural products and the building industry for Luzenac America. While employed by Luzenac America, he received patents for two products. One patent was a spray to keep apples free from damaging sun rays and insects. Another patent was a product that kept fertilizer from crumbling as it rolled on a conveyer belt. Greg's position required him to travel internationally. Later, Greg was hired by the Koch Brothers who owned several industries in the United States. Greg became Vice President of North America Agronomics Business Services. Greg and his family were glad that his work travels were confined to the United States. We were very proud of Greg.

Matt earned the Eagle Scout Award in 1998 during his senior year in high school. We were present for the ceremony. He was also baptized that year. We were very proud of Matt, and more accolades were to follow after high school graduation. In 1999, Matt received an appointment to the Air Force Academy. Susie assisted him with the lengthy application. In 2003, the family attended Matt's graduation in Colorado Springs. The ceremony was spectacular, with the F-16 fly-overs and hundreds of caps thrown in the air at the end to celebrate. His first assignment was to be part of the team in Cheyenne Mountain, also known as NORAD. Matt and Jenise met while visiting from their cars at a stop light in Colorado Springs. Their lovely marriage ceremony took place at the Air Force Academy Chapel. Matt had been a member of Sabre Drill Team in college. What fun to see him and Jenise pass under the arched swords with a slap by the last member. In 2005, little James was born, followed by Noah in 2007. More great-grandchildren to love! There was an article in the Fort Collins *Coloradoan* about one of Matt's assignments. He was part of Operations Enduring Freedom, Iraqi Freedom, and the Joint Task Force Horn of Africa. Matt was in charge of security at his base in the United Arab Emirates. In 2012, we attended Matt's impressive promotion to Major at Warren Air Force Base in Cheyenne, Wyoming, where he was stationed. Matt showed us his office and around the base. We were proud grandparents!

Tom was married to lovely Joy Aschermann in October. Our pastor, Jeff, and Deacon Dr. Trewartha of St. Elizabeth Ann Seton Parish, presided. Tom and I were privileged to read scripture.

In November, Josh was all-conference in football and was presented an award for special team's player of the year at Liberty High School in Colorado Springs.

Andy, Bill's son, left to serve in Belgium at NATO Headquarters. Andy served four years in the Army and then was employed at the Pentagon in Washington, D.C. He married lovely Valy. They had two children, Kiera and Tim, whom we count among our great-grandchildren. Patrick, Bill's youngest son and wife, Mashawn, became parents of Jada. Susie loved being a grandmother (Mimi) to Jada and Tiana. They had previously lost a baby boy at birth which was heart-breaking. Pat and Mashawn later became parents to two more lovely daughters, Nalanni and Danica. We kept being so blessed with more and more great-grandchildren. Pat was serving in the Air Force. In March of 1999, he graduated from the leadership course at the Air Force Academy and was later promoted to Staff Sergeant. We are so proud of Andy and Pat's service to our country. Pat was career Air Force and retired as a Master Sergeant. In April 1999, Todd and Donnie became parents of Sidney Ann. Gracey Rose was born in 2001, and Alexander Troy was born in 2003. What a delight to welcome these little great-grandchildren and enjoy visits throughout the years.

Josh played on Liberty High School's state championship football team in March of 1999. We loudly cheered when he walked across the stage for his high school diploma. We were proud of his academic achievements. Josh had several visits from football recruiters and decided to attend Adams State College in Alamosa.

Susie is Diagnosed with Cancer

In June, Greg, Tina, and Tiana moved to Parker, Colorado, which was closer to Greg's work and Colorado Springs where Susie and Josh lived. The last six months of 1999 were very difficult for our family. Earlier in April, Susie met with Bill about finances. Unfortunately, Bill had moved out and would not allow any of our family to know his address or phone number. The meeting went OK, which Susie said was an answer to prayer, and Bill agreed to continue with his part of the mortgage payment and some landscaping for their lovely home. On June 9, Susie had exploratory surgery where a large malignant tumor was found. She had stage two ovarian cancer. The doctors performed a complete hysterectomy. What was supposed to be minor surgery turned into a 6-1/2-hour major surgery. Susie's surgery was at the Air Force Academy Hospital. They were so kind to furnish a large room for the family with sleeping facilities that night. Susie's surgery brought a process of numerous tests, scans, doctor appointments, and a minor surgery to insert a Medi port for the purpose of infusing chemotherapy.

A few days after arriving home from the hospital, Susie's boss, Ron, and his wife brought dinner to the three of us. They shared how important Susie was to them, both personally and as an employee. They spoke about the way she performed her job with the love of Jesus. Susie worked for the Navigators, an interdenominational Christian ministry, as the Entity Financial/Personnel Administrator and the Office Team Leader. We left for a few days to take care of business items. Susie's many friends made schedules for visits, meals, house cleaning, and errands. Josh was always eager to care for and protect his mother. Greg also gave much time in caring for Susie. Jake helped until he left for his coaching job. Susie always looked forward to his upbeat phone calls. On June 26, Susie's birthday, her beautiful blond hair fell out in handfuls. She cried in my arms. A few days after the shock, Susie and I went to a wig store. We laughed a lot as she paraded around in some of the ridiculous wigs. She finally chose one, but later decided to wear comfortable hats and bandanas. Greg, Jake, and Josh shaved their heads in support of their mother. In September, Susie went back to work and ran a 5K Race for the Cure while she was still undergoing chemo. She surprised the family and her doctors. She and I had been taking daily walks before the race and she began to outpace me. After her last chemo treatment, tests showed she was in remission. We celebrated with family and friends at Greg and Tina's on Thanksgiving Day. Susie wrote, "I am thankful for the incredible support, encouragement, care, love, and concern from my family, friends, my co-workers, church family, and neighbors. I am ever grateful to my parents, who took care of me for weeks, and the loving acts and care from my children, grandchildren, brothers, and in-laws who cheered me on and gave purpose to endure the chemotherapy and its debilitating side effects. Our God is faithful. My walk with Him is deeper than I ever imagined, and He truly has been my comfort, my shelter, my tower of refuge, and strength." Susie returned to work full time as she continued doctor appointments and tests. In June of 2000, we celebrated her one-year survival.

In December 2000, Susie had serious surgery at University Hospital in Denver, with recuperation at Greg and Tina's in Parker, Colorado. Cancer had reared its ugly head again. Tumors were removed without serious consequences, and doctors said she should respond to chemotherapy again. She did respond. Praise God! By June, tests showed she was in remission. Susie began to run, work out, play softball, and continued working. She said she was living one day at a time and giving God glory for each day. Cheryl Olson, Susie's best friend from school days in Fort Collins, sent daily emails to a long list of family and friends. Cheryl supplied updated information and Susie's prayer requests. She encouraged Susie with visits and phone calls. The emails sent by Cheryl gave Susie rest in not having to answer calls and emails. We continued to pray for healing and shrinkage of a tumor still present in her abdomen. By September, the tumor showed improvement, but scans in November showed the cancer had metastasized. Susie insisted on attending Josh's last football game in Alamosa. Her friend, Diane, drove her. What a display of strength and love for Josh. On November 12, Susie waited for decisions from nine doctors who were in conference about her condition. She asked prayers for the doctors' decisions, peace for her family, and for the right combination of pain medication so she could get back to work and exercise. Most of all, Susie asked that she be yielded and surrendered to God, the lover of her soul. She had another surgery and began part of an experimental clinical trial. She remarked that it may not help her, but perhaps it would help others. The chemo brought indescribable pain and other side effects. On December 13, family and friends set aside a special day of prayer and fasting. Susie went back to work!

In May of 2001, Tom woke me at 2:00 a.m. saying he was ill and thought it was his heart. I told him to take an aspirin while I got dressed. That morning, the surgeon placed two stents in Tom's right coronary artery. Susie was at the hospital by 7:00 a.m. to see her dad. In June, my dear Aunt Agnes passed away in Longmont. Sandy, my cousin, asked me to sing for her service. I visited with my brother afterward. Bill, Tom and I often met in Longmont to play golf and visit Aunt Agnes. Bill sometimes came to Fort Collins, where we enjoyed playing on Southridge Golf Course. We had set up a tee time for the following week. That did not happen because Bill had a tee time in heaven. After playing golf, he died from a heart attack while changing his clothes. My brother was buried at Fort Logan Cemetery. I spoke at his service. In August, Tom's sister, Mary Jane, passed away. She was suffering effects from a previous stroke. Susie went with us to her service in El Paso, Texas. People often ask why sad events happen in twos or threes. I don't believe we will ever know. We fell into the arms of God with our sorrow.

Ande graduated from high school and desired to work in some aspect of the medical field. She became a phlebotomist and remained a faithful, caring sister to Casey, who was in a foster home. Ken and Cheryl preferred home care for Casey. Social Services only allowed two weeks, yearly, and Respite Care would not help because Cody was in the house. Cheryl offered to take Cody to the basement or out of the house, but it did not make a difference. I thought there had to be a misunderstanding. Investigating in our community about care for children like Casey, I finally decided that the State of Wisconsin was in the dark ages.

We enjoyed Alicia's activities during her school days, especially softball and soccer. During high school, she was in Civil Air Patrol and became a junior fire fighter. Alicia graduated from high school in 2003. We watched her blossom into a confident, beautiful woman. Our family had a special memory about Alicia. At age 12, she was Mary in our church Christmas Pageant that I was directing. Her brothers, Tom and Matt, were shepherds. As the choir was singing *Silent Night*, Alicia called out to our pastor who was near her, "Jeff, I dropped the baby Jesus." Jeff said, "Pick him up."

Alicia picked up the baby and the pageant continued. We loved listening to her beautiful voice when she sang solos. After graduating from high school, Alicia received appointments to West Point, the Merchant Marine Academy and the Naval Academy. After Alicia and her dad studied the situation, they discovered that if she attended the Merchant Marine Academy at Kings Point, New York, she could choose her branch of service upon graduation. Alicia excelled in every aspect at the Academy. As an EMT, she was credited with saving the life of a man who fell from a scaffold during ship repairs in San Diego. We were proud grandparents as we attended her graduation. Alicia was sworn into the Air Force by the Brigadier General. She was stationed at Offutt Air Force Base and became a navigator. Mike, a close friend during Academy days, introduced his brother, Bill Mikulak, to Alicia. Their romance blossomed and they were married on June 18, 2011. Before the beautiful ceremony, Bill, Alicia, and the pastor parachuted out of a plane. Alicia encouraged me to jump with them, something I had always wanted to do, but Tom was adamant that I stay on the ground. Bill had a wonderful sense of humor, and the family enjoyed the delicious meals he presented. Bill was a trained chef and qualified in many other work areas. Alicia served her second assignment in England, followed by one in Colorado Springs, Colorado. It was great to have Bill and Alicia in Colorado, especially after little Amelia arrived on February 7, 2020. Another great-granddaughter! On Alicia's next assignment at a base in California, she was promoted to Lieutenant Colonel—a tremendous accomplishment. She made the family proud.

Our children knew we did not turn our TV on in the mornings. I will never forget the calls we received from Ed, Susie, Ken, and David on September 11, 2011. When we turned our TV on, we watched in disbelief as planes piloted by middle eastern terrorists flew into the World Trade Center, killing three thousand people. The bravery of survivors, rescuers, and first responders saved many lives. Later, we heard about the plane crashing into the Pentagon. Then news came of Flight 93 that had been hijacked by another set of middle eastern terrorists. Passengers called loved ones, and one person called 911. One man was heard telling his wife goodbye on the phone. His last words were, "Let's Roll." Even though the terrorist pilot was rolling the plane back and forth, the crew and passengers were making their way to the first-class section and the cockpit. When the black box was unearthed after the crash, authorities could hear the last few minutes of chaos. They also learned the plane was to target the White House. The terrorists crashed the plane in Pennsylvania rather than have the passengers take control. Those brave crew members, attendants, and passengers gave their life for our country.

Susie's Valient Battle

In November 2001, a stent was placed in Susie's liver. She began experimental chemo at University Hospital in Denver. Greg, Tom, or I were with Susie for each infusion. Several friends had nominated Susie for carrying the Olympic Torch for a segment in Colorado Springs. Returning from work on January 16, 2002, she found a package containing her Torch Relay uniform. It was below zero on February 2. I helped Susie out of bed and into her relay uniform. Then I took pictures of our beautiful daughter and asked how she was feeling. She hugged me and said, "Mom, I can do this", and I said, "I know you can." To everyone's surprise, Susie ran her segment as people lined the streets cheering her on with clapping and yelling, "Go Susie, go!" At the end, she talked with people and signed autographs for children. The Navigators held a breakfast reception. For two hours, Susie sat in a chair as people stood in line to talk with her. She was exhausted, but so happy for the honor. One of the friends who had nominated Susie to carry the torch purchased the torch for her because she was such an inspiration to her community. The torch was placed near the fireplace in her home.

Susie runs with the Olympic Torch

The parade of family, friends, and co-workers continued as they fed us, tending to errands and housekeeping. We were grateful for these godly people who demonstrated their love and faith in so many ways.

On February 7, Tina and Carol went with Susie to the Anschutz Cancer Center in Denver to meet with Dr. Echardt, who told them Susie was holding her own but there was some fluid buildup. So many decisions for Susie to make: what treatment course to choose, when to have fluid drained, what to eat, how much to eat, what supplements to take, keeping track of many appointments, and dealing with her hair falling out again. I purchased a knee pillow that would aid her comfort while watching TV in bed. I lost count of the comedies and wholesome movies we watched together. We took a few evening and night drives, and there were times, usually after midnight, Susie asked for a hamburger. She knew a hamburger place that was open for 24 hours. When we arrived home, she would take two or three bites and put the rest in the refrigerator. The chemo was causing extreme pain and cramping. During those times, she would squeeze my hand very tight, sometimes leaving a bruise. Tom would cradle her in his arms. Cheryl was steadfast in sending Susie's prayer requests out to over 100 friends and families.

Through all of this, Susie continued working. The following is an excerpt from a letter Susie's boss. Ron sent to the Navigators Military Division. "In Susie's role as Director of the Navigators' Military Ministry which includes more than 150 staff serving all over the world, she is a treasured partner in the Gospel who has always served the Lord with immeasurable excellence and grace—a beautiful and balanced combination of Christ-like character and exemplary competence and professionalism. As a gifted Personnel and Financial Administrator, Susie is an invaluable servant and resource to not only those of us in the Military Division, but recognized as an expert and resource to countless leaders and administrators of other ministries throughout the U.S. Navigators' Headquarters

Building. Susie is now a single mother supporting her son, Josh, who is in college. I want to share with you that we have opened a ministry account for Susie. As we receive adequate funds, Susie will begin to draw extra salary each month to meet financial needs for her and Josh. You are already a giant support to Susie through your friendship and prayers for which she is very grateful. Susie has faithfully and sacrificially served others for years. Any amount God leads you to give will be gratefully received. Thanks for your love and support." The funds came pouring in, making it possible for Susie to take care of financial needs and purchase medications which eased her mind. Later, it became necessary for her to work part time from home. She was so brave as pain and fatigue began to take a toll on her ability to perform. She told me that chemo brain was awful to deal with.

Josh came home from college for weekends when he could to care for Susie while we went home to catch up on bills and Tom's work. I was moderator for our church, which is equivalent to a board chair in other churches. We were grateful for all the faithful prayers offered and how others took over my duties as we cared for Susie. Understanding how much Susie cared for those who depended upon her, we urged her to consider giving the computer and files to her wonderful boss, Ron. Ron and his wife, Patti, came to pick them up. We all cried!

Susie received funds from friends and family allowing her to order supplements recommended by the Block Cancer Center in Chicago. They were designed to help with neuropathy and discomfort from swelling. Even with Susie's work insurance coverage and Bill's military insurance, some meds and many supplements were not covered. In May, Susie's doctors gave the OK for her to attend a Navigators work-related conference in Washington, D.C. Greg, Tina, and Tiana ordered plane tickets and took care of Susie the entire time. During the conference, Susie received a special award for making a difference in many lives and for her never-ending courage in the face of never-ending challenges.

Susie's next challenge was to be well enough to attend Jake and Beth's marriage in June. On June 8, Susie was taken to Memorial Hospital for biopsies. Marilyn came to stay with her for four days. David showed up for many of Susie's surgeries and hospital stays. When he was born, Susie had called him Robbie. Each time she got a glimpse of him coming through the door, she would smile and say, "Mom, here comes Robbie." Susie also looked forward to Ed and Ken's phone calls, and treasured a poem Ed wrote for Valentine's Day. Susie preferred the Air Force Academy Hospital, so she was transferred back after completion of tests and surgery that relieved pressure. Her new pain routine was helping. Heather, one of Susie's nurses, painted her fingernails and toenails, which made her feel good. The doctors were dubious about Susie being able to attend Jake and Beth's wedding in Fort Collins on June 29, since it would be risky. I had a conference with them and asked if there was any way they would allow her to go. They had been calling everywhere in Colorado Springs to find a special medicine she would need, with zero results. Tom, Greg, Jake and Josh had left for Fort Collins the day before. I asked Tom to call our family doctor for help. Praise God, Dr. Smith found the medicine at Poudre Valley Hospital. My next concern was the trip. Susie could lay in the back seat of the car, but she would need to be turned a few times because of the discomfort. Heather, her nurse, asked the date of the wedding. The next day on June 27, Heather told me that she was able to change her schedule and would be going with us on the 28th. When

Susie at Jake and Beth's wedding

circumstances are bleak and there seems to be no way out, God shows up with His love, grace and mercy. What a blessing to have Heather's help. She and Susie slept in our Craftmatic beds that are very much like hospital beds, with Heather tending to Susie's needs. Jake and Beth were married at our home church, Heart of the Rockies Christian Church. Beth was a beautiful bride. Tina was one of her bridesmaids and four-year-old Tiana was a darling flower girl. Jake, Greg, and Josh looked handsome in their tuxedos. I was privileged to sing. Susie looked beautiful in her blue dress and jacket with her snazzy wig and makeup. Tiana sat on her lap during the ceremony. Susie was beaming! At the reception, Greg, Jake, and Josh took turns dancing with her in the wheelchair. Beth joined them and then all three boys dipped Susie while dancing. Heather made sure that Susie ate and had rest times. Susie was quite exhausted when we returned home at 10:30 after being on the go since 3:30. Quite a miracle!

The next day, we took Susie to our farm where she grew up. She always loved our big house. Greg pushed Susie in her wheelchair into and around the house and through the gravel to the barn. (In 1996, the City of Fort Collins had purchased the top 35 acres, where they established offices for the Department of Natural Areas. The area is called The Nix Farm Natural Area, chosen from names submitted by the Fort Collins community.)

On July 6, Susie moved to Greg and Tina's and put her house up for sale. That was difficult for her. The time came for Greg to call Hospice. They placed a hospital bed in the living room. I rarely left her side during the day except for the two days we returned home at Tom's insistence. On our way, I asked Tom to turn around and go back. He refused saying that I needed some rest, and we had a pressing business item to take care of. During that short period, my mind was constantly on Susie. At night all three boys slept near her and took turns administering the morphine. During the night, Susie would call out whose turn it was. Unbelievable! On July 21, the Hospice nurse said the end was drawing near. I stepped to the deck and called to Josh, Greg and Steve, Greg, and Jake's dad. They had been fixing fence. Josh and Steve came running while Greg had the tractor in full gear. Tom took the car to pick up Jake and Beth who had gone for a walk. The family surrounded Susie, expressing our love for her. Greg, Jake, and Josh told her it was OK to go. Tom read scripture from Revelation and John—*John 3:16*, "For God so loved the world that He gave His only son, that whoever believes in Him shall not perish but have everlasting life." *Rev 21:4*, "He will wipe every tear from their eyes. There will be no more death or mourning or crying or pain, for the old order of things has passed away." At 1:45 p.m. on July 21, five days short of her 50th birthday, Susie passed into the loving arms of Jesus. Tiana kissed Susie's hand, laid down beside her and began to rub her face and arms with lotion. It was as if she was anointing Susie for entrance into heaven.

Two memorial services were held for Susie. The first was at Woodmen Valley Chapel in Colorado Springs where Susie and Bill had served on the Worship Team. Greg, Jake, and Josh asked me to sing "How Great Thou Art." I could hear Susie saying, "Mom, you can do this." Beth and Tina read scripture. The other service was on her 50th birthday at Heart of the Rockies Christian Church in Fort Collins. We were told that over 600 attended the service in Colorado Springs and nearly 200 in Fort Collins. I also sang for the second service. Dave sang, "I Can Only Imagine." He said, "Mom, I saw you reach with all you had to sing and knew I could do it, too." Ed and Ken shared memories of their sister. Pastor Brent from Woodman Valley captured all of Susie: her zest for life, serving in a way that brought honor to the Lord, faithfully carrying out her role and responsibilities with grace and love, ministering to others, commitment to her faith, friends, family, and the Navigators, how she yelled at the top of her voice at CSU football games, her sense of humor and infectious laugh, an inspiration to all. Susie's dear friend, Cheryl, spoke about their friendship through the years and how lovingly Susie mentored her girls. Mike Howland, CEO of Christian Service Charities in the United States, made a special trip to share a few words. He talked about Susie's incredible courage and how she was an inspiration to representatives of other charities, and it was his privilege to present her with the award for Outstanding Courage at the conference in Washington, D.C. Susie was not perfect and had her faults, as shared by her boss, Ron Holechek. "Susie would be the first to admit her faults. She was acutely aware of her shortcomings, and experienced significant grief and regret whenever she failed her Lord or others. She was quick to ask for prayer support during those times." In October, the National Military Staff Conference met at the Navigators' headquarters. They planned a special time to honor the memory of Susie to help bring closure to the last chapter of her life. Tom and I were invited to attend. The tribute was beautiful. We were blessed by the expressions of sympathy and emails offered by Susie's co-workers and friends. Our family received over 350 cards and letters. I have chosen one to share that was written by Patrick, Susie's stepson. "I am taking Susie's death very hard. I have several fond memories of Susie and loved her as if she was my mom. She helped me through high school and taught me things I will never forget. Susie introduced me to God and was the spiritual leader in our home. She was so genuine. One who cared about the Lord first and then her family. When I heard the news, I thanked God for bringing Susie into my life. She was a nurturing mother when I needed one the most. I will miss her! May she rest in peace."

As I wrote this section of my memoirs, tears cascaded down my cheeks. In fact, it took two weeks to complete. Parents never expect to outlive their children. During our daily prayers, Tom and I held each other as we cried over the loss of our beautiful Susie. The world was not the same as we began our journey on the road of grief, sometimes laughing and sometimes crying, during love's chain of memories. There remained a hole in our hearts, an indescribable emptiness. Through it all, we gave thanks that Susie was no longer in pain. We knew that God shared in our suffering. We continued to pray for strength and courage as we nestled in God's comforting arms, promising not to be consumed by grief. *Lamentations 3:21-23*, "Because of the Lord's great love we are not consumed, for his compassions never fail. They are new every morning: great is your faithfulness, O Lord, our God." This is a quote from the fall Navigator Frontline News Bulletin: "Susie always kept running. She may have slowed down some, but she ran until God said, 'Your race on earth is won, Susie. It's time to come home.'"

> Lament for our Daughter:
> Our Beloved Susie
>
> *We cling to each other as we cry. Tears come at all times.*
> *Sometimes, we stop in the middle of our prayers to weep.*
> *You are absent, Absent from our lives: family dinners,*
> *Holidays, games, shared laughter, long walks and talks.*
> *We long to see your dancing blue eyes and hear your voice.*
> *We long to watch your feisty spirit in action.*
> *We long to watch and hear you praise the Lord in song and dance.*
> *We long to watch you hold and enjoy playing with little Tiana.*
> *We cherish times with Greg, Tina, Tiana, Jake, Beth and Josh.*
> *Thank you for the legacy left through them.*
> *You were so brave as you battled each chemo, surgery and heartache for three years.*
> *Through it all, your faith in God never wavered.*
> *Yes, we are relieved and grateful that you*
> *Are no longer in pain. In God's house there is no pain.*
> *But, our heartache remains.*
> *You have left a hole in the world that you filled with the Love of Christ.*
> *Only God knows the number of people you led to Jesus through your joy-filled faith and witness.*
> *Memories of your birth, your childhood, your baptism,*
> *Your adulthood, your love, thoughtfulness, courage and your*
> *Beautiful smiling face are etched in our hears forever.*
> *Good bye, sweet girl, until we see you in our Father's house.*
>   *Our Deepest Love,*
>   *Mom and Dad*
> *--2002*

In August 2002, we hosted the Nix family reunion at the YMCA camp near Winter Park. Darius and David entertained us with the auctioneer's song. Each time we gathered, the host family chose a charity to support. This year, it was for cancer research. We all missed Susie very much and shared memories of her. In November 2002, our pastor, Jeff, conducted a tree planting ceremony at our farm in honor of Susie. The City of Fort Collins allowed us to place a marker for Susie at the entrance to the area in front of the house. Later, the Men's Prayer Breakfast group built a playground on the south side of our church in memory of Susie. It has been wonderful to watch children, including those in the surrounding neighborhood, enjoy the playground.

Life Goes On

We traveled with Ed and Marilyn for Parents' Day in 2002 at the Merchant Marine Academy in Kings Point, New York. Alicia was the plebe representative charged with keeping the company in order. It was obvious that she had the respect of all. She out-shined many of the men in performance. In quietness and sorrow, we visited Ground Zero, remembering 9/11/2001. Later that night, we made our way to the top of the Empire State Building where we gazed out over the bright lights of New York City. When Alicia was home for fall break, she challenged me to do pushups. She did not know that I had done pushups for years. When I beat her, she said,

"Grandma, I have a new name for you and it is a compliment. You are my bad-ass grandma!" For different reasons, Tiana and Anna dubbed me the same. I learned to graciously accept.

Ed and Marilyn moved to a beautiful new home on Canby Way in Fort Collins in 2003. We had organized and enjoyed family gatherings for fifty years during Thanksgiving, Christmas, and birthdays on the farm and at our homes. Now Ed and Marilyn opened their spacious home for family gatherings. The great-grandchildren especially enjoyed the electronic piano and the pool table. There was some reminiscing about past Christmases, especially the carol singing. Susie would be at the piano, Greg and David on guitars, and I took my place at the organ. It was great fun as we jammed on some of the songs. Having the family together was always important to Tom and me. As years went by, some family members were separated by miles and sharing holidays with in-laws, and gathering everyone was not always possible. Even so, we considered it a blessing when twenty or more would gather.

Ken, Cheryl and family visited in October. We so enjoyed Donnie, Ande, Cody and Casey. Ken and Cheryl were still searching for more help in caring for Casey. Andy, Kiera, and Tim, along with Pat, Mashawn, Jada, and Nalanni, visited during Thanksgiving week. What a joy to spend some time with those great-grandchildren. We took them all to the farm and later, Jada enjoyed swinging at our church playground that was built in memory of Susie.

Tom and I stepped back from some leadership positions at our church and in the community as we planned to spend a couple of winter months each year at the Palm Creek Golf and RV Resort in Casa Grande, Arizona, and visit relatives in that area. About an hour after I resigned my church position, I was asked to direct the Sunshine Singers by my friend, Liz Case. I will never know how she found out so quickly. I told Liz I could not do it since we would not be around all winter. She said, "Work out a schedule that fits your time and we will adjust." I was blessed to direct a chorus of wonderful women for sixteen years, ages 42 to 83. We performed 12-14 concerts within a span of two weeks during the Christmas season and late spring. We were welcomed by service clubs and many facilities that provided independent or full-time care for seniors. Liz announced our concerts until she became ill and was diagnosed with cancer. Tom and I were part of a team that took Liz to her treatments. She was doing well, but collapsed and died one day at home. Liz was a dear friend who served her community. One of our delights was seeing Liz at CSU athletic events and games wearing her red shoes. We missed our long-time friend!

Our friends and neighbors, Kathi and Neal Buckner, told us about Palm Creek Golf and RV Resort in Casa Grande, Arizona. We enjoyed spending three winter months there for several years. We visited family, played golf and bridge and participated in exercise classes. I enjoyed riding my bike in the vicinity. We became acquainted with several people from many areas of the United States and Canada. TGIF gatherings were most enjoyable. Our first year at the resort, we were preparing to tee off on the front nine when the starter asked if another couple could join us. We saw their Colorado pins and asked where they lived. They said, "Fort Collins." From that day forward, we enjoyed Havyn and Terry's company. Besides participating in resort activities, we played bridge and golf together, had meals at each other's fifth wheels, ate out, and did some traveling. We continued our association through the years after arriving back home in Fort Collins. We made many friends at Palm Creek.

On May 2, 2003, the Navigators' Military Division invited our family to a Living Memorial Tree Dedication held for Susie on the grounds at Glen Eyre in Colorado Springs. The program read, "Susan Marie Nix Bennett, Beloved friend and faithful administrator went to be with the Lord on July 21, 2002. We were blessed by God through her." Scripture was read. Our family turned the earth with a shovel and shared remembrances along with Susie's boss, many friends, and colleagues. Susie's boss, Ron, and his wife, Patti, kept in touch with us. Unfortunately, a few years later, Patti died from cancer while she and Ron were serving the Navigators in California. Four years later, Ron was diagnosed with cancer. Both of our dear friends who showed such loving compassion for Susie died from the same dreadful disease. They would always hold a special place in our hearts.

During the summer, Tom returned to the hospital for two more stents. Ed, Marilyn, and I lifted the surgeon and Tom in prayer while we waited. The surgeon thanked us for our prayers as it was a long, intricate surgery. BY HIS HAND! Tom now had five stents in his coronary arteries. Each day during our prayer time, we gave thanks for the doctors, nurses, radiologists, and others in the medical field who cared for us. Tom's recovery was remarkable. He continued serving on two of his favorite community boards. Dear to his heart were the Salvation Army Advisory Board and the County Council for the Aged. When an announcement was made that city funds for transporting the aged had been cut, Tom organized a transportation team for the aged and handicapped in our church. He also met with the city-wide Faith Council encouraging other churches to do the same. Tom began a Caring Hearts program and a weekly Men's Prayer Breakfast early in the life of our church. Still serving as Elders, we looked forward to the monthly Healing and Wholeness Service, calling on the sick and doing our part in the communion service at one of the care centers.

As a surprise to us, Greg arranged for Tina and Tiana to spend time with us in Arizona. It was delightful to have them. Greg flew down midweek to surprise them. Tiana was advanced to second grade. She was reading on a tenth-grade level. She continued to do well in academics throughout school. During high school, she was Homecoming Baroness and played volleyball and basketball. Most of her activities centered around choir, musicals, and drama. It was a delight to watch her perform! She graduated from high school in 2015. Tiana lived with us her first year of college, which we loved. She began a major in music and earned high academic grades. It was a treat to hear her beautiful voice at concerts. Along toward her junior year, Tiana felt a calling to attend school for her medical assistant degree. After graduation, she became a medical assistant at the Fort Collins Skin Clinic. Later, she enjoyed her job as a pulmonary medical assistant at Medical Center of the Rockies in Loveland and Poudre Valley South Hospital in Fort Collins. She began work on a business degree. We were very proud of Tiana.

Medical Center of the Rockies held a special place in my heart as I was selected to be on a 24-member community advisory board in building the hospital. Each member contributed ideas and concerns. Several of us had been hospitalized more than once. Our first suggestion was to have private emergency rooms. The Advisory Board appreciated that many of our ideas were accepted: the emergency rooms, entrance, reception area, chapel, quality of size and comfort of furniture in waiting areas and hospital rooms including the beds, and much more. We voted on furniture that had been brought to a large warehouse in Loveland. It took a long period of time to try and judge each one. The last part of our journey included the food. We spent an entire evening tasting the food. There was so much good food that it was impossible to sample all of it. What a privilege to serve the community in this way. It was exciting to walk through the hospital on opening day!

In 2004, Ken had a heart-breaking experience for which he took part ownership. He and Cheryl parted ways because of her interest in someone else. It was difficult for Ken, and so hard on the children. Cody called us, as in the past, when things were upsetting at home. We prayed with him, giving hugs and kisses over the phone. Ken went to Milwaukee where he had a rough time not knowing if his next meal would be provided until he found a job with a communications business. Donnie took care of Casey for two months until she was placed in another foster home where she received excellent care.

On January 2, 2004, we were at the hospital awaiting the birth of our great-grandson, Luke. We sat in the hall with the two sets of grandparents—Ed and Marilyn and Joy's parents, Dave and Judy Aschermann. What a delight to see Luke right after his birth and a treat to know that we would see him often as Tom and Joy lived on our side of town. Another exciting event occurred this year when Josh graduated from Western State College. He received his bachelor's in psychology and sociology with emphasis on clinical counseling and criminal justice. The trip to Gunnison was beautiful. The graduation ceremony was impressive and the celebration gathering was great. I thought of how Susie would have loved to have been there. We were so proud of Josh. Later, Josh lived in Las Vegas where he managed security guards at one of the large casinos. We enjoyed visiting Josh, meeting his friends and getting acquainted with his Rottweiler, Cecil.

On July 1, 2005, Jake and Beth called from Indiana to tell us that Paige had entered the world. We went to Indiana to hold and snuggle beautiful Paige while enjoying our time with Jake and Beth. On September 6, 2005, we learned from our grandson Tom that Samuel was born. He had a smile on his little face. There would be two babies in town for grandmothers to cuddle. On November 9, Matt and Jenise called to tell us that James Thomas had been born at Fort Carson. How God blessed us with the arrival of these little ones. We prayed for each one daily from the time they were born.

We enjoyed the Nix family reunion in Salida, Colorado, hosted by the Joe Nix family. From there, we spent time with Greg's family at Lion's Gate Condos in Winter Park. That week we enjoyed two little foster children Greg and Tina were caring for. Jake was 3 years old and Maddie was 2. Their parents were methamphetamine addicts. This was the second time Jake, Maddie, and their siblings had been taken away from the parents. They were darling children. We loved the way they ran to us for hugs.

We had purchased our two-week time share in 1977. We usually traded our second week for time shares in other states and countries. This was a wonderful and inexpensive way to travel and not worry about the high cost of lodging, since our yearly upkeep dues were minimal. Susie and her husband purchased a time share, also. That week was always great fun. After Susie passed, Greg, Jake and Josh owned the condo. Later, Jake and Josh sold their interest to Greg. Tom had congestive heart failure and in 2009 experienced an episode that required a trip to the clinic in Granby. The doctor advised him to stay out of high altitudes. We missed our times at Winter Park, but as with other experiences, we adjusted. We were delighted that Jake and Beth wanted to purchase one week of our time share. We sold the second week to an acquaintance from California.

Dave, Deb, Jordan, and Anna visited us often. Anna loved to play with our many yard animals. Because of living in the country near LaSalle, Deb was on the go a lot since the girls attended school in Greeley. She made sure Jordan and Anna had a cultural education as well. We so enjoyed watching their performances in the Nutcracker each year. Jordan danced from age 6 to 18. She met with friends weekly at the church, where they made bracelets to benefit children who had been impacted by 9/11 in New York. The bracelets were mailed to schools in New York. The Greeley newspaper had an article with a picture of Jordan making bracelets. For some time, Dave's computer screen displayed a picture of Jordan playing at a basketball tournament in Estes Park. Jordan graduated from high school in 2011. While a student at Colorado State University, she was part of the leadership development community where she met Danny. There was a big party at the Rio Grande Restaurant in Fort Collins when she graduated from CSU in 2015 with a degree in communications. She and Danny chose Jacksonville, Florida, as their place of residence. Jordan worked for a law firm and was advanced to the position of Digital Marketing Manager.

David and Anna had a tight bond. David taught Anna many songs as she was growing up, which blossomed into her singing at school events and as a member of the church worship team. We loved hearing her sing. It warmed our hearts to witness the close relationship Anna and David built. Anna had abundant energy and many activities during school. In high school she became interested in Future Farmers of America (FFA). Tom had been an FFA member in high school and was presented with the State Farmer's Award. He and Anna had many talks and sharing sessions. Anna's activities were like a whirlwind. She was on the executive committee for FFA, president of the national honor society, president of the art club and on the executive committee for FFA. The meat judging team went to nationals in 2015, where Anna received recognition for her skills. Anna loved plants and flowers and was top florist of her FFA chapter. She was also in welding class, where she made gifts. Tom was a recipient of a few creations.

My faithful prayer partner and good friend, Marilyn Ferguson, had cancer and moved to stay with her family in Kansas. We corresponded often and made a trip to visit when Marilyn told us she was ready to leave this earth. After our visit, we spoke and prayed together daily until she went Home. Marilyn's memorial service was held in Fort Collins. I spoke at her service, telling of her godly servanthood and joyful spirit. My, how I missed her. I thought of other friends who had gone on before that we missed.

We welcomed five more precious great-grandchildren in 2007. We sat outside the birthing room again and welcomed Micah, who was bright-eyed and active. Another boy for Tom and Joy! Matt called with word of Noah's birth in San Antonio, where he was stationed. Then, we received a call from Jake and Beth telling us of Clare's birth. Greg and Tina adopted little Jake and Maddie. Tom and I were privileged to attend the proceedings. Jake and Maddie sat on the judge's lap for pictures. Greg, Tina, Tom, and I surrounded them. A case worker took pictures. Sadly, when Tina called asking for prints, the Court had lost them. No picture memories of such a special day!

In addition to our five little additions, Tom and I celebrated our 60th Wedding Anniversary held at the Senior Center in Fort Collins. Linda Hall made the punch and baked the cake. Linda, whom I had hired to teach at Irish Elementary School, was like a daughter to us. Friends from church and PEO made and served the food. We felt so special. We were surprised with a musical number by the Sunshine Singers. I was in the seventh year of directing the wonderful women's choir. Ed and David spoke words that filled our hearts, and we spoke our hearts to each other. "Dearest Patsy, you have filled my life with your love, kindness, and understanding for 60 years. Many of those times I did not deserve it, but you were always there with your smile, words of wisdom, and encouragement, and your prayers. I thank God for you and love you with all my heart." My message, "Dearest Tom, I cannot begin to express the depth of my love for you and thank God every day that He chose us for each other and how grateful I am for our oneness in Him in our marriage. You have filled my life with your love, encouragement, understanding, protection, friendship, and funny antics. I love you more than words can express. "

Our good friends and former Fort Collins neighbors, Neil and Kathi, became realtors in Casa Grande, Arizona. They told us of a new housing development not far from Palm Creek Golf and RV Resort. After Kathi showed us a home for rent, we decided to advertise our fifth wheel for sale and rent the house for our three-month stay the next year. We asked God's guidance, as we did with our larger and more serious decisions. There were countless RVs of all types for sale in the area, which we thought would affect finding a buyer. With Kathi's expert advertising skills, we sold our fifth wheel in a week. We did very well on our yard sale. We packed the pickup with our remaining goods and headed to Montrose, Colorado, where we visited niece Gay, and her husband, Rich. Before returning home, we stopped in Rifle, Colorado, to visit high school friends, John and Neva Downing.

2008: Our Travels Continue

In January 2008, we drove to Arizona, looking forward to staying in the new home we rented. As always, we enjoyed our visits with Joe, Lora, and their family. It was nice to be near our friends, Neal and Kathi. We enjoyed evenings at their beautiful home, days of golf, and eating at our favorite Mexican restaurant. Kathi and I took advantage of an exercise program. The four of us attended worship services together at the First Christian Church in Casa Grande. The last five weeks of our stay, I developed a serious case of pneumonia. When I was almost over it, I became ill again. I thought pneumonia was pneumonia, but I was told by the doctor that seven different types existed and I had a second one complicated by my asthma. We ran a humidifier day and night as I downed heavy antibiotics, used my inhaler more often and spent a great deal of time in bed. When I recovered, the asthma specialist suggested that I not spend extended time in Arizona. He stated that a breeze is usually blowing, sending spores airborne. We also experienced dust storms in the vicinity every year. Tom reminded me that I became ill with pneumonia in the 70s while we were visiting family in Arizona. It was good that we sold our fifth wheel the year before. We did enjoy 35 years of trips to every state and Canada, pulling our home on the highways and byways, making friends with hundreds of people, and the years we spent at Casa Grande Golf and RV Resort. We had fond memories of Ed and Marilyn, and Bill and Susie making trips with us. We returned to Arizona later for short visits with Joe and Lora.

In the fall of 2008, we drove to visit Ken in Milwaukee and were pleased to find he was doing well. We drove up north to Chilton to see Cody and Casey. Ande arranged for us to visit Casey in her foster home. Casey seemed very happy. We expressed thanks to her foster parents. Cody, a handsome teenager, was so enjoyable. After our visit, we headed for Indiana to visit with Jake, Beth, Paige, and Clare. It would be our first time to see Clare, who was two, and we had not seen Paige for four years. Clare was a cute, energetic child who liked to climb on things. The higher, the better! Paige was a darling five-year-old. We enjoyed our visit very much in Jake and Beth's lovely home in Granger, Indiana. Jake was a high school volunteer football coach. They were fortunate to have an experienced coach like Jake.

Unfounded Child Abuse Charges

The last of October, Tina called to say they needed our help. Maddie had experienced abdominal pain on her right side and was in Children's Hospital in Denver. We quickly packed our bags and headed for Denver. The doctors ruled out appendicitis. They found a problem with Maddie's bladder and decided a blow caused the injury. They performed a test by filling her abdomen with water as she was held down, which could have made her condition worse. They were no visible bruises on Maddie. However, Tina noticed a bruise on her pelvic bone after doctors finished their examination. Tina told the doctors how Maddie fell hard on her plastic pumpkin while trick or treating, but they paid little attention. Tina was accused of child abuse. We sat with Tina and Greg down the hall from Maddie's room. They would not allow Tina to be with Maddie. We thanked God that Maddie did well with the surgery. Tom left to stay with Tiana and Jake at their home in Kiowa. I was allowed to stay 24/7 with Maddie during her recovery. Greg was able to spend a couple of nights with her. Two days after Maddie's surgery, Greg and I were asked to meet with a social worker and the sheriff in another area. The social worker (we will call her Florence) looked surprised when she saw us. I am sure she was expecting us to be Hispanic. From the beginning, we felt the charge was racially driven. Beautiful Tina is Hispanic, American Indian, and Caucasian. The social worker had an unpleasant, almost hateful look, and threatened to take the children away and place them in different homes. Greg asked why she wanted to take the children he loved. Florence asked how he could take care of them. I spoke up and told her Tom and I would take care of the children while Greg was at work. Florence laughed and asked what kind of experience I had as a caregiver. It was difficult not to retaliate, and I asked the Holy Spirit to guide my words. After mentioning about being a mother, grandmother, and great-grandmother, I shared about my teaching career and how Tom and I provided a home for young men and boys who experienced homelessness or other types of trauma. I also wanted her to know that Tina was a college graduate with a degree in Exercise Physiology and Wellness Management. After more conversation, Florence said we could care for the children, but Tina would not be allowed in the home. We were grateful when Maddie was able to come home. She celebrated her 5th birthday without her mom. Such heartbreak for all, especially Tiana, Jake, and Maddie who wanted to see their mother. I would find 11-year-old Tiana playing with her Barbies in a dark corner of the downstairs family room. She showed amazing maturity in understanding the situation. Being deprived of her mother's presence took its toll on her little heart. Tina was staying with friends from church. Many friends and neighbors wrote letters vouching for Tina and her mothering skills, as well as Greg's love and care for the children. Also, how Tina lovingly cared for children in the nursery at church. Florence did not want to hear or investigate anything good. It was as if she was driven by a force of hate. *Ephesians 6:11-12,* "Put on the full armor of God so you can take your stand against the devil's schemes. For our struggle is not against flesh and blood, but against the spiritual forces of evil..." Pastors and elders of Greg and Tina's church and our church were offering prayers without ceasing. Arrangements had been made for Maddie to be interviewed. Tom took her to the designated place and waited in an outer room. After an hour, a door opened, and Maddie came running. She jumped into Tom's arms, crying. She said, "Papo, they are trying to make me tell lies about mommy." Tom was furious but kept his cool and asked if he could take Maddie home. They questioned her for another 35 minutes. As Tom and Maddie left, Maddie said, "Those people are mean. "

One can only imagine the agony Tina was experiencing, away from her family. Greg's working hours were filled with concern for Tina and the children. Word had spread throughout the entire community. In spite of everything, Tina held her head up high, greeting everyone with a kind word and smile, as always. We were blessed by Greg and Tina's friends and neighbors who brought food and offered to clean the house. Around Thanksgiving, Tina was able to see the children—her only visit during the six weeks she was kept from them. During that time, Tina passed a lie detector test and was submitted to a psych test that lasted for three hours, which she passed. In March, charges against Tina were dropped by the county. The sheriff remarked there was no evidence from the beginning of Maddie being abused. Florence was not satisfied. She filed charges at the state level. It was as if an evil force was driving her. Greg, Tina, and I took Maddie to the most well-known and respected urologist in the state who told us that Maddie's problem could not have been caused from an outside blow but rather from weakness that occurred in the womb, as her birth mother was on crystal meth. Maddie, Jake, and their siblings were subjected to meth daily as well as to countless addicts who frequented their home. Greg and Tina were blessed with a competent lawyer. In May, Tina was exonerated from charges filed at the state level. What a halleluiah day for this sweet family, celebrated by our entire family and others who prayed for victory. Thank you, God, our refuge. We appreciate social caseworkers who protect children from abuse. However, those who are bent in persecuting the innocent need to have established guidelines, view the evidence, and listen to counsel. There is talk, nationwide, about the need for establishing specific rules and guidelines for social workers. We experienced one who was driven to destroy a family. Greg, Tina, and I went for an appointment with the doctor who had accused Tina of child abuse at Children's Hospital. I took Maddie to play. The doctor told us he made a mistake, but would not say so outside of the room because it would ruin his career.

2009

2009 was a year of many surgeries for Tom. In February, he had extensive neck surgery with a four-month recovery time. Tom could withstand a lot of pain, but our family was concerned with this surgery. I tried to make him comfortable as I administered his medications, but he remained in terrific pain. Tom said he should not have agreed to the surgery. In March, he expressed regret that he could not shop for my birthday card and order the red roses for my birthday—the first time since we were teenagers. After recovery, Tom could not sleep at night because of hand and wrist pain. Two carpal tunnel surgeries gave him relief. During recovery from these operations, Tom was diagnosed with prostate cancer. After having gold seeds planted in his prostate, he began eight weeks of radiation and hormone treatments, which were very uncomfortable. After the radiation, his PSA count was normal and remained there. As I cared for Tom and took him to radiation and doctor appointments, he never complained. When life batters us in ways we least expect, God gives us strength for each day as He floods us with peace, love and rays of hope. BY HIS HAND, He leads us into each tomorrow.

We were grateful that Tom's brother, Joe, continued to recover from a stroke. He and Tom had loud phone conversations since they both had hearing problems which was caused by difficulty in the stapes, inherited from their mom. Stapes is a stirrup-shaped bone in the middle ear that transmits sound vibrations. When we moved to Front Nine in 1992, Greg installed surround sound in the family room. At that time, Tom turned the volume up high. If I was sitting upstairs in the recliner, I received a massage! Tom had corrective surgery that was not successful, but with advancement in hearing aid technology a few years later, Tom could hear well. He no longer needed to turn the TV and radio on full volume. One day he said, "Patsy, you are talking too loud. " How wonderful to communicate with Tom in my natural voice.

In the fall, our church released the Director of Music and asked if I would help. I was blessed to direct the Christmas Cantata and lead the children in their songs. It was a busy but joyful time. The women's choir I directed had twelve performances in the two weeks leading up to Christmas. I continued as the church's Director of Music for the next two months until a person was hired to fill that position.

2010

In 2010, we spent time catching up with our close high school chums who lived within 150 miles. We had lunches, picnics, golf outings, card games, and reminisced while we shared pictures of families. Of course, the guys loudly relived every football and basketball game.

Tom and I continued involvement with family, church, and community activities, which brought us many blessings. Tom was regaining his energy from his surgeries, so we returned to workouts twice a week at the club. Patrick, who was stationed in Germany, called to say that little Danica was born. We had another beautiful great-granddaughter. Our sixteenth great! Tom gave me a new set of golf clubs for Christmas. I gave the old Montgomery Ward clubs to Goodwill and was convinced the new ones would improve my game! One of the songs sung by the Sunshine Singers for our Christmas concert was, "Bless That Wonderful Name of Jesus." As we expressed thanks for the way God looked over us, we were reminded that Jesus brings hope, healing, joy, and peace not only at Christmas but every day of the year.

Tom and I talked often about how blessed we were to be citizens of the U.S.A. In our travels abroad, we arose every morning with thanks and remembered those who died for our freedom. We expressed gratitude for our three grandchildren serving in the Air Force: Matt, Alicia and Patrick.

We also celebrated one of Matt's accomplishments. He completed his MA degree in Theological Studies with Distinction.

We were drawn to Deborah, a young woman in our church. She reminded us of Susie in some of her mannerisms and deep faith. Her seven-year-old nephew, Corbin, was quite ill with liver failure.

Deborah asked if we would offer a healing prayer for Corbin. When Deborah brought her sister and Corbin to our home, we held hands as we asked God to cleanse our thoughts to keep our minds clear and pure before Him. Before we laid hands on Corbin, I asked if he understood what we had prayed about. He said, "Yes, you were asking God to clean us." Tom asked Corbin, "Do you believe Jesus can heal you?" Corbin gave an enthusiastic "Yes!" I could just see Jesus smiling. We prayed for Corbin's healing. Each ensuing test over the next three months showed improvement in Corbin's liver count. His faith blessed us as we continued to pray. What a time of rejoicing when baffled doctors pronounced him cured! God, in His mercy and love, healed that little boy. We saw Corbin the next year and later when he was a strong, healthy adult. Thanks be to God! The next two and a half years, we began prayers for Deborah as she was diagnosed with breast cancer. We were present at her home, chemo treatments, and hospital stays. A few friends asked how we could do that after experiencing Susie's three-year battle with cancer. The answer was simple. Our love for Deborah. God saw fit to heal Deborah by calling her home in 2015. In our sorrow we turned to God for His comforting care as we prayed for her family.

2011

During 2011, we spent a weekend in Colorado Springs to celebrate the wedding of Bill and Alicia. Alicia was a beautiful bride. What a joyous time with a beautiful ceremony, lots of good food, drinks, and dancing. We welcomed wonderful Bill to the family as we enjoyed becoming acquainted with his relatives.

Our hearts were overwhelmed with grief by the loss of our beautiful granddaughter, Casey (Ken and Cheryl's daughter), who dealt with several handicaps. She passed into the loving arms of Jesus on February 2, 2011. Doctors said she would not live past her twelfth birthday, but she fooled them by gracing the family with her presence until she was eighteen. We loved being around Casey, who had sweet smiles and became excited when she heard Ken's voice as he came through the door after work. Casey inspired everyone with her determination, infectious giggle, and sparkling blue eyes. Once again, we fell into the consoling arms of Jesus.

In April, Ken was hospitalized. He had pneumonia with complications brought on by malnutrition caused by alcoholism. He was in ICU for several days. His friend, Matt, had taken him to the hospital. We were grateful for the countless prayers said for his healing. Tom and I talked with the doctor or nurses every day about his condition. They said they would let us know if we should come. After ICU, Ken spent another week in the hospital before he was transferred to a rehab center. We were grateful for the numerous prayers that were answered. I flew to Milwaukee to be with Ken. I was shocked when I first saw him. In time, he began to look more like himself. Fortunately, I was able to stay with Ken's friend, Matt, and his wife, Michelle, who lived a short distance from the rehab center. They had a huge Rottweiler they called King. When King was lying on the floor one day, I reached down to pet him. He let out a sound like a soft growl, so I stopped. I was a little uneasy. When Matt and Michelle came home from work, they said the sound was a purr because he enjoyed being petted. King and I became friends. A neighbor knocked on the door one day when King and I were alone. Even though King knew the neighbor, he stood up on the screen, showed his teeth and growled. He was protecting me. Matt, Michelle, and I cleaned Ken's apartment, and I purchased some items he would need. I stayed for ten days. It would be another ten days before Ken was released to go home. During my stay, Jake came to see if I was alright. He had driven from a business meeting in Chicago. We checked Ken out of rehab and went to dinner. I felt so blessed to think that my grandson came all that way to check up on me, When I left, Ken was feeling much better and anxious to get home.

Throughout the years, Ken called often, asking us to pray with him. In addition, he wrote letters expressing gratitude for our unconditional love and especially that of Jesus. We knew Jesus would never let him go. It would be years before he repented and became sober. WE were grateful for the prayers of many, along with Cody's love and care. Thank you, God, for your mercy and healing touch!

In March, we went to visit Joe and Lora. Since Lora's Alzheimer's was progressing, Joe had help with her baths and house cleaning. Those sparks of sweetness and fun in Lora appeared now and then. Joe Jr., who was attentive to his folks, loaned us his good vehicle during our stay while he drove an old Jeep. Judy and John gave help and support for their dad. During her stays, Judy prepared and froze meals for her parents.

In August, we attended my 65th high school reunion in Boulder and stayed with our close friends, Dick and Peg. My class had a reunion every five years, which enabled our committee to keep track of folks. Each year, we missed those who had passed away. Joann, my best friend from junior high school days, was no longer with us.

2012

In May of 2012, Heather, who had been Susie's nurse during her last months, began organizing a 5K Race in memory of Susie. Heather invited us to attend a dinner to meet some of the nurses who were members of the Honor Society of Nursing in Colorado Springs. They would become one of the sponsors of the race. N-X Ranch, owned by Greg and Tina, were also among the sponsors. The 5K Race was held on June 9 at the Memorial Park in downtown Colorado Springs. The theme was "Shattering the Silence." Everyone was given T-shirts that had a quote by Susie: "Have an impact on others that outlasts your lifespan on this earth." Two of Susie's favorite Bible verses surrounded the quote: "But as for me, I will always have hope… *Psalm 71:14*, "Press on toward the goal…for which God has called me." *Philippians 3:14*, A huge arch was decorated with colorful balloons. The proceeds were donated for Research of Reproductive Cancers and a Susie Nix Nursing Scholarship. It was a special day for our family, friends, and others who loved Susie.

Fun with Great Grandchildren

On November 12, we waited again outside the birthing room at the hospital with the other grandparents: Ed, Marilyn, Judy, and Dave. We were excited to have the first glimpse of beautiful Emily. Tom and Joy's family—Luke, Samuel, Micah, and Emily— was now complete. We had been blessed to spend time with our grandchildren: Greg, Jake, Josh, Tom, Matt, Alicia, and Anna throughout the years, and to watch them perform in music and athletics. Now, blessings flowed to have four of our great-grandchildren nearby. We grandparents took turns babysitting and spoiling Luke, Samuel, Micah, and Emily. As the children grew, I loved picking them up after school and visiting Dairy Queen or the Dollar Store. Tiana, Jake, and Maddie loved the Dollar Store, too. The children would usually run up and down each aisle, filling the basket. At that point, I informed them that they had gone over their limit. It took a long time for them to return some items as they decided on the keepers. Joy often left to take care of patients at Poudre Valley Hospital before the children were home from school. We grandparents would stay until Tom arrived home from work. Tom was employed as a machinist for Mountain Secure Systems until he accepted a machinist opening with Walker Manufacturing, which was closer to home. We were very proud of Tom. When we scheduled sleepovers, the children slept in the living room on a blow-up mattress, close to our bedroom until they grew old enough to sleep downstairs. As an adult, Alicia told us of going to sleep with chimes from the grandfather clock, and how I woke them each morning by playing the piano. Tiana was our first great-grandchild. When she was little, she would run in the front door and ask for mac and cheese, even if it was breakfast time. We had a bear carved from a tree sitting on our front porch. One of Tiana's first words was "Bear." She coined her name for us. We were "Mamo and Papo" from that time on to the great-grandchildren. Jake and Maddie would run to hug us and make a beeline for the toy box and dolls. As all the girls grew, they loved playing with Barbies. The boys ran for the trucks and cars, especially ones that made a lot of noise. Anna loved our yard animals. She had fun rearranging them and playing at the park.

Tom's left knee that was replaced in 1998, showed wear and tear so the doctors did a partial replacement. Tom was in the hospital for three days. On the last day, the care worker on the orthopedic floor informed me that we would need to pay for all of Tom's rehab. I had already given $2,700 that was required before he could be admitted. The case worker explained that Tom was an outpatient the first day, inpatient the second day and outpatient the third day. I asked how that could be. She said the hospital could not reach his doctor during the third day to declare Tom an inpatient so Medicare would not pay for rehab. Needless to say, I was upset. I called for a patient advocate. Things went round and round until I asked to see the senior case worker. After filling her in on everything that happened, she apologized and assured me that she would call rehab to get things straightened out. I asked about the $2,700 I had already paid. The case worker, who gave me her phone number, was a great help as I received a message about reimbursement. I asked God to bless the case worker's kind heart.

The fiasco did not end there. Because of surgery, Tom had to be off his diuretic. After his first night in rehab, I noticed intense swelling in his abdomen and legs. In the past six weeks, fluid had been drained from around his lungs twice. I spoke to the nurse and got some run-around that he was being treated only for post-knee surgery. I asked for a scale to weigh Tom. His nurse said she would take care of it. It was near time for a shift change, so I never saw her. I searched the building and found the scale on wheels. As Tom stepped on it, the needle pointed to a 35-pound weight gain. I called Tom's cardiologist explaining the seriousness of his condition. It was another six hours before a nurse entered the room with a diuretic. I was told the doctor's orders were never transferred from the hospital. A comedy of errors all the way around! I spent most of the days and late nights with Tom. His weight stabilized, and his condition began to improve. On the eleventh day, the therapist and nurse said he was ready to go home. I was called to the social worker's office who said Tom was not ready to go home and that she had talked with our family doctor. Something seemed fishy, so I called our doctor. I went back to the social worker's office to tell her I did not appreciate her lie and to whom did I need to make a report. God knew that I was very angry and exhausted. I asked the Holy Spirit to temper my speech. The social worker told me Tom would be dismissed the next day. As is customary for a dismissal, we had a meeting around a large table with the therapist, activities director, head of nurses, and the social worker. All were in agreement to dismiss Tom except the social worker. I was ready to speak up when Tom said, "I did not receive proper care the first three days in your facility. It was my wife who saved my life. Right now, I am questioning the professional treatment from the social worker today." Tom was dismissed to go home. I thanked the Holy Spirit again for guiding us through this journey and for Tom's recovery. When we walked through the door of our home, we held hands as we thanked God. We asked Him to bless the rehab staff and nurses, also those who made errors at the hospital. God is the changer of hearts!

In 2013, Matt and Lauren were married at their church in Cheyenne. It was a beautiful ceremony and reception. We welcomed lovely Lauren to the family. James and Noah lived with their mother, Denise, in Colorado Springs. It was always a treat to see them.

2013

Nine months of 2013 were challenging for Tom. Atrial fibrillation and coronary artery disease produced several complications. The third beta blocker reduced the rapid pulse, and he began to feel better. It was difficult for him to give up playing golf. We enjoyed many years of playing together, both in Fort Collins and on our travels. At times, I had a hook when hitting the ball. During those times, Tom called me the "happy hooker"! The men's golf group that Tom had organized several years before missed his company on the course. I ordered Life Alert for Tom. After a while, he laid it on the end table in the family room where he spent a lot of time. When I scolded him, he said, "I don't like it around my neck. It bothers me." It was to no avail when I reminded Tom of the times I was gone. He was the same with his cell phone. Wherever he went, it was always left in the car. He did have difficulty touching the numbers. (Tom had large hands. He wore a size 17 ring. I loved the feeling of my hand being nestled in his.) I knew where he was most of the time, so if I needed to reach him, I called one of his friends or the Elks Club where he sometimes played cards. The radiation that cured Tom's cancer caused bleeding from his colon. He was hospitalized for the first surgery relating to this problem. He recovered ahead of schedule. We were grateful for God's unending love, presence, and help.

After attending Christmas Eve services at church, the family gathered for the traditional chili, different kinds of soup with accompanying salads, and desserts at our home. We purchased a new chair for Tom. It was a recliner that had three different modes of massage plus heat. The great-grandchildren tried it out. They approved whole-heartedly of the chair! I was reminded how the grands and greats loved to operate our electric beds. Whenever they came to visit, they made a beeline to the beds. They raised the head and foot as far as they could to be squeezed in the middle. Then they lowered it and turned on the massage. Most of the time, I would have to track them down to help re-make the beds.

Between Christmas and New Years 2013, Tom took a tumble down five stairs. The only damage was a gash on his forehead that required 6 stitches. Tom experienced three more falls at home. Since he could not get up on artificial knees, I went to our neighbor's home. John, a burly guy who had played baseball on the team coached by Tom several years earlier, came to help. John would place his arms around Tom's chest and lift him up. He made it look easy. We were so grateful for John's help.

We continued to enjoy three different bridge groups. Tom insisted I continue playing golf in the ladies' league at the Southridge course. As I went out the door, he would holler, "Keep your head down!"

Tom and I took a few short trips to see friends during the year. We would also take walks along the ditch with a retriever to gather golf balls. Tom had been gathering golf balls from that ditch for years. It was a big deal for the grandchildren to help him fish for balls. After the balls were cleaned, they were separated into three piles. He placed the good ones in egg cartons, which he gave to our grandsons or friends. He kept unusual ones with logos in a jar. Most of them were placed in a bucket, which Tom donated to the golf course for use by kids who were learning to play. Tom was back in the hospital again for surgery on his bleeding colon. As he recovered, we added one request to our prayer time. We desired to live long enough to see our oldest great-grandchild graduate from high school.

Ande, who lived in Wisconsin with her husband, Russell, called to tell us that Frankie had been born. Another beautiful great-granddaughter!

2014

In 2014, Tom came home from playing bridge with the guys, handed me the keys to the Journey and said, "Here are my car keys. I am through driving. Call David and tell him to sell my vehicle." I asked what happened. He explained that he was stopped at the light on Lemay and Horsetooth. He had fallen asleep momentarily and was awakened by the car honking behind him. I hugged him to say I was so sorry but very proud of his wise decision. I had done most of the driving over the past two years, but Tom did enjoy driving to play bridge with the guys. During all of Tom's health problems, he rarely complained. Because of our respect and love for each other, he followed my advice—except for the Life Alert! Of course, there were times he broke out with teasing to give me a bad time. I just smiled and said, "I read you like a book so you may as well give up." One time Ed was visiting with his dad in the family room. Tom yelled for me. Ed said, "Dad, what do you need? I am right here." Tom said, "I know, but I want your mother." When I reached the bottom of the stairs, Tom said, "Where would you have been if I had not called you?" I got back at him later by adding bitters to his bourbon and 7-Up. Keeping a sense of humor and enjoying little pranks was fun, healthy, and always prevalent in our marriage.

Ande called in October to tell us about the birth of Leni. Another beautiful great-granddaughter! When Frankie and Leni were old enough to join 4-H, I loved watching videos of barrel racing goat tying, pole bending and other events. Both girls won awards. They won saddles and buckles that were almost as big as their bodies. Ande, Russell, and the girls moved from Green Bay, Wisconsin, to Webber Falls, Oklahoma.

Our dear friend, Dick Rogers, passed away. He had struggled with heart problems for the last few years. He called to tell us goodbye the day before he died. We assured Peggy we would be there for her. Dick and Tom, best friends, were groomsmen for each other's weddings. The four of us had enjoyed decades of friendship that included many travels and much laughter.

2015

In 2015, Tom experienced some improvement from his many health problems, even after a bout with pneumonia. The family was amazed at his strength and determination. We continued to enjoy bridge groups, family gatherings, and attending worship services at church. It was difficult for us to give up our 45-year worship ministry to care centers and rest homes. Our dear friend, Betsy, offered to continue leading the church team for worship service at Rehabilitation and Nursing Center of the Rockies. Life is filled with transitions, and God reached out through His Holy Spirit to guide us through each one.

Alicia and Bill left for England where they would be stationed for the next three years. They were able to visit other countries during that time and filled us in on the habits and interesting slang of the Brits. I looked forward to Bill greeting me with, "Hi, Love."

Matt was honorably discharged from the Air Force. He and Lauren lived with Ed and Marilyn for five months while they made future plans. They returned to Cheyenne where Matt became the Human Resource Manager for the State of Wyoming. Lauren also worked for the State of Wyoming as an accountant.

Our great sadness of the year was the passing of Tom's brother, Joe, and his wife, Lora. Joe's heart condition escalated, and Lora had been ill with Alzheimer's for several years. Joe died first. Then, it seemed that Lora wanted to be with him. They had been together in a care facility for some time. Both were buried at their beautiful ranch near Gardner, Colorado. Unfortunately, we could not attend either service. Knowing of Tom's illnesses and that his heart could not tolerate high altitudes, nephew John called to remind us that we should not come and the family understood. We were able to see part of the service via a phone video. We had so many good times at the ranch and in Arizona visiting with Joe and Lora. We also had great memories of the many visits by their family to our farm. Tom and I talked about other remembrances of Joe, and I recalled the fun Lora and I had through the years, from having mud fights in our bathing suits, to our late-night sharing after the family was tucked into bed. We looked backward to remember all these things, but Joe and Lora were in God's house for the forever future. We expressed our deepest love and sympathy to Joe, Jr., Judy, John, and Jack. We were consoled by our ever-present Lord.

One evening Tom asked me to look at his toe. It was badly damaged, which sent us to the emergency room. I asked what happened. The only explanation was a weight he had dropped on his toe at the exercise club. The neuropathy had escalated to a point where Tom had almost no feeling in his lower legs and feet. Tom had treatments at the wound center twice a week for three and a half months.

Tom and I had asked God to allow us to see our first great-grandchild graduate from high school. God is Good! What a happy time, and we were so proud of Tiana and her accomplishments. Tom was not feeling his best when we attended Tiana's graduation party. Greg and Jake helped Tom navigate the stairs. We were blessed even more, as Tiana lived with us during her freshman year of college. It was quite a transition for her to adjust being away from family, especially her mom. There was a place in town that held dances for young people. Tiana told us about dancing different styles and the people she met. We also enjoyed attending the concerts and watching her perform in a play at CSU. Tiana had a beautiful voice. Later, she decided to become a medical assistant. She was an MA for a skin clinic in Fort Collins, and secondly, she assisted pulmonary doctors at the hospitals.

Stairs were becoming an issue for Tom, as the family room downstairs was his man cave. Before the year ended, he wanted to check out the Worthington, an independent living facility. I had toured two other facilities, but we liked the atmosphere at the Worthington. We had also been luncheon guests of friends who lived there many times. The only available apartment was too small for us, as it was not easy for Tom to maneuver with his walker. On the way home, I told Tom that I would investigate a stair lift so we could stay in our house. The lift was installed within a week and proved to be of great help. The grandchildren rode it up and down and said it was too slow for them.

I began to experience frequent and severe atrial fibrillations, diagnosed as supraventricular tachycardia. On January 10, 2016, surgery called an ablation corrected the problem. I was the oldest person to have the surgery. Tom and I thanked God for the surgeon's skill and those who assisted. Over our life span, Tom and I saw and experienced incredible advancements in medical science and technology.

On January 26, Matt and Lauren announced the birth of beautiful Amber. Her birth was a milestone for us, as she was out 20th great-grandchild. How wonderful to have these precious great-grandchildren: Tiana, Jake, Maddie, Luke, Samuel, Micah, Emily, Paige, Clare, James, Noah, Amber, Sidney, Gracie, Alex, Frankie, Leni, Jada, Nalanni, and Danica. We were very proud of the way our grandchildren and their spouses were raising these dear ones, providing love and guidance in a Christian home.

Our close neighborhood friends were Kitty, Lila, Judy and Suzanne. We knew Lila before she moved across the street from us. She and Tom had worked together in real estate. Judy also lived across the street. One winter, she saw Tom struggling to pick up the newspaper from the icy driveway. From that time on, as Judy walked her dog, Sadie, she laid the paper in front of the garage door. Kitty, the latest arrival from Illinois, was like a sister to me. Cheerful Suzanne, who lived next door, brought delicious food to us. These thoughtful friends were a blessing. We women enjoyed a weekly movie club at Kitty's home.

It was a privilege to direct the Sunshine Singers for sixteen years and work with our outstanding accompanist, Carolyn. The choir had grown to 45 members, and I would miss each one. I resigned to spend more time at home with Tom. The chorus had a wonderful retirement party where they presented me with a beautiful clock which sits on top of my piano.

It was a joy for Tom and I to attend school programs and athletic events that involved our four great-grandchildren in town plus Tiana, Jake, and Maddie in Elizabeth, Colorado. During the year, Tom's energy level prevented him from participating in many events. He shared that it was time to ask someone else to be in charge of the Elk's dinner bridge group that he had organized 35 years earlier. We were grateful when a couple volunteered to carry on.

We were raised to look our best for church services. One Sunday morning Tom asked if it would be OK not to wear his tie. A bolo tie served the purpose quite well. We had a fun ritual on Sunday mornings. Tom would ask which tie matched his shirt and coat the best. I would ask which earrings he liked. He always chose the dangling type. During the service when we stood, I helped Tom to his feet. Men at church were quick to take care of his walker. On one Saturday, the Men's Prayer Breakfast group brought the breakfast meeting to our house, which pleased Tom.

Tom was an avid fan of Andy Griffith who was an actor, comedian, television producer, southern gospel singer, and writer, whose career spanned seven decades in music and television. In the early nineties, I searched for CDs of the Andy Griffith Television Show. I finally found the first four episodes in Canada. Later, the other episodes became available in the United States. After watching the Matlock series on television where Andy was a criminal defense lawyer, I purchased those CDs for Tom. It was his habit to watch two episodes every day. His favorite quote from the Andy Griffith Show was "What a tangled web we weave when at first we do deceive."

2017: Moving to the Worthington

In early 2017, Tom was insistent that we visit the Worthington again. I called Jodie, the manager at the Worthington. She was excited to tell me there was a vacancy made for us. When we arrived, Jodi took us to the third floor. The location was on the west side with a view of the foothills, which was perfect. It was a two-bedroom, two-bath apartment with a good-sized den. Tom moved about with ease. We made a deposit for the apartment.

We called Ed to ask that he place our home for sale. A contract was signed within three weeks. We had lived on Front Nine for 26 years. There was a lot to do in organizing a garage sale. Men from our church moved furniture from the basement to the garage. Ed and Marilyn pitched in to help. Most of the work was done by Kitty, Lila, and Judy. Those dear friends helped for three days, pricing the furniture and tools that family did not take, and placing other items on different tables in the garage. We had accumulated a lot in 26 years! (Several friends asked if it was difficult to part with so many things. My answer was no. It is just stuff.) Ed was our roaming security officer during the sale. Grandson Tom, was the cashier. Marilyn, Kitty, Lila, and Judy made themselves available to answer questions. It was awesome to watch Greg, Tina, Tiana, Jake, and Maddie move my piano up the narrow stairway. They were in top physical shape from participating in Cross Fit exercise. How grateful we were to family and friends!

Kitty and I had measured furniture for our move. We cut out exact measurements from black plastic and laid it on the apartment floors. It was a quick, efficient way to find out which items fit and an easy guide for the movers. Tom's man cave was the second bedroom, which we decorated first.

Tom was feeling blue in our apartment at the Worthington because he could not help with the garage sale. The second day of the sale, I brought him to Judy's house across the street, where family could pop in to visit. Sadie, Judy's dog who never responded to men, jumped on Tom's lap when he sat down on the recliner. When Tom ate lunch, Sadie sat by his chair. She was his constant companion for the day. Sadie knew Tom did not feel well!

In May, I was rushing to attend our great-grandchildren's spring program. The family was already seated. Walking fast, I tripped over the doorsill which catapulted me across the hall. Striking the wall, I fell with all my weight on the left side. I was in terrific pain as I asked two students to tell someone from the Nix family. God was on the scene. In an instant, a man who identified himself as a medic began to examine and comfort me. Luke was the first family member to appear. Ed and Tom were right behind. The medic told them I most likely had a broken hip. I was grateful when the ambulance and medical team arrived. They immediately injected something for pain. I was taken to the surgical prep area at Poudre Valley Hospital where I waited for the trauma surgeon to arrive. He had an emergency that preceded mine, so the wait was long. I suggested that Ed and Marilyn go home. The surgeon arrived to explain that I had fractured my hip and femur. He showed us the rod that would be placed from my knee to the hip. At this time, my daughter-in-law Deb, Dave's wife, appeared to say that she would be staying with me. Deb slept in a chair that night and was with me the next day. God blessed me with wonderful, caring, daughters-in-law whom I loved as my own. After a thirteen-day stay in a rehab center I went home. Since I did not arise early for the first week, Tom brought breakfast from the dining room. He carried it on his walker seat. Tom would open the door to our apartment and call out, "Breakfast is being served!" Having two meals a day provided by the Worthington was great. We ate breakfast and lunch in the dining room, enjoying conversation with friends. I had a wonderful physical therapist. I did not want to be married to the walker, so I was diligent with my exercises. In two months, I was able to drive and walk without assistance. Tiana went with me on my first drive. I made a wrong turn onto a street which I readily corrected. We had a good laugh and Tiana kept the secret. She was a great help to us during my recovery. She appeared to help with numerous things, and we loved her presence.

Anna graduated from high school in May. She was recognized for several achievements in her classes and activities including the National Honor Society. We were so proud of Anna. Unfortunately, I was not able to travel and missed her graduation and the fabulous party Dave and Deb arranged to honor her. Tom garnered enough strength to attend the celebration. Ed and Marilyn looked out for him during the festivities and brought him home early. Anna left in September to attend Sam Houston College in Texas, majoring in criminology.

We celebrated three milestones in the span of one year—our 70th wedding anniversary and both of our 90th birthdays. Because of Ed's organizational skills, each party was fabulous, with lots of family and friends to greet. We were pleased our anniversary party was hosted by the City of Fort Collins Natural Areas at our farm. Tours were conducted for those in attendance. The farmhouse, tenant house, and barn had been placed on the Historical Register. A memory stone for Susie had been placed in the garden.

The city purchased the last 40 acres of our farm in 1998, and we were delighted that the natural habitat and buildings were preserved. On our anniversary, we shared these memories. It has been a blessing to stand side by side through the ups and downs; raising our children, enjoying grandchildren and great-grandchildren. We have shared our tears and heartaches, our disappointments and joys, our successes and failures, our mistakes and mischievous acts. We have laughed and cried through our experiences and those of our dear children. We have shared our deepest thoughts. We have been quick to forgive. Most importantly, we have shared our love and dependence on an awesome God.

At the Worthington, we had access to a private dining room and chef-prepared meals. In December, we hosted two separate dinner parties for 44 friends and family who had helped us pack, move, assisted with the garage sale, brought meals, called on us when we were homebound, drove us to appointments, prayed with us and served communion when we could not attend worship services. We were steeped in love by godly friends and family. *John 13:34* "A new command I give you. Love one another..."

Tom continued to play bridge with the guys. Each week I drove him to Mulligans Pub where they played. Our friend, Gary, brought him home.

Life After Tom

In January of 2018, Tom returned to the hospital for transfusions. He refused another surgery for his bleeding colon. Arriving home, I asked again if I could help with his socks and shoes. Even though the task took a long time, he insisted on doing it on his own. He also refused to use the chairlift to stand up. I told him he was stubborn, but brave and wise. With each passing week, Tom's health declined. The end of January, he returned to the hospital for more transfusions. Upon returning home, Tom continued watching two episodes of Andy Griffith and Matlock each afternoon. When the doctor asked about his diet, Tom said, "I eat oatmeal for breakfast, soup for lunch and a fruit smoothie with a little ice cream for supper. Either before or after supper, I drink bourbon and seven up." Our doctor said, "That sounds pretty good!" A couple of my friends remarked that Tom was eating too much sugar. My response was that at 90 years of age, he should eat what he wants. We had an appointment with our family physician in February. He was so kind and loving as he explained the transfusions were not helping and there was nothing more he could do. Tom looked at him and said, "Darn, I was hoping to play more bridge." Dr. Cawley instructed me about medicines Tom should continue taking and which ones to discontinue. He said he would also arrange for hospice care.

I got Tom's walker from the trunk of the car when we arrived at the Worthington. We took the elevator to the third floor in silence. When we entered our apartment, I hugged Tom and said, "I love you so much, and I am not ready for this." Tom said, "You and I have climbed many steps together, honey. The only difference this time—Jesus is waiting for me!"

Our family was such a blessing. We had calls from those who did not live nearby. Our close friends, Linda Hall, Janet Wright, and Tom and Marlene Norman were the last ones to visit us. Tom and Marlene were there for each of Tom's hospitalizations. Our pastor, Melissa, came several times. Tiana spent time with us. On February 24, Tina, Jake, and Maddie came to stay for three days. Tom had decided to have a catheter. He said Tina and I were up with him too much at night. On the 26th, Tina and Maddie left for home, but Jake stayed two more days. It was beautiful to watch fifteen-year-old Jake help his Papo and even empty the catheter bag. Greg came on the 29th. On March 1, Joy came to check on the catheter because hospice had a problem anchoring it. On March 3, Tina was back to stay for three days. On March 6, Alice and Bev from church stayed with Tom while I attended a party for my 90th birthday that Ed had arranged at our church. I was grateful to visit with the many friends who came, but I missed having Tom by my side. Ed planned to spend the night with us.

Later that afternoon Ken called. The only words he spoke were, "Mom, I am so sick." I called 911 here and asked the operator to connect me with 911 in Milwaukee. She said that was not possible. I hung up and dialed again, receiving the same answer. Ken lived near the university, and I remembered there were two police precincts in the area. The first one I called said they could not help me. I asked to be forwarded to the other precinct. A caring sergeant who answered the phone told me not to worry. I appreciated that the Hospice Chaplin was here and offered a prayer while we waited. I received a call from the hospital saying Ken had been admitted and someone would call again after he was examined. I called Cody and asked if he could drive to Milwaukee to check on his dad. He said, "Don't worry Grandma. I will be there in two hours." Such a relief! I was so proud of Cody for the way he took over. He said his dad needed to be near him. When Ken was checked out of the hospital three days later, Cody moved him to Chilton. He had found an apartment in an independent living facility for his dad.

Dave spent all day on the 7th with us and had short visits with his dad when he was awake. I told him I thought Tom would be going home to Jesus in a couple of days. Our doctor had told us we would have Pathways Hospice, but somehow we ended up with a hospice whose office was one hour away. Their visits were sporadic. The nurse had informed me that she was leaving on a trip with her husband. I assumed a different nurse would be coming, but no one else showed up. On March 8, Anna came to spend the night. She had flown in from Texas three days before. She stood by Tom's bed and sang several hymns. He reached out to hug her. Anna and I were watching TV at 10:00 p.m. when Deb showed up. I administered Tom's morphine and anxiety meds every four hours. At 4:08 a.m., he swallowed the liquid medications. I expressed my love for him. His breathing became shallow. At 4:25 a.m. on March 9, 2018, he peacefully drew his last breath. After a few minutes, Deb, Anna, and I stood in the living room with our arms around each other as the tears fell.

Ed and Matt accompanied me to the mortuary to make funeral arrangements. I was glad to be busy with notifying family and friends of my beloved Tom's death. There was also insurance, organizations, credit cards, businesses, and charities to notify. I worked through all of it with a numbness. My mind was in a fog as I tried to concentrate. It is difficult to explain the emptiness that surrounded me, especially in the evenings. A hundred memories flooded my mind. Little things like gently rubbing oil on Tom's face or reaching out to hold his hand before falling asleep. I did give thanks to God that Tom was no longer in pain, but I felt like part of me had been amputated. An unexpected yearning for Susie became prevalent.

Once a week Tiana and I watched movies. I loved her company. Later, she spent 10 days with me while waiting for an apartment. My sons called to check on me. I felt so deeply blessed when Ed and Dave, individually, expressed that I was their best friend. Ken said I was his angel and best friend. I gave thanks while hearing those sweet words as I remembered the mistakes I made as a parent.

Tom's service was on May 20, one day short of his ninety-first birthday. Anna and Tiana sang, "How Great Thou Art." Ed, Greg and Matt shared memories. On the front of the bulletin were words Matt wrote about his grandfather:

An athlete and a farmer
A warrior and a veteran
A husband and a father
A grandfather and great-grandfather
A Christian and an example
A patriot and a patriarch
A man of great legacy

David shared memories about his dad and sang, "I Can Only Imagine." I dedicated Tom's cap to our friend, David H., a cap that Tom wore especially on workdays at the church. It said, "Everyone is entitled to my opinion." Our pastor, Melissa, was a great help in having the bulletin printed and organizing the service. Her meditation offered words of encouragement, as she captured all of Tom—his witness of love for others, his servant heart, sense of humor, and mischievous acts. As people left, there were many comments that Tom would have loved the celebration of his life and how uplifting the service was. Forty-eight family members were among those attending the service. We were blessed by their presence and all others. The family visited over lunch and into early evening with memories of Tom. As I prepared for bed, grief and tears shook my entire body. I fell into bed, exhausted. In the morning, I was awakened by a bird's song. I smiled and prepared to face another day without Tom, leaning on God's strength.

The rest of 2018 was a blur. I continued my activities, doing necessary chores, attending worship service, praying with and for friends. Needy friends and acquaintances seemed to spring up everywhere. I thanked God for sending them into my presence and prayer life. There were times voices sounded as if they were in a tunnel. Then, during conversations, my heart and mind would think of Tom and Susie. Settling down in the evenings, I was grateful for the TV or texts that filled some of the void. My friend, Kitty, who was like a sister, called or sent texts of understanding with words of comfort and love every week for several months. Her husband had died from a heart attack when they lived in Illinois. Ed, Ken, and Dave often called or sent texts. The most difficult and lonely day of the week was Sunday. Tom and I had been together in worship services since we were teenagers. Tears flowed from time to time. I thanked God for a husband who was devoted, knew my heart so well, encouraged me, and demonstrated his love for me. My heart and mind

---

Lament for My Husband
My Love and Best Friend

How I miss you, Tom. My world is empty and the silence is deafening. I know that seventy years of marriage, plus the three years of dating, writing letters, and being together was a blessing, but it still did not seem long enough. Funny thing that in all of our sharing there was more to say before you slipped away. I wonder if I told you enough times how much I loved you? I miss our talks, praying together and holding hands. Love's chain of memories brings smiles and tears as my heart aches with indescribable emptiness. I long to feel your touch, to see your smile and the mischief in your eyes. Times of laughter, love, hugs, arguing, sharing, understanding, forgiving and praying together flood my mind. Just being together, enjoying each other's presence. The way you teased me and your thoughtfulness. Roses for every occasion with expressions of your love. I am so grateful for you, my godly husband. You lived your life with integrity, humility and humor, sharing the love of Jesus with countless others. You were a Christian example and witness to our immediate and extended family. You faced each diagnosis with courage and grace as you expressed concern for me. Tears flow as I sit in your chair and cradle your picture, longing to hear your voice and feel your touch. I cannot explain my grief. I know God shares the depth of my grief, and I pray for His strength as I experience each day without you. I give thanks that God granted us seventy years of marriage, but the hole in my heart remains. Goodbye, my love, until we meet again in God's heavenly realm.

— 2018

became buried in those blessings and there were more times I experienced joy in the Lord through the heartache.

Then, suddenly, I was not the person I thought I was, as Satan attacked me. I had difficulty sleeping and asked God to take my negative and guilty thoughts away. I read about others who had similar experiences after the death of a loved one. I was in misery as I waited on God. Actually, I felt as though I was in a deep pit. This was foreign to me. I had left a crack in my armor that allowed the father of lies to creep in. Time passed before the Holy Spirit convicted me of self-pity. Throughout my life experiences, I never remembered feeling sorry for myself. I asked for an explanation. When and how did I wallow in self-pity, Lord? The Holy Spirit made it clear that I was undone about all the attention Tom received after his death. Most people did not ask how I was doing. They expressed how much they missed Tom. I realized, more than ever, that countless others were grieving Tom's passing with me. They missed his presence, hugs, witness, and sense of humor. In my sorrow, I had left negative thought cracks for Satan. and he had his fun making me miserable. I confessed my sins and asked God's forgiveness. I prayed for him to renew my mind and heart and spirit. Another two weeks passed before I felt God's warm hug as He delivered me from that dark pit. *Psalm 18:1*, "I love you, O Lord my strength. The Lord is my rock, my fortress, my deliverer."

We had a surprise visit from Jenn and Thomas. Thomas was eight and we had not seen him since he was a baby. He was so cute! We visited the farm and took a picture of Thomas in front of the sign, "Nix Natural Area." Ken's adopted son, Johnathan, had abandoned Jenn and Thomas and disappeared, running away from his responsibilities as a father and husband. Such heartache! Tom's health had prevented us from visiting them in Arizona. We were grateful that Jenn's parents provided them with a loving home. I always smile as I prepare a birthday card for Thomas each October and look forward to the time Jenn and Thomas can visit again.

Dave and Deb's daughter, Jordan, and Danny became acquaintances in their freshman year at Colorado State University. They came for Christmas which was a treat. We enjoyed Christmas Eve dinner at the Olive Garden with them, Ed, Marilyn, Dave, Deb and Anna. Anna gave me a bear dressed in a Navy uniform. She asked me to touch the bear's hand. Anna had recorded Tom's voice saying, "I love you very much, honey." What a wonderful gift. I cherish listening to Tom's voice—often.

My grief widened as dear friends, Marilyn Goodrich and Linda Hall passed away. Marilyn and I had been close friends for 60 years. Ed, Marilyn, and I spent time with her as she celebrated her 90th birthday. She died shortly afterward. Linda was like a daughter to Tom and me. She was always there, insisting on taking charge of food for our anniversary celebrations. She lit up the room with her joy. Linda fought stage 4 colon cancer with courage and grace as she continued to help others until she became bedfast. I cherished the years, and especially the last month, I spent with her.

A big event in 2019 was the wedding of grandson Josh and beautiful Karen in Hawaii on the island of Maui. Greg and Tina were so kind to pay for my airfare and lodging. Josh arranged lodging in a lovely, spacious beach house on the oceanfront for Greg, Tina, Tiana, Jake, Maddie, and me. The house was near the ocean. I usually arose before the others and enjoyed my first cup of coffee on the deck. I observed many changing moods of the ocean, the dancing sunlight beams across the water, ships in the distance, swooping birds and their calls. I thanked God for the peace and beauty that surrounded me. A gentle breeze touched my cheek as I thought of Tom and Susie. After a few minutes, Greg and Tina joined me with their coffee. The beach house was a short distance from Jim's lovely home where Josh's dad's wonderful party ensued. We became acquainted with Karen's large family. On June 13, Josh and Karen were married in Jim's beautiful yard on the oceanfront. Additional family members who joined in the fun and festivities were Ed, Marilyn, Jake, Beth, Page, Clare, Alicia, and Bill. We enjoyed food, fun and reminiscing. I grew fond of the White Russians bartenders Greg and Jake made for me. What a joyous time! The flight home was good. I spent the night at Greg and Tina's. Whenever I visited Greg and Tina, Tina would pick me up in Fort Collins and bring me back home. Since I had decided not to drive on I-25 South, she was always willing to make the two-hour drive, both ways. Tina was like one of my own and I was blessed by her love and kindness.

During the year, I met Hannah and her two children who had moved into a new Habitat for Humanity home. Our church matched funds that were given in memory of Tom and donated many hours in labor to build the home. Tom would be so pleased that memorial funds and lots of love labor by our brothers and sisters in Christ honored him in this way.

A Pandemic

In March 2020, our nation and the world began to deal with an outbreak of coronavirus disease (COVID-19) that began in China. The virus was costly as it ran amuck for over two years with statistics of nearly four million deaths worldwide. Supplies like toilet paper, disinfecting wipes, hand sanitizers and masks flew off the shelves. Our busy nation was almost silent. As with any pandemic, nations were thrown into turmoil and fear. Hospitals ran out of rooms and supplies to care for the sick. Doctors, nurses and other health care employees worked overtime which led to exhaustion and depression. Families were unable to visit their ill loved ones or be with them as they passed away. Nurses and doctors held the hands of the dying. Families were isolated at home while students began virtual education. Many parents worked from home while tending to their children. Teachers were on overload as they did their best to instruct online. Lockdown occurred. Some businesses never recovered. Because of the isolation, families were unable to gather. Everyone hungered for social interaction. With caution, our family did gather from time to time. I disinfected everything with Clorox wipes upon entering my vehicle and even wiped all the groceries as I unloaded them. I had been in the habit of wearing masks at times and opening doors with gloves or my coat sleeve because of my asthma.

I was looking forward to the day we would be free from COVID and its many variants. I thought of deaths that occurred during my lifetime from other pandemics/epidemics that involved smallpox, mumps, chicken pox, measles, diphtheria, typhoid fever, flu, polio, tuberculosis, malaria, and AIDS. I express gratitude for those who worked tirelessly to develop vaccines. While an epidemic refers to disease across a region, a pandemic refers to disease in many countries. The one difference of past epidemics was that the ill were quarantined to their homes unless they needed hospital care. After closing for a few weeks early in the pandemic, schools and businesses reopened.

A COVID vaccine was developed in December 2020. Adults received two injections and a booster over a period of time, with a second booster recommended in 2022. The vaccine was made available to teens and children. One can read about the turmoil, unrest, and atrocities that occurred in our country during this year and the following ones. My heart ached as "America the Beautiful" acquired deep ugly stains and scars. I prayed for our nation and our government officials to remember the principles on which our government was founded. I prayed for all parents and schools to teach responsibility, patience, kindness, acceptance and love for one another, for understanding that there are consequences for bad behavior. I prayed for God to heal our broken nation.

Leading an Open and Affirming Discernment Team

I was asked to gather and lead a discernment team for our church. Our task was to communicate with each member of the congregation to determine if Heart of the Rockies Christian Church would become Open and Affirming, a movement to welcome everyone, recognizing that God made all of us in his image. I told our pastor and the elders I would pray about this. I jokingly told them that most churches send 92-year-old members out to pasture. During the third day of asking God to lead me, I happened to find the following poem I had written years earlier:

> We Are Those Who Call Ourselves 'Christian'
> God, you have blessed us, adopted us and poured out Your favor upon us.
> We see how incredible You are! Or do we?
> Release from us the chains of prejudice, fear, hate, indifference, and apathy
> When will we learn that all are Your children, made in your image?
> When will we learn to seek understanding for those who are different?
> When will we learn to reach out to those who are shunned?
> When will we learn to grant mercy to wounded souls?
>
> Help us to respect each other's uniqueness and strive for unity of all-encompassing love.
> Forgive us, Lord! Teach us through your Holy Spirit of truth.
> Let us truly love, accept, respect, and embrace all of Your children,
> For through this, You are glorified.

The caring, competent, praying team I served with set about providing education, meetings, a Sunday School class, an evening virtual class, group and individual visits, contacting each member of the congregation. We established a timeline of one year to complete the task. Because of COVID, it took a few months longer. The congregation voted unanimously to approve our new welcome statement that was all-inclusive.

Heart of the Rockies Welcome statement:

Heart of the Rockies Christian Church (Disciples of Christ) welcomes into membership, full participation, and leadership, all persons regardless of race, ethnicity, gender identity and expression, sexual orientation, age, economic status, physical or mental ability, familial status, and faith history.

As an Open and Affirming congregation, we reach out to those who have known the pain of exclusion and discrimination by the church and society.

The Holy Spirit moves among us to create a sense of belonging to encourage love and acceptance of one another. We share the joys and challenges of what it means to grow in our love for God and our service to others. Our community is shaped by God's life-giving, life-changing unconditional grace. In turn, we strive to become a living expression of God's love.

Our Kids' Memories

Over the years, whenever our family gathered, Ed, Susie, Ken. and Dave would share memories. Here are some of their offerings: Dad was showing Pete how to operate the forklift. Somehow, Dad managed to drive it into the ground, breaking several teeth. Mom learned to repair most things around the house. She rarely asked Dad to fix anything because it would be in worse condition after his efforts. One Thanksgiving, the kitchen sink backed up. Mom got the wrenches and Dad insisted on helping. Ed said, "Dad, I can do that for you." Tom said, "Just get out of my way." Ed and Mom stepped out to the yard, laughing because they knew what was about to happen. Tom managed to twist the pipes into a tangled mess. The plumber's words were, "What in the ___ happened here?" Dad insisted on showing Ed how to ride his new Vespa scooter. He was traveling fast, turned too sharp and crashed into the fence. Mom was bouncing around in that blow-up Suma wrestling contraption trying to lose weight. She lost her balance, rolled into a corner and had to call for help. These stories remained fresh, causing much laughter. Other memories: Visits to the Museum of History in Denver, the zoo, the Cheyenne Mountain Zoo in Colorado Springs and the newly completed Air Force Academy Chapel, fishing trips to Red Feather Lakes, visits to relatives in Arizona and Oklahoma, the week vacation in Bella Vista, Arkansas at Christmastime, as well as extended visits by our cousins every year. One time we chose sides to have a dried cow pie fight. Dave threw one that was not quite dried hitting Roxie in the face! Other times remembered were going to Sunday School and church, Mom and Dad always there in support of our interests, activities and careers. Mom, building our confidence by teaching us to perform and speak in front of audiences. Mom reading Bible stories to us at bedtime. The smell of Mom's cooking. Dad pulling us in the toboggan behind the tractor on snowy fields. Being free to bring friends home without asking. Mom and Dad teaching us a strong work ethic. Ken saving a kitten's life by using mouth-to-mouth resuscitation. Ed backing our Rambler station wagon out of the garage into the feeder box which ruined the back window and cargo door. Susie insisting the dress she made for band was a perfect fit. Mom tried to guide her in making the side seams wider. When Susie first stood up at the next concert, her dress ripped down the back. Ken and Dave chasing and teasing Susie until she doubled up her fist and punched them. Ken and Dave's smoking episode. A neighbor had given them a pack of cigarettes. As punishment, Ken had to smoke in front of Mom and David in front of Dad, until the cigarettes were gone. Their stomachs paid the price. Digging for old bottles at abandoned mining sites, as well as extended visits by our cousins every year. God's miracle of transformation that took place in Dad delivering him from anger issues. The love our family had for one another.

Sidney graduated with an associate degree in English from Texas Tech in Lubbock. She married James Bradford after completing her BA at Texas A & M with a teaching certificate. I am very proud of Sidney. Gracey attended Temple College in General Studies. Alex joined the Marines, hurt his back and was dismissed. It was disappointing for him.

2020

The year 2020 was a year of celebration. Bill and Alicia's beautiful, healthy baby girl, Amelia, arrived on February 7. Alicia had the flu a few days before Amelia was born along with some complications afterward. Bill was right there to see that she had proper care. We were grateful for her recovery.

After Tom died, Tiana and I looked at Affinity Apartments where I put my name on the list. Residents were not confined to the building. They offered several amenities with a welcoming atmosphere. My apartment was on the west side with a view of the foothills. On June 1, I moved to Affinity Apartments. I was back on the east side of town where Tom and I lived for 27 years, close to family, church, former neighbors, bank, shopping, and the golf course. I hired Kid Gloves to move me. Their service was packing and unpacking. They put everything away in my new apartment and hung pictures. To my amazement, they placed books in their original order in the bookcase. I was happy with my new location. Tom, Joy, and family lived two blocks away. Ed and Marilyn were seven minutes away.

Tom and I enjoyed watching Jake, (Greg and Tina's son) wrestle and play football from grade school through high school. He graduated from high school in June. I was proud of him. I thought of how much Tom and I enjoyed visits from Jake and Maddie: sleepovers, playing rummy and other games, shopping, visits to the Discovery Museum, playing in the park, and trips to the Dollar Store.

Anna initiated an invitation to their farm for a July 4 celebration. Dave, an expert cook, manned the grill. Anna and friends set up tables in the barn. Everyone brought food. It reminded me of the good old-fashioned potluck dinners that were held at the church. I also thought of Jessie, a widow who was a member of First Christian Church at the corner of Mulberry and College. She always brought baggies and a large purse to take food home. When a couple of women loudly complained and thought it bad manners, Tom said, "This is one way we can take care of the widows as we are directed in the scriptures." We never heard another complaint, and other widows of meager means began to bring their containers to the pot luck dinners. We were sure God was smiling. Everyone enjoyed the fireworks, food, and hospitality of Dave, Deb and Anna while celebrating the birth of our nation.

My Sisters Find Me

In early July, I received a call from a person who said, "Hi Patsy, this is someone from your past." I thought the caller might be a high school or college chum, but she said, "Patsy, this is your sister." I was so excited and asked, "Are you Jackie or Yvonne?" She said, "I am Yvonne, but my name was changed to Meredith. Jackie's name was changed to Cheryl." No wonder I could not find them years ago! Meredith lived in California and Cheryl in Kansas City, Missouri. It had been 72 years since I saw those darling girls when they were two and three years old. I was 20 at the time. I then had a phone conversation with Cheryl. Both sisters asked about my brother, Bill, who had passed away in 2001.

My sisters Meredith and Cheryl (seated)

I wanted to know how they found me. David, Cheryl's grandson, indicated an interest in building a family tree. Cheryl and Meredith said, "Find our sister first." David found my name listed in the census. His real find was a picture of Tom and me celebrating our 70th wedding anniversary, which one of our grandchildren had placed on Facebook. Later, David saw Tom's obituary. He called my church and asked if I was still alive. When told I was alive and well, he asked if I was able to talk on the phone. This 30-year-old was wondering what condition I was in at age 92. Because of security, our church administrative assistant did not give him more information, but David found my phone number. My sisters and I thanked God for bringing us together. I had plans to cancel my landline the following week. We were grateful to David for his diligence in searching for me.

Later in July, Matt made arrangements for Cheryl, Meredith, and David to meet my brother's family at Old Chicago in Cheyenne. My sisters were so excited about their new-found relatives that included Ed and Marilyn, Matt, Lauren and Amber. It was also special for Ed and me, since we had not seen my brother's family for some time. I missed my sweet niece, Pam. The boys said she was the glue that held the family together after their dad died. Meredith and Cheryl were also thrilled to meet other members of the Nix family during their visit. They expressed regret about not getting to meet Bill and Tom. The three

My grandnephew, David

of us had so much to share. Their journey in life held lots of bumps, bruises, neglect, and abuse. Both Cheryl and Meredith were intelligent, talented women. They had successful careers. Cheryl was a speech pathologist, working with children. Meredith held CEO positions for two different companies. I was very proud of them and their accomplishments. We spent hours on the phone getting caught up. We each mentioned our irresponsible dad, whom we had forgiven. After all, we would not exist without him.

The next year, my sister, Meredith, came for a two-week visit. My other sister, Cheryl, and her grandson, David, came later for a week. I hosted a reunion of the Nix and Bennett families on July 24. Affinity Apartments, where I live, has a family/game room for gatherings. There were 30 in attendance. Meredith and Cheryl were happy to meet additional family members. We especially appreciated that David had copied many old and new pictures for everyone. We ate and thoroughly enjoyed visiting for three hours. I loved getting caught up with my sisters.

Losing Dave

I had been concerned about my son, Dave. He told me how much worse the pain in his legs had become. It was evident the circulation was poor. Dave was stubborn throughout the years about seeing doctors. It was difficult at this time, since he was at the car dealership in Denver six days a week. However, when he experienced some dizzy spells, he found a doctor in Denver who prescribed high blood pressure medication. I told Dave the blood pressure medicine would work better if he gave up drinking so much beer. He just smiled and said, "I love you, Mom." I so looked forward to our lunches together. In addition, I enjoyed once-a-month breakfasts with Dave and his best buddies from early school days. Mike and Kevin would pick me up for a trip to Greys Restaurant in Ault, Colorado, where we met Dave and Ray. The guys had made visits to our farm in their growing up years. The breakfasts were delicious, and the conversation was entertaining. It was special to witness how much the guys care about each other.

In December, Anna graduated cum laude with a degree in Criminal Justice. She had been on the Dean's list each year, coordinated tours of prisons and detention centers and was the youngest presenter at the National Conference for The Association for Treatment of Sexual Abusers. Deb and Dave flew to Texas for Anna's graduation. I found out later that Dave was unable to walk and needed a wheelchair for the trip and the graduation ceremonies. Our family was able to see the graduation exercises remotely, which was a treat. I was very proud of Anna and her accomplishments. I called Dave with more urgent concern about his health. As usual, he smiled and told me not to worry. Deb and Anna were also frustrated he did not take his condition more seriously.

In March 2021, Josh called to announce Karen had given birth to a baby girl. Little Maile was my twenty-second great-grandchild. Josh was faithful to send pictures, texts, and videos. I appreciated technology that allowed me to follow her growth. I was also blessed with pictures and videos of Amelia that Bill and Alicia sent. Bill, Alicia, and Amelia came to Fort Collins in May to say goodbye. The family joined them for breakfast at Lucille's, Bill's favorite place to eat. Alicia's three years were up at Peterson Air Force Base, and her next assignment would be in California at Edwards Air Force Base. Bill secured a job at the base which would be convenient for them.

It is amazing how God leads us to pray for those we never meet personally. I have prayed with many throughout the years during a phone call. The latest occurred when I called Caremark, the business that supplies medications through my health insurance. As I talked with the young man, he remarked about the kindness in my voice. I thanked him and asked how his day was going. He began to tell me he was bipolar and suffered from anxiety attacks. I recalled the many times Ken would call when he was having an anxiety attack, and we would pray together. I asked Angelo if he would like me to pray for him. Afterward, I assured him I would continue praying for him each day. I smile as I lift his name from my prayer box. Soon after, God prepared nurse Diane's heart when I made a trip to urgent care. I was in great pain with an intestinal infection. I asked Diane how she was and thanked her for taking my vitals. She asked, "How can you smile and think of others when you are in such pain?" I told her it was because of Jesus in my life. She left the room and quickly returned. Diane pulled a chair up and sat down facing me. She said, "I want to thank you. I am a believer, but I have been backsliding for a long time. I am going to ask God to forgive me and restore my dead spirit." We gave thanks to God for His love and allowing us to meet each other. His plans carry blessings unnumbered.

Donnie, Ken's stepdaughter, graduated from Texas A&M with a degree in Liberal Studies after receiving her Associate Degree in Business Administration. She updated me as she progressed through school while holding down a job. Donnie returned to school after several years, which was quite an accomplishment. I was very proud of her. Donnie and James, her husband, stopped for a visit later in the year. It was delightful to hug them and catch up on family news.

On June 1, 2021, Deb called to say that Dave had passed away. She was at yoga exercise in Greeley when Dave's boss called to say he had not shown up for work. Deb hurried home and found Dave face down behind his pickup. He was preparing to leave for work when he suffered a heart attack. Deb attempted to revive Dave without success. The medics also tried. I can only imagine what Deb went through at the time. I called Ed. He sent an email to our family. Matt called and said he would drive Ed and me to be with Deb at the home place between Kersey and LaSalle. Matt always shows up during a crisis. Deb had called the sheriff and was talking with her and the deputies when we arrived. Her good friend, Marcy, was with her. During the next four hours, we stood in the road or visited in the car to support Deb. No one was allowed on the property because of the investigation. All the while, my heart was breaking. Deb told us the doctor had recently increased Dave's high blood pressure medication. We later learned he had fallen twice within a week at work. Matt and Ed communicated with the deputies. The coroner arrived and took Dave's body. We left after Deb's sister and brother arrived. On the way home, we remarked how Dave disliked seeing doctors. If he suspected he had the flu or other illness, he picked up penicillin from his veterinary friends. I offered to write and pay for Dave's obituary. I sent copies to Deb, Anna, and Jordan, and also to Deb's sister and mother. What I wrote received approval from everyone. I was so devastated that writing the obituary was difficult, but I was glad to help in that way. Deb's father had died a short time before, so she and the girls were still dealing with his death. These facts did not lessen my overwhelming grief at losing my youngest son. When I gave birth to my children, I had no idea I would lose any of them. I should have gone first.

Lament for My Son
My Beloved David

Tears come at all times as I try to cope with the reality that you, my youngest, sweet son is gone. I cry out to God in my grief that is felt in every part of my entire being. You are absent from family and holiday gatherings where you were always joyful with smiles and a joke for every occasion. In the place where you were, there is a void too deep to describe. Another hole has been carved in my heart. I loved your smiling face as I sang to you. You were my baby who hummed tunes before you could talk. At age 5, you showed me a bumble bee sitting in the middle of your hand and said, "Mommy, look at this friendly bee. God sure knows how to make beautiful things." Because you loved the farm and all the animals, you wanted to stay home and work with Dad instead of attending kindergarten. At age 13 your first music compositions were praise songs to God. You wrote and shared other songs about love, life and memories. I long to hear you sing and play the guitar. I miss our talks and your smiling face. Memories of your birth, childhood, baptism, teen years, adulthood, kindness, thoughtfulness and love are etched in my heart. Also, other memories of the wonderful father you were to Jordan and Anna. You were thoughtful with calls or arranging lunches after your dad died. Dad and I were so proud of your accomplishments: top award at the county fair and citywide music competitions; national championships at wrestling and rodeoing; top salesman awards at car dealerships and one hundred percent customer satisfaction that covered four states. You used all the talents God gave to you. Throughout trials in your lifetime, you held tight to Jesus. Only God knows the number of low-income families you helped to own a vehicle because of your astute business skills and lovingkindness. You truly loved your neighbor. I never heard you speak an unkind word about anyone. As I leaned on God for strength, I remembered the last line from one of your songs: "I am free. No worries now. It is easy to see what Jesus has done for me." Because of what Jesus has done for us, I will see you again, my dear son, in our heavenly home.

--2021

Torrents of tears blurred my sight as I wrote about David. I was doubled over with grief. My mind was also flooded with memories of Tom and Susie. When one loses loved ones, tears are triggered by memories and photos. Other times, they fall while driving the car, looking at beautiful sunsets, watching TV, listening to music, singing hymns, and other reminders. They even come as surprises, unannounced, while shopping for groceries or engaging in other life events. Through my tears and heartache, I thanked God for holding me close. Life is never the same, but God continues to comfort and lead me BY HIS HAND as he floods my soul with rays of hope, grace, mercy, and love, giving me strength and joy for each tomorrow.

Ed and I spoke at Dave's service. Among those attending were several nieces and nephews which warmed our hearts. Although Ken was not well, he flew in from Wisconsin. Ed and I were so happy to spend time with him. Cousin Dennis picked Ken up at the airport and stayed with him the entire time. They were best friends. We later learned Dennis has been diagnosed with stage 4 colon cancer. Anna spoke about her dad and sang, "I Can Only Imagine." Dave had sung the same song for Susie's and Tom's services. Dave's boss handed me a note that read, "Dave was a treasure in my life and so easy to work with. He always performed his job with joy."

Three weeks after David passed into the arms of Jesus, I received word that my nephew, Jack, was found dead in his home. Jack was the youngest son of Tom's brother, Joe, and his wife, Lora. He and David were best buddies when they were little. Jack became a recluse, but his sister, Judy, with husband, Darius, visited him on occasion. I continued to send Christmas cards through the years with no response. When Jack's next-door neighbor realized she had not seen him for some time, she called the police. Jack was diabetic. It appeared that he had fallen, hit his head and died the same week as David. Our family grieved his passing as we prayed for his siblings.

July 4th was Dave and Anna's favorite holiday. Anna was able to come home for the weekend. She and Deb planned a family and friends potluck celebration, including fireworks, in honor of Dave. We had a wonderful time listening to the booms and seeing beautiful art fall from the sky. The children loved their sparklers. Anna's boyfriend, David, who was a police officer, assisted in many ways throughout the evening. Our family was quite impressed and gave a thumbs up to Anna for her choice.

In December, Anna passed her final exam and graduated from the police academy, passed her state exam, and was officially commissioned and sworn in as a law enforcement officer in the state of Texas. She made the family proud. Anna began her rookie police officer status by working the night shift in College Station, Texas. My daughter-in-law, Deb, a woman of deep faith, continued to deal with the loss of Dave, her dad, and mother. Losing those loved ones within a year also remained fresh for Jordan and Anna. Deb lived with Anna while she searched for an apartment in Texas. I looked forward to each of Deb's visits as we shared coffee or lunch together.

2021

Over a period of two years, Ed and Marilyn had been sharing their desire to live in Cheyenne, Wyoming. Ed reiterated about high taxes and congested traffic in Fort Collins. In September of 2021, Ed and Marilyn purchased a home in West Cheyenne. I was glad to help with packing. Their new home has miles of open space where antelope and deer often wander up to their fence. The home is spacious, larger than their former home. Marilyn enjoyed painting in her expansive art studio. The neighbors were welcoming. All things led to a slower pace of life and enjoyment of living in a smaller community. Matt, Lauren and Amber already lived in Cheyenne, and Matt and Lauren's offices were one half mile away.

On July 8, 2021, I attended my 75th high school reunion at Boulder High School. My good friend, Judy Partain, accompanied me. There were ten of us—so happy to see each other. We knew of three other classmates who could not attend. The assistant principal of Boulder High treated us royally. We were shown the new additions of the school. We met in a nice area of the cafeteria and enjoyed eating lunch from Chick-fil-A. Our group thanked Lynden Peterson for arranging our reunion. After each person shared what happened in their lives since our last reunion five years ago, we had a songfest. I had fun leading the singing. We sang songs like Mairzy Doats, One-Z-Two Z, Swinging on a Star, Don't Fence Me In, You Made Me Love You, This Land is Your Land, Whistle While You Work, God Bless America, and the Boulder High School Fight Song. Everyone sang with gusto! Our graduation class was closely knit. We had a reunion every five years. After a wonderful afternoon, we said goodbye. There were no frowns or regrets as we parted company, only hugs and smiles, knowing we would see each other again and sing with gusto in heaven.

The following weekend, Meredith and I left for Winter Park. Greg and Tina had invited us to stay in their condo for two nights. We drove over the Trail Ridge Road, enjoying God's beautiful creation around every curve. We stopped at the summit, where Cara, Meredith's granddaughter, was employed for the summer. It was a treat to meet my grandniece, and we visited more the next weekend in Estes Park. We relished our time with Greg, Tina, and family while enjoying our visit with the Hunters: Greg's dad, stepmother and their family. A tradition on Thursday evening is to gather at Hernando's Pub, where we enjoyed good food, drink and fellowship. Friday morning was a busy time. Checkout was 10 a.m. so after the vehicles were loaded, we hugged goodbye and asked God for safe travels.

In August, my niece, Judy, called to tell me that Joe (Tom's brother's son) had a brain bleed. Joe, his wife, Rosie, and family operated a Christian Ministry for men without fathers at the ranch near Gardner, Colorado. Rosie offered updates and I was able to speak with Joe a few days after his surgery. God answered our prayers as Joe gained strength each day and recovered. *Isaiah 26:3* "He will keep in perfect peace all those who trust in him, for in the Lord Jehovah is your everlasting strength."

Delightful times occur when Judy comes to visit. On one occasion, she forgot her cell phone and wandered around Fort Collins trying to find Doug's Diner where Ed, Marilyn, and I were waiting. It is a laughable matter each time we talk or see each other. I am so grateful for the thoughtfulness of my nieces and nephews and pray daily for them.

My niece, Roxie, daughter of Tom's sister, Mary Jane, and her husband, Lester, came for a visit. It was so good to be with them. They stayed in the guest suite at my apartment building. Roxie has been faithful in keeping family events and pictures. She never misses remembering me on special holidays with cards. We reminisced about the many times the family gathered at our farm and at reunions. I shared stories about Mary Jane that Roxie had never heard. I found one of the letters

Mary Jane sent to me when she was in the service and gave it to Roxie. Later, I found another one, which I mailed to Roxie. She made copies for her siblings, Gay, Dennis, and Lora.

Dennis was going through surgeries, chemotherapy, and radiation during the year. Each time we talked, he was upbeat, thanking God for walking beside him and the blessing of his family. Giving thanks to God in difficult times brings peace. Dennis enjoyed talking about our farm and the many times Bob, Mary Jane, and family visited us. He recalled getting into mischief with Ken and David: they engaged in escapades along the river like darting across the flume to the other side, which was against the rules; swimming in the river on hot summer days. They escaped from the world along the riverbanks. Dennis even remarked about the make-shift treehouse in the oldest tree where Ken and David hid him for over two weeks when he ran away from home. They tried to shoot mice that were invading the animal feed with BB guns. They hurried through chores so they could be about more mischief. Our family continued to pray for God to sustain Dennis through the coming months of treatment and surgery.

Ed and Marilyn hosted the family for Thanksgiving in their new home in Cheyenne. Ed prepared the turkey, ham, potatoes, and gravy. It was very tasty along with all the other food everyone brought. The family gathered at Tom and Joy's for a potluck at Christmas. Wonderful aromas filled the air from different soups. We also feasted on hors d'oeuvres, salads, rolls, and many desserts. My delight was watching the great-grandchildren open their packages. The next joy was wishing Ed a happy birthday and singing the Happy Birthday song to Alicia over the phone on Christmas Day.

2022

The year 2022 began with surgery for me. A pacemaker was implanted to assist with my irregular heartbeat. My cardiologist had encouraged the surgery for two years. I thought I was feeling OK since I continued to walk a mile every day, engage in other exercises, and participate in church and community events. I was diagnosed with congestive heart failure. Tina and Greg took me to MCR Hospital in Loveland at 5:30 a.m. on January 10. Greg waited while Tina stayed with me during recovery. I was able to go home around 3 p.m. Greg and Tina stayed overnight. I was so grateful for their love and thoughtfulness. My good friend, Judy Partain, took care of me for four days. I was recovering nicely but was told not to lift my left arm above elbow level for six weeks which prevented me from doing the smallest chores. Trying to dress was a challenge and laughable. A contortionist would have done it well. I learned to function well only using my right arm. Judy came back twice to make my bed. She is such a dear friend and is considered part of the family. Grandson Tom, called often, as always, to ask if I needed anything. He and Joy brought groceries countless times to my apartment and refused reimbursement. I thought of *1 Timothy 5:3* that speaks of children and grandchildren taking care of their families. When I was back to normal, I realized the pacemaker made a great deal of difference in my breathing and stamina. My good friend, Jane Shouse, had a pacemaker, and she suggested that I invest in a medical alert system. I dragged my feet because I did not want the item dangling around my neck. During the next two months, I saw my regular cardiologist, the surgeon, and technicians, who tested my pacemaker. A checkup with my oncologist revealed near normal counts for carcinoid tumors. All was well. Thank you, God.

In March, Ed organized a gathering for family and close friends at BJ's restaurant for my 94th birthday. Such a joyful time. Afterward, Ed remarked how he, Susie, Ken, and Dave thought Tom would outlive me. Ed was referring to the twelve major surgeries plus illnesses I had, including three bouts of pneumonia. During those times, I asked God to protect my children's emotions and strengthen their spirits. I was thankful for their resilience and faith as God encouraged them with His steadfast love and protection.

Spring, fall, and Christmastime brought delight in attending the great-grandchildren's programs and concerts in Fort Collins. I recalled the joy I felt in teaching K-12 music, supervising the school district music program and directing church and community choirs. I was also given the privilege to work with preschoolers in town. I thought of Josh and Emily in their preschool programs. Josh was a shepherd. At one point in the program, he took the bandana from his head, twirled it and threw it into the audience. Emily lifted the bottom of her dress to wipe a runny nose!

Tom and Joy continued to check in with me and ask if I needed groceries or help with anything. I was very appreciative of their thoughtfulness and help. Calls, texts and holiday cards came from other loved ones which made my heart sing.

Ken endured another serious surgery. This time, it was on his neck. After recovery, he received minimal improvement on the nerve pain in his legs and arms. After experiencing disappointment and poor treatment at a pain clinic, he began searching for a pain doctor who was noted for up-to-date pain treatment.

Dave's close friends from kindergarten days are so good to me. I enjoy being with them periodically for lunch. Mike sent a text the last week in May, remembering that Dave would be gone a year on June 1 and we should have breakfast that day. Mike and Kevin picked me up to meet Ray, Billie, and Rusty at the restaurant. As we sat down, I noticed an empty chair in honor of David. We all missed David and his joyous presence. Billie presented me with a dozen beautiful red roses. As I placed them in a vase at home, they reminded me of the beautiful red roses Tom gave me for every special occasion.

On June 3, Alicia was officially recognized as a Lieutenant Colonel in the Air Force. We were able to watch the ceremony virtually. We listened to the accolades spoken about her achievements over the past fourteen years. Wow! Our family is so proud of her. My heart was warmed as she spoke appreciation to the following: her husband and best friend, Bill, who was holding precious Amelia, her parents, brothers, and Bill's parents. I cherished her words about me. Alicia spoke of those in the Air Force who contributed to her advancement. Of course, I was not surprised at her accomplishments. Alicia showed leadership qualities, determination, and integrity from her childhood years. She is trustful, talented, fun-loving, and thoughtful with a kind heart. She can be tough when merited—just the type of leadership we need from those who are protecting our country. The only thing that would have made me happier is to have watched the ceremony in person so I could give Alicia a hug.

In June, Luke, Maddie, and Paige graduated from high school. I was so proud of these great-grandchildren and count it a privilege to be alive. Luke said, "Not everyone has the opportunity to enjoy being around their great-grandparents." I was not able to attend Paige's graduation in

Indiana. Luke attended Liberty Commons, an outstanding charter school in Fort Collins. The graduation ceremony began with a pledge to the American flag, followed by singing The Star-Spangled Banner. It brought back memories of a time when all graduation ceremonies began the same way. Luke sang a solo with the choir. He participated in choir and played trombone in jazz band and the advanced band. Naturally, it was a treat to attend the concerts where Samuel also played in the advanced band. Luke enrolled at Front Range Community College in Fort Collins. Maddie's graduation, held at the convention center in downtown Denver, was also impressive for all who were homeschooled. Maddie, an athlete, participated in basketball, volleyball and track. A talented artist, she enrolled at The Rocky Mountain School of Art and Design in Denver. Paige, a talented athlete, played lacrosse and ran track. She enrolled at Auburn University in Alabama.

Every once in a while, a grandchild would ask if there were slang words when I was in high school and college. I shared a few: Everything was swell or hunky dory instead of "cool." Old cars were called a jalopy. We said words like pshaw, fiddlesticks, holey moley, jeepers creepers, jumping jehoshaphat. Dream boat was a handsome guy. Cookie was a cute girl. Drip was someone boring. Yuck was having to do homework. Cutting a rug was dancing. hot diggity dog meant wow. What's buzzin' cousin? meant how is it going? Holy mackerel meant very impressed. Knuckle sandwich meant punching someone. Cable is a slang word meaning upset or angry). *Ah Nee Ah* means really). Phrases we heard often were, "Straighten up and fly right. I haven't seen you since you were knee high to a grasshopper. Close the door, were you born in a barn? Wear your best bib and tucker. Don't take any wooden nickels. Get the lead out. Use some elbow grease on that job. You sound like a broken record. Quit your bellyaching, and so many more. Tiana asked how outhouses were cleaned. I explained that when one filled up, another deep hole was dug and the building was moved over it. Then, the previous hole was filled with dirt. She said, "Gross!" In those days, we used magazine pages for cleaning. We called the Sears Roebuck & Co. catalog "Rears and Sore Butt. "

My days are filled with family, golf, bridge groups, lunches with friends, activities at the Affinity where I live, PEO meetings, Bible study, Elders' meetings, calling on the sick, praying for others, and worshiping with brothers and sisters in Christ on Sundays.

Texting and talking with family is always special. I especially love the pictures of Bill, Alicia, and Amelia and the frequent videos and Facetimes from Josh, allowing me to watch Maile grow. At a year and six months, she looks into the phone and says, "Hi Mamo." I have been so blessed by my heavenly Father!

In July, Josh, Karen and Maile came for a visit. How exciting to lay eyes on Maile and hold her. We drove to Wyoming for a visit with Ed and Marilyn. Ed treated us to lunch. At the restaurant, Maile was checking things out while Josh kept up with her. She stopped at one table and put her hand up for a high-five. She's a very active little girl. In the vehicle, it was a treat to sit in the back seat by Maile. Their visit was much too short, but I was grateful for the time we had together.

Women at the Well, a group in our church, meets monthly for dinner. We were sitting in a beautiful area outside a restaurant when my friend, Karen, began to choke. She stood up, walked a few steps and bent over attempting to dislodge the food. I asked if she was alright. She shook her head, no. It was the first time I used the Heimlich Maneuver. Thanks be to God, it worked. At church the next Sunday, Karen thanked me for saving her life. We both knew the thanks belongs to God who gave me the ability to help.

Jake and Beth invited me to stay in their condo at Winter Park the end of July which included my friend, Judy, who was kind enough to drive on busy highways. We had stayed in Greg and Tina's condo the previous year. Jake, Beth, and the girls came every other year, so it was a chance to spend some time with them. My cardiologist was not keen on my going to a higher altitude because of the pacemaker. He finally agreed. I promised at the sign of any trouble, I would head back home. I was able to tolerate the high altitude, even while taking a walk each day. Thank you, God. Paige and Clare who had separate rooms, doubled up, so Judy and I could share a room It was wonderful to be with Jake, Beth, and the girls as well as Greg, Tina, and family each day, and the extended Hunter family. Jake had become owner of Results Unlimited Company where he had been employed for years. Beth is now Senior Associate Athletic Director at Notre Dame. I am proud of their achievements.

In August, Cheryl, Meredith, and I hosted another family reunion at BJ's restaurant in Fort Collins. Meredith was the cashier. Cheryl made balloon figures for the children. She had performed as Petunia the Clown at community events and church for many years. Everyone enjoyed pizza, lemon thyme chicken with rice, salads, and soft drinks. Deb, Joel and Susan, Laurie and family, Pat and Danica, Rose and Julie's husband, Jim, joined us for the first time. Others attending were David P., Tom, Joy, Luke, Samuel, Micah, Emily, Danny, Ryan, Sam, Bill, Barry, Patrick, and Sheila. It was a wonderful afternoon of visiting and taking pictures. We were already looking forward to next year's gathering. Meredith had broken a bone in her foot. She was wearing a boot which did not stop her from going and doing. As always, I felt blessed to be with both of my sisters and great nephew, David, who had searched for me, making it possible for Cheryl, Meredith, and me to see and enjoy each other after being apart for seventy-two years.

A short time after the reunion, Joe and Linda Cowan presented me with 12 copies of my poetry, thoughts and prayers in book form, the number I would need for my immediate family. Previously, Linda had asked if she and Joe could publish my poems. Those two dear friends in Christ worked tirelessly in editing, typing, and choosing graphics. Linda had medical problems stemming from previous surgery for an artificial heart valve. I was especially grateful for her astute work as I witnessed her faith and joy in the Lord. The three of us sat in the lobby of the apartment building where I lived, as I looked through the book. It was beautifully done. A friend from Bible study asked what we were doing. Joe showed her the book. She said, "You know, Patsy, there will be more than your immediate family who would like a copy." I stopped at Legends who put the book together and ordered more copies.

Ken called to tell me that he could not walk. We were so hoping the neck surgery was an answer to his pain and mobility. He found it difficult to use the walker which had been his companion for the past eight years. My silent reaction was, "Oh No!" Ken said he felt led to find another doctor. I asked the Lord to please guide the search and told him softly that I did not want to lose another child. The Spirit with me said, "Be thankful and think of me." *Col 3:2* 'Set your minds on things above, not on earthly things." I thanked God for His abundant blessings and asked His help to keep my thoughts on Him and my eyes on Jesus.

Ken did find a different doctor, whose goal was to help patients walk. It was a hallelujah day when Ken called to tell me he could walk, unassisted. He went on to explain the doctor had helped numerous sedentary people walk by installing a spinal cord stimulator that is programmed to the nervous system. Ken said, "I cannot stop praising God, Mom! I am also grateful for the wonderful doctor. After eight years, I was able to visit with Cody's friends at his barbeque." Cody occasionally invited friends and their families for an outing. He cut and patched plastic barrels together to pull younger children behind the tractor. Ken was delighted to ride with him and walk along the river. Cody also had carts for the older children. He is very thoughtful of others, including the care and love he extends to his dad. Ken was able to attend the church where he was active years ago. He shared his good news with the pastor and others.

On September 30, I enjoyed a visit from Cherie, Meredith's daughter and my niece, whom I had not met. I did spend time, previously, with her sweet daughter, Cara. Cherie shared about others in her family. I hope to meet them some day. I loved our time together.

Ken experienced a setback. During church services, he collapsed and spent two days in the hospital. His family doctor thought atrial fibrillation had caused the problem, but scans and tests of his heart were good. After being home for a day, he experienced other problems. His hands swelled and he had no appetite. I prayed with him. Another two days in the hospital with further tests convinced doctors that Ken was showing signs of an autoimmune disease. He was to see a rheumatologist as soon as an appointment could be made. In the ensuing days, the hand swelling decreased, and Ken was feeling better. He said, "Mom, I am praising God and thanking Him every day. I can still walk and notice some improvement in the leg and arm pains. God is so good." *Psalm 63:4,* "I will praise you as long as I live, and in your name, I will lift up my hands."

December brought more family health concerns. My sweet daughter-in-law, Marilyn, was diagnosed with sudden onset aggressive leukemia. Ed first cared for Marilyn at home, which proved to be difficult. With encouragement from the children and a caregiver friend, Marilyn entered the Davis Hospice Center in Cheyenne. It's a beautiful facility where patients have suites instead of rooms. On Christmas Day, fifteen family members gathered in her suite. We were pleased when Marilyn recognized us as one by one we went to her bed—a blessing, because she had been struggling with dementia. (Ed and I recognized signs of memory difficulties in 2016. In 2018, Marilyn was diagnosed with mild to moderate cognitive impairment. As the disease progressed, Ed began to do all the shopping, cooking, cleaning, and lovingly caring for Marilyn.) Alicia and Amelia flew from California. What a treat to see them. As I watched Alicia try to keep up with two-and-a-half-year-old Amelia, I said, "She reminds me of you at that age!" Bill had driven from California with their dogs, Poseidon and George. I was delighted with a two-hour visit from Bill, Alicia, and energetic, darling Amelia before their return to California.

Ken

On December 15, Cody took Ken to the hospital in Appleton, Wisconsin. Tests showed he had pneumonia, RSV, and type 2 flu. The doctor was having difficulty administering the amount of oxygen Ken needed because his CO2 levels were high. Cody was with his dad most of the time. The doctor and nurses were not encouraging. After a few days, the doctor told us that Ken would not make it. Cody and I, through tears, were trying to make a decision. We told the doctor to go ahead with disconnecting Ken's life support, and we waited to see what God would do. The next morning around 5:15 a.m., Ken began to rally. In another two days, he was released from the hospital. The doctor said, "You have a Christmas miracle." We could not express enough gratitude to God for the miracle of his life. Cody and Angela give loving support to Ken. The two of them also spend Sundays with Ken and keep track of his needs.

Ken's recovery was slow. Because of the trauma his body experienced, the nerve support for his legs ceased to function. Ken needed the walker for support again, which was discouraging. We continued to thank God for the miracle of his life. We understand living in a sinful world means Christians are not exempt from suffering and tragedy. Our hope is in God who sustains us, granting peace, love, and strength.

2023

In January 2023 granddaughter Anna received an award for enforcement efforts for drivers under the influence. She continues to work the night shift as a police officer in College Station, Texas. I pray daily for her safety. My good friend, Terry, picks me up for dinner and bridge the first Thursday of each month. On January 4 at 5:00 a.m., Terry accompanied me to eye surgery, such a dear friend. For years, Terry, Judy Partain, Linda Hardy and I have played golf together. We are a happy foursome!

On January 16, fourteen family members gathered in Marilyn's suite for her seventy-fourth birthday. It was one of her good days. She looked beautiful and enjoyed the party, flowers, and cards from family and friends. She recognized us. We will have memories through the many pictures taken. I spent the weekend with Ed. He continued to deal with a painful back and foot.

In February, six of David's close friends took me out to celebrate Valentine's Day and my upcoming March birthday. They presented me with beautiful flowers and a box of candy that measured fifteen inches by two feet. I never saw so many chocolates! Even though I shared with friends, I ate far too many. The lovely card was signed, "All Your Stepsons." David would smile at the way they show such love for me. I am even on their text thread which is so enjoyable. Sometimes I enter in, but it is such fun to read about their lives, what is on their minds, and the way they feel free to express themselves knowing I read every word! I am truly blessed.

My dear friend Judy had not seen Ed and Marilyn's home, so she chauffeured us to Cheyenne. Judy was impressed with Marilyn's beautiful paintings in the art studio. I am glad to have three of them on my walls. Ed treated us to lunch before we visited Marilyn at the Cheyenne Hospice Center. She was asleep when we arrived. After forty-five minutes, she began to stir, opened her eyes and said "Hi." She was disoriented that day and began to search through everything in the room for something she could not identify. Ed asked, "Marilyn, can I help you find something?" She said, "I don't know." This action, along with others, causes high frustration for those with dementia. Ed offered his calming suggestion for her to sit down and visit. She gave us hugs and we visited for a short while before leaving.

On March 4, Ed planned a big party at BJ's Restaurant for my 95th birthday. Always thoughtful, Ed never forgets special days and events and treated everyone to a buffet. I never dreamed God would grant me such long life. (I express thanks to Him every morning, praying that what I do and say pleases Him.) The party included 22 family members and long-time friends, Ed and Becky Harper, Joe and Linda Cowan, Kitty Voss, and Judy Partain, who made my birthday very special. We all missed Marilyn's presence but had good reports that she was doing better. A surprise was Alicia's presence. She had flown in the night before, treated me to dinner and spent the night. It was so special to have that time with her. Besides that celebration, the management of Affinity, where I live, had a special time to recognize birthdays. In addition, I was overwhelmed with texts, calls, cards, and lunches with friends. It appears that longevity gives people more cause to celebrate in case one is not around for the next one. Smiles! Speaking of age, Amber was gently passing her fingers over my veins in my hands. She asked if they hurt. I assured her that they did not hurt and explained that with age the skin grows thin, making veins more prominent. I have told many of my younger friends that with age one dries up—inside and out. The most disappointing "dry up" I experienced was that of my singing voice. I sang my last solo for worship service when I was 92. Since then, much as I try, the dryness caused from age and asthma medications prevented me from soaring through the music. While singing along in church, there are time my voice stops. It is then that I sing with my heart.

Alicia is Deputy Commander for AFOTEC Detachment 5 which involves operational tests for all fixed and rotary wing aircraft (except fighters) that the Air Force is acquiring. She is being transferred to Washington, D.C. Her future job in Washington, D.C. will be a Division Chief for a study group conducting research on a variety of technical and military operational issues. Bill, Alicia's husband, has been the Industrial Project Manager for Pratt and Whitney, where they do testing on the F-35 engines which have taken the place of the F-16 fighters. His next job in the Washington, D.C. area will be managing the engine mock-ups for CTOL/STOVL engines for Pratt and Whitney. Bill and Alicia have both been recognized for excellence in their professions. Our family is proud of their achievements.

Ed gave constant updates to the family about Marilyn who has many good days at the hospice center. She certainly fooled the doctor who said she would not live past January. The family was looking forward to celebrating Ed and Marilyn's 50th anniversary on May 5.

Family and friends celebrated Tiana's graduation on March 24 in the Agave Room at the Rio Restaurant. The burritos and margaritas were delicious. Ed, Judy, and I took an Uber to Tiana's party. Ed had previously received the news that he would be a recipient for disability from the Veterans Association, retroactive to September. He would finally receive help with PTSD and injuries that occurred during his service in the Vietnam War. Wanting to share his good fortune, he offered to pay for additional drinks. Tiana received her BA in Business Management, having made straight As while working full-time. I have always admired her determination and tenacious spirit. During her busy schedule, Tiana made time to keep in contact and plan dinners out. It was delightful to see nephew John, his wife Frances, and their twins, Monica and Audrey. John has suffered with pain for years after receiving a mesh implant during surgery, which caused more surgery with added intense pain. John, a man of great faith, rarely complains. We are praying a new procedure involving a nerve implant will allow John to walk without pain.

Heart of the Rockies Christian Church (Disciples of Christ) celebrated 30 years of ministry on Palm Sunday, 2023. I was privileged to share on video about the founding of our church and the music ministry. During this same time, I served on the Spiritual/Prayer Team for a capital campaign. Since the beginning, Heart of the Rockies Christian Church prayed about sharing our nine acres in some way to help the needy in our community. Throughout the years different ideas were explored. In 2022, our church donated land to a partnership that included CARE Housing (72 affordable apartments); L'Arche Northern Colorado (two homes for people with intellectual disabilities to thrive in a community atmosphere); and Fort Collins Habitat for Humanity (nine homes). City leaders were so impressed with our plans that Heart of the Rockies Christian Church was presented with the Human Relations Award. A ground blessing was held in March 2023, and groundbreaking took place in October 2023. What an exciting time for Heart of the Rockies Christian Church!

CARE Housing and our church will combine resources to build a Heartside Hill community center to be used by all. It will include a large fellowship hall to be used by the church and others. With additional funds from the capital campaign, our church building will be remodeled and enlarged to better serve the congregation and the community. We give thanks to God who opened every door, to the leadership of our pastor, Melissa St. Clair; to numerous church leaders who spent hours, days, and months on the project; to prayer warriors who never ceased to pray; and to a congregation who is moving forward with a vision.

Great-granddaughter Emily was baptized on Resurrection Sunday, April 9, 2023. Emily shared with the congregation why she wanted to be baptized. She told how her mother, Joy, led her in accepting Christ as her Savior at their dining table. We had a family luncheon following Emily's baptism. Thoughtful Ed presented the ladies with beautiful Easter lilies. With a grateful heart, I again thanked God for blessing me with grandchildren and spouses who raised their children in Christian homes, teaching about the importance of following Jesus. Ed brought me home. We visited for a while and hugged goodbye. As always, he said, "I love you, Mom, call you tomorrow. "

Losing Ed and Marilyn

The next day, thinking about my age, the happy occasion of Emily's baptism, and wanting the pleasure of presenting my memoir book to family and friends, I was preparing to write the ending, until I received the crushing news from Matt that Ed was killed in an automobile accident two miles from his home. I cried, "Oh no!" several times. I prayed for Matt who had to deliver the news to his family and to all of us. I prayed for Tom, Alicia, and their families. We knew Ed must have suffered a stroke or heart attack. He had been taking heavy blood pressure medication, and he let me know the previous week that he did not feel well. His blood pressure was dangerously high. I urged Ed to call 911, but he decided to wait. He assured me the count had gone down and he was feeling better. It was later confirmed that Ed died from a heart attack. Swerving to the right, his vehicle hit a guardrail and fell into a ravine. A passerby and medics performed CPR to no avail. The coroner reported that Ed died within 30 seconds to two minutes after the heart attack.

I could not grasp the news that my first-born was gone. My entire body and mind were engulfed in grief that had no description. Ed, my steadfast, thoughtful, loving son, left a space that could not be filled. Much as I tried to make sense of what had happened, I spiraled into a deep grief. Tom's death was very hard, but I had difficulty making sense of saying goodbye to Susie, David, and now, Ed. I know we live in a world where the unimaginable and unexplainable are everyday realities, and grief comes, uninvited to everyone. As Pastor Melissa said, "Although death does not have the victory, it does still sting." My heart hurt as I prayed for Tom, Matt, Alicia, and their families. God knew I was wondering why I had been granted such a long life. I was not only wrapped up in grief over Ed, but memories of Susie's and David's deaths came flooding into my heart, and I longed to feel Tom's arms around me. Clearly, I heard these words, "Let Your Faith Rise." I stood up and with humility and asked God's forgiveness for allowing myself to sink into a dark place. *Romans 12:12* came to mind, "Be joyful in hope, patient in affliction, faithful in prayer." I listen to the radio station K-Love whenever I am driving. Two weeks after Ed died, a song I had never heard was sung. It spoke of difficult times and a broken heart. It ended with these words. "God is not finished telling your story." Tears rolled down my face as I pulled into the Safeway parking lot and I sat there weeping. I gave thanks to God for lifting me out of the shadows and asked him to grant me the grace to calmly accept His plan for my life. The song "Under His Wings" filled me. "Under His wings, what a refuge in sorrow. How the heart yearningly turns to His rest! Often when earth has no balm for my healing, there I find comfort, there I am blessed. Under His wings, under His wings. Who from His love can sever? Under His wings my soul shall abide, safely abide forever. *Psalm 91:4*: "He will cover you with His feathers and under His wings you will find refuge; His faithfulness will be your shield and rampart. "

Family and friends gathered for interment of Ed's ashes with full military honors on Friday, April 21, at Cheyenne National Cemetery. It was a cold, windy day. Alicia wrapped her arms around me to shield me from the shivering cold. Tears fell as I accepted our country's flag on behalf of my son, which I placed with Tom's flag in the study. Ed's memorial service was held at Heart of the Rockies Christian Church on April 22. The church was overflowing with those who knew and loved Ed. We were so appreciative for the support from family and friends. Our immediate family was blessed by the attendance of 36 other family members. Matt and Alicia spoke about their dad, offering stories of his deep faith in Jesus. Anna shared memories about her uncle and sang, "I Can Only Imagine."

> Lament for My Son
> My Beloved Ed
>
> *I cannot wrap my mind around the reality that you, my oldest son, reached heaven ahead of me. I am consumed with grief. The hole in my heart has widened and deepened. You will be absent from family gatherings where your sense of humor shined, especially when you were helping cook the meals.*
>
> *From the age of three, you loved to sing and make up your own tunes. Sometimes you would sing your prayers as you knelt beside the bed with head bowed and hands folded. Dad and I were so proud of your accomplishments in music, sports, studies and the keenness with which you learned during your school years. My mind travels over it all: your birth on Christmas Day, your childhood, baptism, teen years, adulthood and your death on Resurrection Sunday.*
>
> *You were dependable, trustworthy, kind, loving and considerate of dad and me. Your tender heart reached out with compassion to help young people and to pay surgical expenses for a friend who had no insurance. You served and loved your neighbor. You were a steady, supportive, hardworking husband and father who never forgot a family birthday. You enjoyed planning events and parties.*
>
> *Dad and I were proud of the accolades you received in college, serving your country in the Viet Nam war, teaching and volunteering in the community. You lovingly cared for Marilyn as she began a decline of dementia. Later, when she was diagnosed with leukemia, you were faithful with daily visits to be with her at the hospice center. You were known as a man of integrity and honesty in your business and in the community. Most importantly was your faith in God and joy in Jesus.*
>
> *You often checked on me after dad died. I miss our talks, texts, phone calls and visits. I miss the way you would sing-song my name as you came through the door. After witnessing and celebrating Emily's baptism on Easter Sunday, you brought me home and carried a beautiful Easter lily to my apartment. I walked to the car with you. We hugged. These were the last words you spoke, "I love you, Mom. I'll call tomorrow." There was no tomorrow on this earth.*
>
> *Because of the promise in Jesus, on a tomorrow that God chooses, I will join Dad, Susie, David, Casey and you, my dear son, in God's heavenly home.*
>
> *--2023*

Jeff, our former pastor and dear friend, offered glimpses of Ed's life and community service. It was comforting to have Ken beside me at the service. I was so blessed with his company and love during the three days he stayed with me. Ken has been faithful, thoughtful, and loving with frequent calls while dealing with his own physical pain and surgeries.

Two days following Ed's memorial service in Fort Collins, the family gathered with Marilyn at the hospice center for a service there. Marilyn looked beautiful. She enjoyed the lovely flowers brought from Ed's service. She wiped away tears as the chaplain conducted the service, which indicated she understood that Ed was no longer present.

The following week, Matt asked if I had called Ed's phone. I had. I wanted to tell Ed that the lily had eight blossoms. Those whose dear ones have passed on often desire to share events with them, even speak with them. Those moments bring tears, laughter, and joy.

On Mother's Day, the family gathered at the hospice center to celebrate with Marilyn. She ate well and enjoyed the attention. Marilyn still had her sense of humor as she called Tom a dork. The name was usually saved for Ed. She did ask where Eddy was. When told he was in heaven, she said, "Oh, yes." As I hugged her goodbye, she said, "I love you, Mom. We sure have good times together."

I was to see Marilyn one more time at the hospice center. On June 8, Matt called to say she had taken a turn for the worse and was unresponsive. On June 9, 2023, Marilyn joined Ed in heaven. I prayed for Tom, Matt, Alicia, and families, who grieved the loss of both parents and grandparents within a two-month period. I, too, was grieving the loss of my son and my sweet, thoughtful, talented, fun-loving daughter-in-law.

The mortuary in Cheyenne was filled for Marilyn's service. The hospice chaplain told of Marilyn's determination, sense of humor, love of art, her quips, and feisty spirit as she spent time directing women in the kitchen on how to make cookies. Alicia, Matt, and Maddie spoke about Marilyn's generosity, her smile, and her love of God through her paintings. Matt drew our attention to one painting. It was four arrows pointing in different directions with the caption, "We are one." Indeed, we are all God's children. We are all one in Christ Jesus. I recalled words to a hymn: "In Christ, there is no east or west, in Him no south or north, but one great fellowship of love throughout the whole wide earth." My heart yearns for Marilyn. I smile as I walk through my apartment, gazing at three of her beautiful paintings. It was touching, through tears, to witness Tom, Matt, and Alicia take part in placing Marilyn's ashes with Ed's at the Cheyenne National Cemetery.

We grieve not for the loved ones who are in heaven, but for ourselves as we know things will never be the same. We miss their presence each day. The hole in our hearts remain, but God swoops in to provide strength and courage to face each tomorrow, that we might glorify Him through loving and serving others.

Grandson Tom picked Josh up from the airport on July 10 and drove us to Cheyenne for the memorial service. Marilyn's 1956 Chevy pickup was purchased by Josh. The pickup purred like a kitten. We cooled by opening the wings and windows. Aside from enjoying the ride, I loved spending time with Josh. Karen, and Maile arrived the next day. Josh's dad and Lucy invited me, Kelly and children (a long-time friend of Josh) to his lovely home for a barbeque. It was such a treat to visit with Karen and to play with Maile. At two years of age, Maile was on the go and "everything is mine" fell from her lips often. Maile sat with me on the piano bench at my apartment, following my fingers and hands over the keyboard. When she played on her own, it was with graceful, light touches. I told Josh and Karen that Maile would do well with lessons.

Continued Visits and Events

On July 13, Jim Louser who had lived with us for five years, came from Wheatridge to take me to lunch. He was excited to visit the farm and relived many memories. The Union Pacific railroad tracks ran along the west side of our farm. Many times, a row of box cars would be dropped off for later pick up. Jim reminded me of the time he, Ken, and David were checking out the box cars. I received a call from Kenny. "Mom, can you come pick us up?" I said, "Pick you up from where?" He replied, "Well, you see, we did not know the box car was hooked up to the train. We are in Loveland." A store manager allowed Ken to make a call. As I drove to Loveland, I gave thanks that the boys were safe and able to jump off the train at Loveland instead of some far-away place! The boys were not happy with our discussion on the way home and the extra work laid out for them.

I enjoyed time with Lauren and Amber on July 15. We had lunch together and Amber had fun shopping at the Dollar Store. Jenise, James, and Noah came for a visit on the 25th. They accompanied Tom to pick me up from the ER where I was being monitored for high blood pressure. It was a treat to see them.

During the past three years, I have been blessed with the back-and-forth frequent phone calls and texts from my sisters, Cheryl and Meredith. My mind often returns to the first time I saw those sweet little girls. I thank God and Cheryl's grandson, David, who brought us together after 72 years. Hosting reunions brings joy when we three sisters gather with the Bennett and Nix families.

Donnie and James came for a visit in August. They shared updated pictures of Laramie, my 18-month-old great-great grandson. Soon after their return to Texas, Donnie sent a picture of Bellamie, Laramie's sister. That sweet baby is my first great-great granddaughter. Thank you, Lord, for another grandchild to love.

In August, I was watching the news about a terrible fire engulfing the town of Lahaina on the island of Maui. Josh, Karen, and Maile lived in Lahaina. I called Josh and was relieved to hear his voice. He and Karen had quickly loaded the Jeep with everything they could and headed up a mountain north of them, which proved to be a wise decision. I praised God and asked assistance for them to escape the island. Josh was able to find space on a plane heading for the mainland. He, Karen, and Maile reached Las Vegas, where they were welcomed by Karen's family. Even though they have a place to stay, they are homeless, wondering about their home on Maui. Pictures of the aftermath were devastating and unbelievable. I prayed for those who lost loved ones, homes, vehicles and businesses.

In October, Ken had another serious neck surgery. Prayers were offered for successful surgery and recovery. The scar extended eight inches from the base of Ken's skull, downward. Recovery was long and Ken did receive some relief from the arm and leg pain. I have lost track of how many surgeries he has endured since his first back surgery at age seventeen. Ken continues to trust in Jesus and praises God as he faces each day with pain. There was excitement in his voice as he shared that he will soon be entering his tenth year of sobriety. *Psalm 106:1,* "Praise the Lord. Give thanks to the Lord, for He is good; His love endures forever."

Joy's parents, Dave and Judy, were so kind to invite me to their family Thanksgiving dinner. I came home with enough food for three meals. I pray for Joy, a woman of perseverance and faith. She has dealt with physical difficulties for some time. I am blessed by the thoughtfulness of Tom, Joy, Luke, Samuel, Micah, and Emily, who all live nearby.

In January 2024, Josh stopped for a visit. He was on his way back to Las Vegas after visiting his other grandmother in Wisconsin. Since the fire, Josh and Karen had returned to Maui twice to check on the condition of their condo. Sadly, nothing was salvageable because of smoke damage. The second time they found their condo completely flooded from a broken pipe. They will return to consult with the HOA and their personal insurance representative. They plan to rebuild and rent their condo in Maui. They purchased a home in Las Vegas. Maile was accepted in a pre-school for high-achieving children. She is very happy in her new surroundings, especially the attention she receives from Karen's family. Josh was hired to teach at the school one block from their home. He will, again, be teaching the beloved students with learning disabilities.

My 96th Birthday Celebration

In January, my sister, Meredith, called to say she would be planning a party for my 96th birthday on March 3. She remarked that Ed always planned my birthday parties, and she wanted to be sure I had a special one. Besides texting family members, she was planning the menu, writing name tags, making calls from California, and ordering food, while holding down a full-time job. On February 28, Meredith arrived. We had a good visit and talked with our sister, Cheryl, who was in the hospital in Kansas City, Missouri, with kidney stones, sepsis and a heart problem. We prayed for Cheryl and asked God to give wisdom to the doctors and nurses who were caring for her. The next three days, Meredith was running errands for party supplies, decorating the venue, and arranging for BBQ ribs and chicken. In the middle of it all, Meredith was talking with the nurses who attended Cheryl. We thanked God when we heard her condition was improving. (Later, Cheryl was moved to a nursing home for care and rehab where she is working hard to regain her strength. Talking with her on the phone is a blessing. Thanks be to God! We look forward to the day she can go home.)

The number of people who had responded to the party invitation was up to sixty. All were family members, except a few close friends: Kitty Voss, Judy Partain, Karen DiRaffael, and Ed and Becky Harper. I was excited because I had not seen some of my family for a long time; and I had not met several of my great nieces and nephews. An added blessing was Ken's attendance. I was grateful to Cody and Angela for bringing him. I would miss Cheryl and other family members who were unable to attend. Meredith outdid herself and the party was a huge success. Nephew John offered a beautiful prayer before we ate.

Closing Thoughts

As I bring these memories to a close, I offer this prayer for my family:

Holy God, I pray that all my descendants who are living and those not yet born become men and women of faith, displaying integrity, honesty, responsibility, trust and gratitude guided by the Holy Spirit while trusting Jesus as their savior. May they hold fast to your word and grow spiritually while sharing the Joy of Jesus with others. May they know Your healing power and Your unconditional love. May they display love for one another and others. John 13:34: "A new commandment I give to you, that you love another, just as I have loved you."

God expects us to serve and glorify Him onto old age and continue to grow in our faith. Wrapped in His grace, He teaches me more every day from His word. As my life continues to unfold, I will lift my hands in gratitude to God for His presence in my life, the guidance of His Holy Spirit and the salvation joy I have in Jesus. I thank Him for my loving husband, beautiful children, grandchildren, and extended family. I thank God for friends and family who have prayed for me and those who shaped my life with kindness, understanding, guidance, generosity, and love. I thank God for those who helped me grow spiritually. I thank Him for inner strength, courage and peace, always drawing me close through storms, heartaches, illnesses, mistakes, laughter, and joy. I am grateful for God's healing touch, mercy, and forgiveness of my sins. I praise God, love of my soul, for the gift of eternal life through the sacrifice of His son, Jesus, my Savior who died on the cross for all. *John 3:16-17,* "For God so loved the world that He gave His only son, that whoever believes in Him shall not perish but have everlasting life. For God did not send his Son into the world to condemn the world, but that the world might be saved through him."

I stand in awe of God and bow before Him with humility and gratitude, for throughout my life He has protected, healed, comforted, guided, and covered me with His unconditional love. My God has walked in front of, behind, and beside me all the way reaching down to lead me . . .

BY HIS HAND

Acknowledgements

I express my love and gratitude to these dear friends and sisters in Christ:

Becky Harper, who devoted four years of encouraging me, typing the manuscript, keeping me on track, asking the right questions for clarity, never complaining when I handed her countless inserts, and maintaining a joyful spirit through unexpected health challenges.

Linda Cowan, my longtime friend, for encouraging me and providing thorough editing above and beyond my expectation while dealing with serious heart problems.

Sue Anderon, a multi-gifted friend, who assisted with final editing, providing suggestions, wise guidance and researching for publishing.

Family

My Family
Mother: Alice
Father: Walt
Brother: Bill
Grandparents: Gladys and Elmer; Rachel
Aunts and Uncles: Reatha, Agnes, June, John, Bud, Russell, Bobby, Gilbert, Art
Foster Parents: Hap and Mae
Sisters: Cheryl, Meredith

Tom's Family
Parents: Ed and Roxcea
Brother: Joe
Sister: Mary Jane

Our Children

Ed and Marilyn's family:

Children: Tom, Matt, Alicia
Grandchildren: Luke, Samuel, Micah, Emily, James, Noah, Amber, Amelia

Susie and Steve, Jim, Bill's family:

Children: Greg, Jake, Josh; Patrick, Andy
Grandchildren: Tiana, Jacob, Maddie, Paige, Clare, Maile, Jada, Nalanni, Danica, Kiera, Tim

Ken and Cheryl's family:

Children: Johnathan, Jennifer; Cody, Casey; Donnie, Ande
Grandchildren: Thomas, Sidney, Gracey, Alexander, Frankie, Leni
Great Grandchildren: Laramie, Bellami

Dave and Deb's family:

Children: Jordan, Anna

In Loving Memory

Tom

Ed and Marilyn

Susie

Dave

Casey

Family Photo Gallery

Eddy 1955 *Susie 1958*  *Kenny 1958* *Dave 1958*

Ed Senior Year  *Susie Senior Year*  *Ken Senior Year* 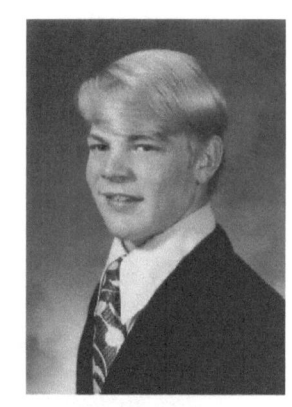 *Dave Senior Year*

Family 1957

Mother's Day 1958

Family 1962

Dave, Kenny, Susie, Eddy 1971

Family 1994

Growing Family 1995

Our Grandchildren

Tom with Michah, Samuel, Luke, Emily, and Joy

Matt with Noah, Lauren, James, and Amber

Alicia with Amelia and Bill

Greg with Maddie, Tina, Tiana, and Jacob

Jake with Paige, Beth and Clare

Josh with Karen and Maile

Patrick with Danica, Nalanni, Mashawn, and Jada

Cody and Angela

Donnie with JJ, Alex, Gracey, Bellamie, James, Sidney, and Laramie

Ande with Bucky, Frankie, and Leni

Jordan and Anna

Jenn and Thomas

My Poetry, Songs and Prayers

Excerpts from the book of *Poems, Prayers & Thoughts of Patsy Nix*

School

School is the craziest thing.
All we do is work and sing
And when gym period comes, I am glad
Everybody's happy and nobody is mad.
Then there is dancing too
But you usually dance so much you wear out your shoes.
Some kids are sour lemons
When they're out of school
But when they are in class—they are peaches to the teachers.
They bring an apple a day to keep the teacher away
(From their ma's and pa's)
I wouldn't want to be an old teacher's pet, no way
I'd rather play pool.
But I guess I'll have to admit,
I'm kinda glad I go to school
To make good friends with the kids,
And learn the Golden Rule.

1940 – age 11

I'm Irish, but American

They rave about the shamrock
And those "Irish eyes of blue"
And a saint by the name of Patrick
Whom they reverence so true

With a wee bit of blarney
The Irish go on their way
With a merry heart they wear their green
True folks of Erin, they.

But I'm an American School Girl
Who loves the red, white and blue
And I think we've a match for the shamrock
Right here at home, don't you?

So here's to the American Beauty
A rose with fragrance rare
And American youth where duty calls,
You'll always find them there.

But we'll wear the green with the Irish
On this St. Patrick's Day
While we fight for the four big freedoms
In the great American way.

1942 – World War II had begun for the U.S.

To Tommy

Remember me, dear Tommy
Wherever you may roam –
Whether you be just a step
Or a thousand miles from home.

My thoughts will all be with you
Each night and every day,
Along with those from Him above
Dear – don't forget to pray.

I'll say a prayer for you each night
As I have done before
And home your future will be bright
What 'ere it has in store.

I'm going ot miss you terribly much
Your smile, the way you talk,
Just everything about you Tommy,
Even the way you walk.

Your thoughtfulness for everyone,
Your jokes, the way you tease,
Just keep on being like yourself
And love me – will you please?

Look at the sunny side of things,
You'll always find a light
And tho' you're far away from me
I'll be with you day and night.

Whatever happens don't give up
I know you'll make the grade
There's someone watching from above
You need not be afraid.

At times you've been unhappy
About things I've said and done.
I'm terribly sorry – please believe
I didn't mean a one.

I'll write you everything I do
About the people I'm around
Gee, it won't be like being with you
I'll be so lonely now.

I'm not much of a poet
But I've tried to make you see
Someone loves you, more than you know
And that someone is me!

1945 -- Tom left for the Navy in May, and he carried a copy of this poem with him the whole time he was in the Navy. It was very tattered by the time he returned!

When It's Over, Over There

Nights have been so long since you went away,
But my heart keeps saying, "You'll come back to me someday"

When it's over, over there
You can come back home to where
Someone is waiting for you
Some one that's true.
While you're fighting over there

Every letter that you write
Seems to keep my world a light
We'll build that cottage for two, plan things to do
When it's over, over there.

I pray every night, to the Father above
To keep you, my love, for me
And I know that He will
Keep you safely until
You can kiss me goodnight tenderly.

So my darling, please sit tight
Think and dream of me each night
We'll have that cottage for two, plan things to do.
When it's over, over there.

I wrote this song for Tom when he was in the Navy in 1945. I sang this song at our 50th anniversary party.

For My Children -- Eddy, Susie, Kenny, David

May I shower you with hugs and kisses.

May I teach you good health habits and the rewards of work well done.

May I help you understand that everyone makes mistakes and chalk them up to learning.

May I show that you can always depend on me in all circumstances.

May I always encourage the exercise of your brain and lead you in analytical thinking.

May I guide you in appreciation of God's beautiful world.

May my actions show the importance of helping others, especially those less fortunate.

May I show clearly, the importance of trust, understanding, integrity and forgiveness.

May I help you learn that God's Word is true, that He is always present and ultimately in charge of your daily lives and that you can depend on the guidance of His Holy Spirit.

May you know how deeply and unconditionally I love you, and help you to understand how much more deeply you are loved by Jesus.

1955

Lord, I Praise Thee

I praise the Lord
For friends and loved ones that increase
As day by day He showers me
With blessings, and a spirit free

I praise the Lord for beauty fair;
For grass and trees, for sky, fresh air,
For laughter of a little child,
For letting me talk with Him a while

And yes, 'tis easy to praise His Name,
Lift up my hands, sing a refrain
When all goes well—but, what if it seems
A door has closed on all my dreams?

Oh, can I praise the Lord for this –
Fatigue and pain; a tight clenched fist.
A quilted sky with a darkened thread,
Thunder clashing 'round my head?

Oh yes? I praise Him now, and more
For Christ, His son, who hung adorned
With nails and thorns, spilling His blood
That I might reap a cleansing flood.

I praise the Lord for joy or pain,
And ask His will, that I might gain
An insight into greater things
He has in store for my whole being.

And though I feel the pangs of pain,
I raise my hands, sing a refrain
To praise His Name and humbly say,
"Lord teach me more, today!"

May 1972 – following a heart attack

Thanks Be to God

As I gazed across our fields, I was awestruck by the beautiful blanket of undisturbed, fresh, clean snow. My world was still and quiet, waiting for a full freshness of winter. It was the same with my soul. I too, was quiet and expectant, waiting for the gentle impress of God's renewal. Waiting to be swept clean by the incoming of His own fresh, undisturbed love and forgiveness.

When I walk alone on the farm or kneel to pray, I receive the rock-solid assurance from my heavenly Father that I am loved, and He knows by deepest needs. My thoughts center with calm confidence in Jesus. Who could be more encouraging? Who could put more flame in my faith than Jesus?

Life is like a symphony, and we are God's instruments. Our Father will play out our lives according to His own orchestration while he takes joy in his obedient children. May my life be a sweet savor that is pleasing to him.

My life has been intertwined with what can be achieved under my Father's care. From early childhood, God led me by His hand. He has poured out His spirit in abundance, inspiring me to serve others. I am filled to overflowing with the joy of His faithfulness and love.

During times of stress, I become lost in awe, wonder and inspiration as I bury myself in God's Word. I become suspended in time with interludes of His grace as he leads me through the valleys to higher ground. I am lifted up. Thanks be to You, O God, my refuge and strength.

Birth is one of God's miracles. How sweet to watch a mother lick her newborn foal, struggling to stand on spindly legs. How joyous to watch a mother snuggle and rock her newborn baby. I think of Mary cuddling the Savior of the World and give thanks for God's eternal gift of love and life.

What a comfort to call You Father. What a privilege to be Your child whom You long to shower with deep, quiet love. I am filled with the joy of Your presence. I have long thoughts about the way You guide and teach me through the Holy Spirit who lives within me. In my old age, I pray You continue to use me and teach me Your ways. May what I do and say be pleasing to You. I cherish the moments You imprint on my heart that You love me, granting mercy, peace, and forgiveness. I cannot utter enough thanks for the gift of hope manifested in Jesus, my Savior and Lord, who died on the cross for my sins and the sins of the world.

Christ Jesus: The Way, The Truth and The Life!